Compact disc at rear of book

THINKING
SOUND
MUSIC

THINKING
SOUND
MUSIC

The Life and Work of Robert Erickson

Charles Shere

With a Foreword by John Rockwell

Fallen Leaf Press
Berkeley, California

Published by Fallen Leaf Press
P.O. Box 10034
Berkeley, CA 94709

Printed in the United States of America

Library of Congress Cataloging-in-Publication Data

Shere, Charles, 1935–
    Thinking sound music : the life and work of Robert Erickson / Charles Shere.
        p.   cm. — (Fallen Leaf monographs on contemporary composers ; 2)
    Includes index.
    ISBN 0-914913-33-6 (alk. paper)
        1. Erickson, Robert, 1917–   —Criticism and interpretation.
    I. Title   II. Series.
    ML410.E767S54 1995
    780'.92—dc20
    [B]   95-32686
                                                                                        CIP
                                                                                        MN

The paper used in this book meets the minimum requirements of the
American National Standard for Information Services—Permanence
of Paper for Printed Library Materials, ANSI Z39.48-1984.

Dedication

See page xviii, and to Gary Samuel, and to the memory of Bill Triest;
they all let me know.

Contents

Illustrations / viii

Foreword / ix

Preface / xiii

Introduction / xv

PART ONE: THE LIFE

Childhood, 1917–1934 / 3

Early Maturity, 1934–1940 / 10

The War Years, 1940–1946 / 19

Interlude, 1946–1953 / 25

San Francisco: KPFA, 1953–1956 / 33

San Francisco: UC Berkeley, 1956–1958 / 41

San Francisco: The Conservatory, 1957–1966 / 46

San Diego: Building a Department, 1967–1975 / 58

Teaching, Travel, and Retirement, 1976–1990 / 66

PART TWO: THE WORKS

I. THE EARLY WORK: MUSIC AND THE MIND, COMPOSITIONS THROUGH 1957

The Early Vocal Music and *The 1945 Variations* / 85

Postwar Transitional Work, 1948–1950 / 89

Breakthrough: Early Mature Work, 1952–1954 / 96

Second Wind: The Early Masterpieces, 1956–1957 / 101

II. THE MIDDLE WORK: MUSIC FOR PERFORMERS; EXPERIMENTS
IN SOUND, 1960–1977

    Further Challenges to the Performers, 1960–1963 / 115

    Finding Sound on Tape, 1965–1967 / 134

    Fun, Games, and Virtuosity, 1966–1969 / 140

III. MUSIC IN ITS PLACE: RHYTHM, MANTRA, AND SONORITY,
1968–1975

    Music Expressing the Environment, 1969–1970 / 157

    The Rhythm of Mantra, 1968–1973 / 164

    Sonority and the Sound Structure of Music, 1974–1975 / 172

IV. CLOSURE: MUSIC AND THE INTERIOR MIND

    Introspection: Solo Music / 189

    Introspection: Small Ensembles / 194

    Introspection: Voice and Violin / 204

    Retrospection: Late Orchestra Pieces; Looking to the
      Mountains / 209

    Back to the Drums / 219

    Strings Again, Two Last Songs, and the Final Chamber
      Scores / 221

Appendix I: Discography / 238

Appendix II: Chronology of Compositions / 240

Appendix III: List of Works by Title / 243

General Index / 254

Illustrations

Frontispiece:

Drawing of Robert Erickson composing, 1955, by Lenore Alt-Erickson.

Following page 81:

Lenore Alt-Erickson and Robert Erickson in Douglas, Michigan, early 1940s.

Erickson as personnel clerk, U.S. Army, ca. 1945.

A page from *The End of the Mime of Mick, Nick and the Maggies* for eight-part chorus.

The score of *Pacific Sirens*.

Excerpt from *Ricercare à 5*, for five trombones.

Stuart Dempster performing Robert Erickson's *General Speech*, April 1995.

Foreword

I admire Robert Erickson and Charles Shere for similar reasons, which have nothing directly to do with Charles's music, which doesn't mean I don't admire it, too. The reason I admire them has to do with how they have shaped their lives, their careers, and their art and—let's be forthcoming—how that shaping reflects and frames my own rather different choices in life. And the reason I admire this book is that in it, Erickson and Shere come together in a way that to me is emblematic of their achievements in life.

Let me explain. The United States is a large, rambling, shambling kind of country. Unlike France or Britain, it lacks a monolithically dominant political and cultural center, no matter how much Washington and New York may attempt to fulfill those roles. Part of the reason is our atomistic, individualistic national mind-set, and part is the sheer geographical expanse of the nation and the location of those two cities at the far eastern end.

Still, the rise of mass popular culture and the binding ties of ever more sophisticated electronic media have eroded the isolated independence that far-distant parts of the country used to enjoy (and suffer from). Our lives, and our culture, have grown more homogeneous. Yet even a cursory glance at our art, and especially our serious music, suggests that a disproportionate amount of this country's major achievements have come not from establishment game-players in the major eastern cities but from cranky outsiders. Those are individualists, a curiously large number of whom seem to come from New England or Northern California, who may well subscribe to the nation's atomistic-individualist temper, but who in doing so deny themselves the short-term creature comforts of mainstream conformity.

Now, however, there is a countercurrent at work, a newly fashionable mind-set that seeks to revitalize individual and regional independence and to assert the value of work and lives that don't easily subscribe to dominant mores as propagated from the old cultural capital (New York) or the new one (Los Angeles). That countercurrent has been particularly evident over the last half-century in the San Francisco area, the home of the Beats, the hippies, queer culture, a new American haute cuisine based on local ingredients, and, not least, an arts scene that holds itself sweetly and defiantly aloof from the official culture—sternly modernist, slickly minimalist, soupily neo-romantic, or whatever—that passes for the dogma *du jour*.

Robert Erickson's career has epitomized that movement in the realm of serious contemporary composition. Like so many Northern Californians, he came from somewhere else. Yet his arrival there in 1953 must have seemed like coming home. Immediately, he plunged into activities that helped define a scene, not so much as a "school" of like-minded composers and their student epigones, but as a playing field for activity in which individuality could flourish. He did that by example as a composer; as a teacher at the San Francisco Conservatory and the University of California at Berkeley (and later at the University of California at San Diego, whose music department for a while functioned as a curious southern outpost of the San Francisco sensibility); and as an administrator, at KPFA radio in Berkeley and at the San Francisco Tape Music Center.

It is Erickson's own music, of course, on which Charles concentrates in this book, and that will serve as the composer's ultimate legacy. Lots of composers stick doggedly to a single, glacially evolving esthetic, as if fearful that a too-sudden shift will destroy their image or their credibility. Others flit about the stylistic spectrum, never finding a voice that they could even contemplate subsequently abandoning.

Erickson's music has evolved over the years, but it retains a core of personality and always suggests a lively questing spirit rather than mere facile opportunism. To my taste, not all his ventures have proved equally successful, which is the price of any true experimentation. But the best of them reach deep, both into themselves and into us, and suggest that Erickson's final place in American musical history, if there's any justice in the writing of that history, may be far higher than it is at present.

That process of reevaluation is already under way, and it is reflected in the near-simultaneous appearance of this book along with Erickson's memoirs, *Hearing Things*, and John MacKay's *Music of Many Means*. Without in any way commenting on the value of other studies, I can speak to the skill of this one and suggest that some of the reasons for Charles's success here relate to his own similar place in American and Northern California culture.

I have known Charles for more than thirty years, ever since I returned to the place I grew up, the San Francisco Bay Area, to pursue graduate studies at the University of California at Berkeley in the 1960s. When he was music director of KPFA then, one of Erickson's honored successors, I produced opera and late-night programs on the station, under his auspices. He became a collaborator (on an opera-review program) and a lifelong friend. A friendship based not just on personal affinity but on our shared interests in music and food, most notably at Chez Panisse, where he serves as a board member (his wife is Lindsey Shere, the restaurant's acclaimed dessert chef).

Charles's life I admire both in itself and as a path not taken by me. He is rooted in Northern California culture and its landscape, like a native oak. He and Lindsey, to my eyes, have created an enormously stimulating and elegant life for themselves and their children, based not on an accumulation of things or power but on a highly proud and personal set of choices about what is important for themselves and the world. And in being thus true to themselves, they have contributed to a regional culture that invigorates not only those who live there but—as with Erickson's music and what we all hope will be its final place in our national culture—the country at large.

This Foreword is hardly about me, but I might mention that Charles (and, through this book, Erickson) fascinates me because I came from this culture and retain warm and continuing personal connections to it. Yet I chose to base myself first in Los Angeles and for most of my life in New York and to involve myself, as a critic for the *Los Angeles Times* and *The New York Times*, as an author, and now as a festival director at Lincoln Center for the Performing Arts, as directly and influentially as I could in the shaping of our mainstream culture. Whether I am doing so in a selfless search for excellence as I (in my crankily individualistic Northern California way) see it, or in a craven quest for power and worldly glory, I leave to others to say. But my perch on the East Coast encourages me to look longingly and admiringly back to my own roots and to the trees, like Erickson and Shere, that have grown from similar roots.

What makes this book fascinating for me is not just its intelligence and writerly deftness, but its success in addressing the thorniest problem confronting all serious music critics. As I understand it, the series in which this book appears is designed for the layman, for those interested in contemporary music who may not have the mastery of terminology to profit from a more technically worded study. That is, of course, precisely the same task that faces any music critic for a daily newspaper, which both Charles and I have been.

This book is instructive in the telling of Erickson's event-filled life, but where it really becomes important is its ability to evoke the music, composition by composition, in language that is both sophisticated and meaningful for someone without a full armory of technical knowledge. This involves primarily the use of metaphor and cleverly descriptive writing; there's no magic secret about it. But it seems to me that Charles has found a language, or better yet can use that language that we all speak, to summon sound-worlds that might otherwise remain unheard.

Of course, Erickson's music need not remain neglected. With luck, prodded on by books like this, it may gradually enter the repertories of our more progressive performing groups. From there, if there's sufficient health left in a music culture in which the present has been dangerously severed from the past, it will flow into the mainstream itself. Which will be good for Erickson's reputation, for the eventual sales of this book, and, just as important, for us already swimming in the mainstream as well.

John Rockwell

Preface

Music arises early in human development. It is a spontaneous response to the child's perception of the world around him. Similarly, social musical response appears early in developing cultures. Chanting, singing, drumming, and dancing seem universal. As a society evolves, its music becomes many things. It is an aid to memory in preliterate cultures, a bonding ritual in religious and patriotic observances, an adjunct to game-playing, and finally, perhaps, an entertainment.

Societies have encouraged and developed the innate musical impulse—one might almost say exploited it—for good reason. Even in our culture, technologically sophisticated and materially secure, musical participation is salutary, for both society and the individual. Listening to music encourages attentiveness, trains the memory, and develops pattern-recognition skills. It sharpens one's ability to detect relationships and to predict the likely course of near-future developments of present events.

In the last century or so, however, concert music, in American society, has gone through two quick and damaging ordeals. In the closing decades of the nineteenth century, largely through the cultural aspirations of a newly wealthy merchant class, it was elevated to a High Art, soon gaining both priesthood and catechism, complete with Lives of Great Composers for the instruction of neophytes. Then, in the fifty years since the end of World War II, waves of technological advances in broadcast and recording widened the audience for music—and by making the canon overfamiliar converted it from art to entertainment.

In recent years, exigencies of marketing and other influences have created a tendency toward large and general concert audiences. At the same time, general publications, including not only daily and weekly newspapers but also more narrowly targeted magazines (such as *The New Yorker*), have felt it advisable to cut back the extent and generalize the appeal of their music coverage. The result has been to further weaken the position of contemporary music within musical life in the United States.

I undertook this book to offset these developments and to introduce a uniquely American voice to the lay musical enthusiast. The book is journalism, not scholarship, and I have limited my research to three kinds of primary sources.

When the book was undertaken, several years ago, Robert Erickson kindly provided his then-unpublished memoirs, *Hearing Things*, giving permission to quote from them at will. He also consented to a number of interviews over the years, and has also permitted quotations from the letters we exchanged from time to time. (Except for italicizing titles, I have left Erickson's orthography alone.) Just as this book was going to press I learned of the imminent publication of Erickson's memoirs, *Hearing Things*, in an edition combined with John MacKay's study, *Music of Many Means*.

I have also relied on such material as came readily to hand in the course of attending concerts featuring Robert Erickson's music, including program notes and occasional reviews. The primary sources have been the scores themselves, nearly all of them now available from Erickson's principal music publisher, Smith Publications, and recordings of the music, both as commercially released and as archived at the University of California, San Diego.

Many people have helped with the writing of this book: I am grateful to Glenn Glasow, Bonnie Harkins, Joe Kucera, Will Ogdon, Tom Nee, Carol Plantamura, and Alan Rich, and especially to Sylvia Smith, Erickson's publisher. Among these and many others, one man above all has given me much to reflect on during the gestation of this book, and two women have been remarkably patient with its exceedingly slow birth. I particularly thank Douglas Leedy, a thorough scholar and a fine composer; Ann Basart, an indulgent editor and publisher; and Lindsey Remolif Shere, the most stimulating, challenging, and rewarding companion imaginable.

Introduction

Robert Erickson is utterly American, and uniquely of our time. His work is nourished by his awareness of his time and place, and so has much to say to us, who share it. And since his work is both sound and fascinating, it is delightful to respond to it.

But Erickson's work is music: he is a composer, and thinks and addresses us in sound. And the classical-musical establishment, now as always in this country, has little interest in its own time and place. Erickson has won a share of honors and grudging recognition. There have even been a few recordings made of his music. But he remains a maverick. To know one's own time, it seems, one must stand a little apart from its mainstream.

Much of the most fascinating and significant music of our century has been made by mavericks. Charles Ives, Edgard Varèse, Virgil Thomson, Henry Cowell, Harry Partch, John Cage, Conlon Nancarrow, Lou Harrison—all of them extended not only musical expression and resources but the very perception of music in our time. And most of them did this from marginal positions, neglected at best, ridiculed at worst, by the established conservators of the art they pursued with such dedication. At the close of the century they are seen, finally, as central to the continuing musical tradition. (Well, most of them. Cage's case will go through many appeals before it is finally settled.) It is time for Erickson's position to be similarly resolved.

Erickson is quintessentially American, and small-town middle-American, self-taught to a great extent, a tinkerer. His parents were immigrants. He did not grow up in a wealthy family, attend an Ivy League university, or move among social circles. He was thirty-four years old when he first saw New York City, forty-nine when he first crossed the Atlantic. He is the kind of man who does not listen patiently to an authority telling him something can't be done or won't work. He knows how to find his own solutions, often home-made, when no conventional one comes to hand.

He has always been fascinated with sounds, and has studied them enough to know that it is in hearing things that we come as close as we can to erasing that invisible line between ourselves and the world around us. The sounds he hears are beyond categories, really, and that is why in his music wit and wisdom, comedy and comprehension are one. Storm sewers, herds of cattle, freeway traffic, string quartets, the twelve-tone system, welding rods, pottery mugs, tic-tac-toe games—all these have entered his workshop. From them he has fashioned a steady production of music, always either at or just ahead of the breaking issues of his day.

The curve of Erickson's career is interesting and instructive. He was among the last generation to learn music the old-fashioned way, a step at a time, folk music first, then the nineteenth-century repertoire, then, as it was being written, the music of our own time. He learned the music with his hands and his ears, playing it, not exclusively with his ears and his brain, via recordings and theory. His own music quickly traversed the principal styles of his century—twelve-tone music, dissonant counterpoint, neoclassicism—and then invented the remaining ones: collaborative improvisation, music on magnetic tape, the acoustical tonality of his final transcendental music. And at all times that he studied music he also studied sound: birdsong; industrial noise; the sounds of wind, rain, and water; the sounds of speech.

He learned how to live with disappointment and hard times. A combination of determination, discipline, and flexibility allowed him to deal with the Great Depression, with the army, and with the distracting politics of noncommercial organizations and university faculties. His patience and apparently innate cheerfulness have been sorely tested, for in his later life Erickson has been an invalid, confined to his own home for fifteen years, essentially bedridden for seven.

The one compromise he would not make was with a principled nonconformity. He found this easier to maintain away from power centers within the American cultural establishment, and so he settled on the West Coast.

Mark Swed wrote, in 1985, that

> Robert Erickson lives and writes music in California for a reason. The San Diego-based ... composer orchestrates better than any other composer alive, and the colors he achieves are those of Southern California sunsets and desert wild flowers and soft blue sky....
>
> But [his music] represents the California spirit by being more than pretty colors. It is the promise of a better world that brings people to California in the first place, and somehow, miraculously, Erickson captures that sense of a new world in sound. For some years the composer has suffered from a debilitating muscle disease ... but his music reveals a joy that transcends worldly pain. Mozart and Milhaud are the only other two composers who have done that as well. ["New Sounds, California Style": Los Angeles *Herald Examiner*, November 2, 1985.]

To many this summation will seem parochial. Erickson is not parochial. His music draws on a respectful awareness and careful study of African, Chinese, Indonesian, and Indian music, as well as the Western European concert tradition. He knows folk music and jazz, and can write as a scholar on computer music, acoustics, the physics of speech, or the music of ancient Greece.

But there is always a sense of place in Erickson's music. He has never forgotten that the first obligation of musical expression is that it be rooted in human emotion; and he is aware that a profound connection to source is at the center of healthy emotional and spiritual life.

I first met Robert Erickson in 1962, when Gerhard Samuel, then the conductor of the Oakland Symphony, suggested I study composition with him. He was undoubtedly instrumental in shaping my own career in the next five years, first at KPFA radio in Berkeley, then at KQED television in San Francisco. We drifted apart after his move to San Diego in 1967, but we maintained an occasional correspondence thereafter.

There is no way I could suppress my own feelings about the man in writing about him, and I will not pretend this is anything but an enthusiastic view of his life and work. In fact I must confess to an agenda: I want to introduce Erickson and his music to a hypothetical layman, an enthusiast for the culture of his or her own time and place—the United States at the close of the twentieth century. For that reason I have begun with a fairly brisk account of Erickson's life, saving extended discussion of the music for a later section of the book. A certain amount of repetition has resulted: I hope the reader will be patient with it.

I hope, too, that any professional musicians reading this will pardon my explaining certain technical elements as they come up—often roughly rather than supremely accurately, and often by way of metaphor some may find far-fetched. I hope professionals will also be patient with occasional discussions of familiar material. To learn of the music of Robert Erickson it is necessary to know something of the other music of his time—of our time. It has therefore seemed useful, now and then, to move beyond his career to the larger cultural context in which it developed.

Ultimately this book is about music, practicality, and occupation. "All music means something," Erickson has pointed out. Useful music—*good* music—must be meaningful to those who hear it. I hope this book at least addresses that meaning, and I offer it, with love, respect, admiration, and humility, to the man who is its subject.

THINKING
SOUND
MUSIC

PART ONE: THE LIFE

Childhood, 1917–1934

The first sounds I remember are the clank and thud of the upright piano overhead. I was playing among the pedals while Uncle Harold and Aunt Albertine were making music. I was somewhere between one year ten months and two years ten months of age. The dates are in Uncle Harold's diary, which Albertine gave to Uncle Andrew, one of my father's several brothers, who gave it to me. I was living with Uncle Harold and Aunt Albertine because my mother had died in the Great Flu Epidemic of 1918. My father's only sister took me in—and probably saved me from an infantile psychosis. *

Earliest sounds are significant to composers, especially to modernists. Igor Stravinsky remembered the sound of the ice breaking up on the River Neva in his native St. Petersburg. Edgard Varèse recalled the whistle on the steamboats plying the Saône in Burgundy. There was water in Erickson's childhood, too, but it is the music of the family parlor that resounds in his earliest recollection. His aunt Albertine and uncle Harold sang often, both at home and in performances for church groups and the Salvation Army—which didn't keep Uncle Harold from singing off-color Swedish songs around the campfire.

Uncle Harold was a piano tuner, and tuned harmoniums as well—the foot-pedal pump organs popular in turn-of-the-century parlors. Along with another uncle, Erickson's father's youngest brother Emil, Harold worked for the Cable Piano Company in Chicago, designing and building player pianos until radios replaced them as the focal point of American home entertainment. The entire

---

*This and all other similarly set (italicized) quotations are from Robert Erickson's memoir, *Hearing Things: Autobiographical Essays*, written between 1973 and 1980 and kindly made available by the composer. Unless attributed, otherwise-set quotations from Robert Erickson and Lenore Alt-Erickson are either from *Hearing Things* or from interviews conducted by the author, 1987–1994.

family was musical and inventive. Uncles Gus and Andrew built violins and spent long Sunday afternoons discussing the secret of the famous Stradivarius and Guarnerius violins, then retiring to experiment with varnishes, hoping to replicate the famous Cremona tone. Gus built his violins on the round dining-room table: "The family ate its meals from a thin new moon of table; violin parts, not to be disturbed, covered the rest."

> *I came out of a little, no place town in Northern Michigan where what we played was band music and Handel's Messiah. I was an outsider right from the beginning, because I lived with a lot of relatives when I was very young. I became quite an assessor of what kind of group I'm in. And one thing I knew was that I wasn't one of the family.*

The "no place town" was Marquette, the county seat of Marquette county, a port town almost centered on the north shore of Michigan's Upper Peninsula. It looks out on Lake Superior, across one hundred miles of open water to Canada. The nearest city of any size is Milwaukee, two hundred miles due south as the crow flies, but twice as far by road in 1917. To this day Marquette seems remote, an anomalous center of trade, education, shipping, and light industry, serving a wilderness whose principal resources are lumber and iron ore.

After his mother, Edith, died in the 1918 influenza epidemic, Erickson lived with Harold and Albertine in Chicago for a year. Then, when he was nearly three years old, he was handed on for six months to other relatives back in Marquette—where the dining table was covered with violin parts. He lived for a while with his father, Charles, in a boarding house "where everyone whistled." Then his father remarried in 1921. His new mother, Ellen Isaacson, also played the violin and sang—everyone in Erickson's childhood seemed to play violin and to sing. She saw to it that he took lessons, practiced an hour every day, and finally, when he was about seven, learned to read music.

During the months that he'd spent living with cousins, the ward of this uncle or that, Erickson had been overshadowed by the older children. They all played violin from infancy; one had "perfect pitch"—could give the name of any note he heard. Recognizing notes, and playing and singing in tune, was literally child's play in this household. Such play doesn't always come easily or naturally, and Erickson was at a disadvantage. Still, there were lots of instruments available: pianos, violins, a cello, zithers, a mandolin, a guitar, the harmonium. Singing and whistling were in the air even when instruments weren't at hand.

Erickson's father played mandolin, and had his own repertoire of Swedish songs. The boy's first compositional effort was an attempt to enlarge that repertoire: his father, perhaps amused, indulgently played it for him. "It sounded terrible to me when he played off the series of mostly big, round whole notes, but I also remember a strange feeling of wonder—'If I make notes then others can make them back to me.'"

As well as all this human music, there were the sounds of nature. When Erickson was ten or eleven years old his father built a cabin on a small inland lake near Marquette. Surrounded by tree-covered hills, with a high rocky bluff at one side, and dammed at the end by beavers, the lake trapped evening silence when the breeze died down: "Against that stillness the report of a beaver tail slapping the water seems to last forever, echoing and reverberating from the rocky bluff, standing in the ear like a sculptured object, fixed and solid."

Water sounds filled Erickson's childhood: the thundering, hissing waves on Lake Superior, heard in stormy weather on the rocky point in front of the lighthouse; and, in gentler weather, the lazy swishing rhythms of lapping waves sweeping the sandy beach. On fishing expeditions to narrow streams, in search of brook trout, no noise intruded to mask the sound of the creek, and Erickson learned to listen to the differences of each individual stream. These sounds would dominate a pivotal composition over half a century later, when the composer used the natural sounds of running water, by way of specially enhanced tape recordings, to accompany *Summer Music* for solo violin.

There was industrial noise in this composer's childhood as well. Some of this merged with natural sounds, becoming part of the environment. On hikes, the family often turned toward a power dam on the Dead River, where they would walk along the flume running from the dam to the powerhouse. "The water vibrated powerfully under foot all the way, and inside the powerhouse, warm and exciting, with all those dials and meters, there was the hum of the dynamos—a complete, head-filling, body-filling sound."

A boy's natural curiosity about machines and machinery led to hikes to neighboring sawmills, where endless clanking chains carried logs up from the pond, sending them to great circular sawblades whose clang and shriek could be heard from far away and became physically affecting, "tickling one's ears," as the boy approached more closely. Clanks and shrieks were already clichés of modernist music: a witty poet complained of the "bang, bang, bing" of Stravinsky's *Rite of Spring* at its American premiere, and Edgard Varèse was soon to incorporate sirens and numerous percussion instruments in his orchestral music. But in the case of Erickson's music it's interesting to note the influence not only of individual mechanistic sounds, but also of mechanical *structures*: the repetitive machines and cycling processes of this immediately familiar industry would resound in the loops and repetitions of his mature music, just as the flywheels and endless belts would be recalled by the reels and tape-loops of his first electronic sound-studio.

Occasionally the natural and industrial sounds collided with music. One of the family friends, a conductor on the Lake Superior & Ishpeming Railroad, was a Frenchman, a fine violinist and an accomplished trick fiddler. He could play "Pop Goes the Weasel" with the fiddle behind his head, or while holding the bow between his knees, or in his teeth. And yet he may have impressed the young Erickson not only for these accomplishments, and for performing them without printed music, but equally for his exotic relationship to the railroad and to its wonderful sounds—"the marvelous sequences of rattles, squeaks, glissandi and sighs as the first jerk of the locomotive was propagated throughout the length of the train," and, especially, the trains of ore cars, each with its own set of internal rattles.

> *There were other sounds, interesting and exciting ones. These have stuck in my mind. I am sure that I never thought of them as music, or possible musical material; nevertheless these memories have had their effects. I was very much aware of the ambiance of forest, snow blanket, echoing rocks and sound over water, and nowadays the ambiance of concert halls and other music environments is an integral part of the music for me. I know that I keep trying to recreate the brilliance and vividness of image that I experienced in sounds like the slap of that beaver tail on a still lake. I measure sounds I hear now against those*

memories; I am alert for sounds that are as memorable, and sometimes
I find myself searching for sounds that mean as much.

Erickson began piano lessons in earnest at seven, the practice hour closely supervised by his stepmother to make sure he was reading the notes and practicing the exercises. Like many budding composers he preferred "fooling around," improvising. "The rest was boredom and drudgery." The boy had wanted to study violin, but his stepmother was concerned with "practical" matters as well as music. She wanted to develop his dexterity, probably concerned because of his left-handedness; and she felt piano lessons would be a congenial therapy. Finally, though, when he was in the fourth grade, he started violin lessons, continuing meanwhile with his piano lessons. He began by studying with his stepmother, and could quickly play duets with her. After a year he moved on to a professional teacher.

He enjoyed the music lessons, but he didn't like practicing. He found football, baseball, the woods, and reading more interesting. When he discovered the world of books, sometime after the third grade, his lifelong passion for reading was instantly revealed. He read everything in the house, from Zane Grey to *The Home Medical Adviser*, and he began making the local public library a regular stop on his way home from school. After devouring the collection in the basement children's library he moved to the open stacks on the main floor, reading all the books about music and much else as well, including Freud (in the eighth grade!) and books on the physicists who had recently described the new world of the twentieth century: Eddington, Maxwell, Einstein; books on wave theory and photons; books on relativity.

The small library helped offset the cultural isolation of Marquette, then a town of fifteen thousand ("counting those in the penitentiary on the edge of town"), 450 miles by road from Chicago. Even now, at the close of the century, Marquette seems closer to Canada than to the United States, owing to relatively clear radio reception across Lake Superior. In the 1920s, though, even radio reception was noisy—owing, it was said, to the rich deposits of iron ore in the soil.

Still, there was music in Marquette—*live* music, perhaps because of the isolation and the lack of today's electronic culture. There was a succession of mediocre touring artists: "has-been singers on a final tour, operas with rickety sets . . . , violinists playing their bon-bons." There was even an occasional glimpse of the modern musical world: Erickson had studied Handel, Mozart, Beethoven, and the romantics at the piano, but that instrument suddenly promised new possibilities after he heard Debussy's "Jardins sous la pluie" played by a young out-of-town musician at the local music club.

Except for such moments, music in Marquette was plain and serviceable. An orchestra of fifteen or twenty musicians played at the Delft Theater, until "talkies" put them out of work. The churches provided choral singing: excerpts from Bach cantatas at the Lutheran church the Ericksons attended, with instrumental accompaniment on special occasions, and Handel's *Messiah* every year, sometimes with soloists imported from Chicago.

And there was the town band. Erickson took up the flute soon after the violin, and began playing in weekly summertime band concerts during his high-school years. The repertoire was conventional: marches, transcriptions, and novelties, and from time to time something "symphonic"—Franck, Tchaikovsky, or Verdi. Erickson's memories of these concerts is significant:

> *In practical terms, symphonic meant chromatic and chromatic meant (unfortunately) out of tune. For a long time I was suspicious of such music, because it didn't seem to make sense. We produced more than a few inadvertent atonal moments. Nevertheless, I consider myself lucky to have had that experience in the city band. I learned to play in a group in a (somewhat) professional way, and I learned how wind instruments sound under varied conditions of player and place.*

Erickson's generation was one of the last to come to music in an orderly, experiential manner, preparing each move in a sequence recalling the historical development of Western music. With the advent of radio and recordings this changed: from the earliest years, everyone is exposed to every kind of music. But a small-town musician in early-twentieth-century America approached music as a practical thing, working hard to play scales in tune, and generally hearing and playing "simpler" music than the late-romantic symphonic repertoire now so firmly in command of the airwaves and the concert halls.

One began with scales. Hymn-tunes and folksongs were content to rely almost exclusively on the eight notes of the familiar scale. "Chromatic" notes, the black notes of the piano keyboard, were exceptional: good for providing "color" (in close-harmony barbershop-quartet styles, for example) but unstable and likely to go out of tune. Musical stability needed wide-set, "consonant" intervals, the kind still associated with such Americana as traditional blues and Aaron Copland's *Appalachian Spring*.

Erickson's ear was undoubtedly trained early. The perfect-pitch games, the years of violin lessons, and the singing had emphasized the role of ear-to-finger (or larynx) coordination. Correct intonation—playing or singing exactly in tune, whether to the keynote or to the other performers—would have been a high priority in his musical instruction.

By the time he was in high school, his experience with wind instruments, whose tuning is not easily adjustable, must have heightened the boy's awareness of the role of tuning in musical expression. The conventional repertoire—the marches, waltzes, and folksongs familiar from his early childhood—was largely diatonic, keeping to the eight natural notes of the scale of their key. (Even today band music is largely restricted to the four "flat" keys most natural to the wind instruments: F, B flat, E flat, and [rarely] A flat.) As the music becomes more "chromatic," as "foreign" notes creep into those scales—"accidentals," the black keys on the piano keyboard outside of the white-key scale of C major—amateur and student musicians play with greater uncertainty, their instruments sounding more out of tune. Little wonder Erickson would be suspicious of the music that produced such results!

Early Maturity, 1934–1940

Erickson graduated from Marquette High School in 1934 and took a job as a printer's devil and proofreader at a local printing company. "Lonesome for music" after leaving school, though still continuing his private violin lessons, he decided on a career as high-school band and orchestra director, and enrolled, still in Marquette, at Northern Michigan State Teachers College (now Northern Michigan University). But the books in the local library had suggested greater musical interest than Marquette could offer, and Erickson had begun composing. He knew he had to find teachers who were composers, and soon traveled south to Chicago to find them.

There he began weekly harmony lessons from May Strong, who had been recommended by a music teacher at Northern State, paying for them out of meager wages earned as a busboy or messenger boy. He soon had to drop his violin lessons as an economy measure, but he continued his harmony lessons until his musical demands proved too adventurous for his conventional instructor.

Erickson had taken a room on the North Side of Chicago, not far from the Biograph Theater, where the notorious bank robber John Dillinger had been shot down by Treasury agents in July 1934. Even nearer, and of greater interest to Erickson, was the neighborhood bookstore, where he struck up an acquaintanceship with the clerk, who offered to introduce him to Park House, a neighborhood settlement house where people gathered on Friday nights for discussions. Soon Erickson was a regular visitor.

Park House, an experiment in communal living, had been established in the early 1930s by Jim Nobel, a former theological student interested in people and in social processes. Named for Dr. Robert Park, a sociologist at the University of Chicago, it provided the residence of a dozen or so people, and was visited regularly by scores more. Residents and visitors had formed small groups devoted to music, dance, drama, books, and art; on Fridays larger gatherings met at dinner to hear an invited speaker.

Here for the first time Erickson, at nineteen, felt close to "a group of people with well stocked minds, people older and more mature than I. I was the youngest person there,... ready to talk, argue and harangue, so exhilarated by ideas, art, music, dance, friends, communal feeling, that during the day, delivering samples for the Bradner-Smith Paper Company, I sometimes felt I was dancing along above the pavement."

The dance group was preparing a concert and asked Erickson to compose its music: the dissonant style he had by then elaborated apparently suited the theme, which he later recalled as a grim message about urban life. One of the dancers, Lenore Alt, made a strong impression on him as he accompanied the rehearsals; a year later, in November 1938, they were married.

Lenore Alt had had a similar childhood to Erickson's. She was born in Cadillac, Michigan, a small town in the inland Lower Peninsula of Michigan, where her father operated a planing mill making use of the local forests. Both of her parents had emigrated from Germany. Her father, William Alt, with his mother and two sisters—ten other children had died in infancy—had been abandoned by his father. William was brought up (in Germany) by an uncle and made to learn shoemaking, which he hated; at seventeen, told by his absent father that things were rosy in the United States, he scraped together the money to leave his uncle—only to find, on reaching America, that his father had lied to him and had already started a second family here, and that the youth would be on his own.

At the age of nine, also because of family dissension and instability, Lenore's mother, Louise, had come to the United States with her mother, a member of a reasonably prosperous farming family. Louise was a craftswoman of considerable skill, always with a piece of yarn or crochet cotton in her apron pocket, always working. "When I began to feel better after childhood illnesses she'd put a particular quilt on my bed. I'd ask whose material this piece or that was, and she'd say this aunt, that cousin...." There was lace work, too, a skill brought over from the old country.

At high school in Cadillac, Lenore had found a teacher in manual training and art who had an eye for people with promise. Lenore "hung around the art department all the time" and spent weekends with four or five friends sketching. After her first year of high school she went to the Chicago Art Institute's summer session with her teacher, taking courses alongside her for the next few summers. On graduating from high school Lenore enrolled at Washington University in Saint Louis, where her older brother, a chemist, was living. Soon, though, dissatisfied with this dislocation, she returned to the Art Institute.

By 1938 she was participating in the Federal Arts Project, painting murals, and living at Park House. When she met Erickson they were both studying ceramics with Eugene Deutsch, well known in Chicago. She was working on a series of pottery mugs of slightly differing sizes and was interested in the sounds they made when struck. The sounds also fascinated Erickson, who used them as the featured percussion instruments in the music he provided for the Park House dance concert.

After their marriage, in November, Lenore hyphenated her maiden name with Erickson's: Lenore Alt-Erickson. "Father said, 'Don't lose your name': I had already exhibited" under it. The Ericksons continued collaborating for the next thirty years, as Lenore exhibited and taught in Michigan, Minnesota, and the San Francisco Bay Area, ending her teaching career only when they settled in San Diego in 1967.

Erickson's strongest musical impressions at Park House came through the opinions of Frank Kearney, "a small, vivacious man, badly crippled by child-hood polio ... , by turns charming, nasty, tender, and occasionally bitter." Kearney, a musical snob, admired a restricted repertoire, mostly Beethoven: the Third, Fifth, Seventh, and Ninth Symphonies; the late quartets, piano sonatas, and piano concertos; the violin concerto, "Archduke" Trio and "Kreutzer" Sonata. Schubert's posthumous B-flat Sonata and C Major Quintet were allowed, as well as Wagner's *Tristan and Isolde* (but not the *Ring*) and much Brahms, but no Schumann, Chopin, Liszt, Italians, or pre-Shostakovich Russians.

In short, Kearney had the taste of a typical musical intellectual of the time. It inclined to the German, though it admitted Bartók quartets. It approved Berg and Schoenberg (though *Gurrelieder* was the only Schoenberg yet readily available on recordings) and excluded Debussy, Ravel, Mahler, Stravinsky, and Sibelius. In spite of this rather narrow field of enthusiasms, Kearney's approach to music impressed Erickson:

He went straight to the heart of the music—its heart to his heart—and he knew when a connection had been made. Most people don't. Many listen for pleasure, very often a vague, diffuse, barely musical pleasure, making small demand on the attention. Frank ... listened to the whole, the parts, the phrases and the nuances. He followed the music, caught up with it, grasped its sense, and experienced it.

Two other musical friendships Erickson made at Park House would provide more professional stimulation: the composers Ben Weber and George Perle. They were studying counterpoint and composition with Wesley La Violette, then a professor at DePaul University; the three may have met at a Friday-night talk given by La Violette at Park House. All three—Erickson, Weber, and Perle—were fascinated by the music and ideas of Schoenberg and Berg. Weber, a year older than Erickson and like him largely self-taught, was already composing with the "twelve-tone technique"; Erickson and Perle, who was two years older, were soon to follow. (Perle went on to become one of America's preëminent theorists of the technique, which Schoenberg had elaborated twenty years earlier as a refinement of "atonal" music, music avoiding conventional harmony resting on keynotes. The technique amounts to a guaranteed equal distribution, throughout a piece of music, of all twelve pitches in the octave, taking chromatic music to its extreme.)

Encouraged by his two new friends, Erickson soon began studying with La Violette, who put him to work writing "Bach style inventions, canons and fugues." But there were no textbooks or introductions to the twelve-tone technique, only a few editions of the mysterious music itself—and those scores were not readily available.

By now employed by a music company, Erickson was able to obtain some scores of music by Schoenberg, Berg, and Anton Webern from Europe. Some of this music—Schoenberg's piano piece op. 33a, for example—resisted his every effort at understanding. Other pieces, studied for hours almost as if they were ciphers, gradually worked their way into his comprehension. It was the familiar process of the time: inherently coherent, complex cultural documents, the products of methodically developed European modernism, slowly revealing themselves to the intelligent and open-minded but isolated American temperament.

Erickson and his friends soon had an opportunity to hear an important twelve-tone work in concert: the American (though Russian-born) violinist Louis Krasner was to play Berg's Violin Concerto in Chicago in 1938. (Krasner had commissioned the work four years earlier, in 1934, and had premiered it in Barcelona in 1936.) The score had just been published, and Erickson immediately ordered it. He studied it, along with Perle, Weber, and a fourth friend, the violinist Irving Ilmer, who played the solo part, Perle and Weber taking turns playing the orchestral accompaniment on the piano. Perle plunged into the analysis of the music: he was later to become the leading authority on Berg's music. (Similarly, Ilmer was later a member of the prominent LaSalle String Quartet, which made a specialty of the quartets of Schoenberg, Berg, and Webern.)

The four friends attended every performance of the concerto by Krasner and the Chicago Symphony (led not by music director Frederick Stock but by his assistant Hans Lange). The orchestral musicians expressed a customary contempt for a "difficult" new score: one cellist later claimed he played "The Star-Spangled Banner" through all the orchestral climaxes, and that it had made no difference. But Erickson was struck by "the whole magnificent sound of the piece, the liquid woodwind passages, the transparent brass writing, the tuba(!), and that marvelous passage where the orchestra violins, like a spreading sunrise, gradually join the soloist."

The adjectives "liquid" and "transparent" suggest that Erickson took in all these details as physical *sound*, not as intellectual concepts or compositional techniques. His small-town- and country-trained observation, and his love of sound, were at the center of this response. Years later Erickson retained his admiration for Berg, considering Berg's drama and color more immediately congenial to American audiences than the structural complexity of Schoenberg and Webern, and Berg's rhythmic and thematic play as related to jazz. The influence of Berg on Erickson probably reached its peak in the *Chamber Concerto* of 1960 and the *Concerto for Piano and Seven Instruments* of 1963.

The intellectual component of this twelve-tone music was slower to penetrate Erickson's consciousness. Berg's *Lyric Suite* for string quartet, completed in 1926, was the only advanced work by any of the Schoenberg circle then available on records, in a performance by the original Galimir Quartet. Kearney took Erickson to visit two young men who had a large record collection, and at their house, late one evening, after he had had to listen to a great deal of Delius, the *Lyric Suite* made its first impression on him. It made no sense to Erickson at the time, but Kearney bought the records, played them over and over, and made Erickson listen again. "Somewhere around the tenth hearing my light went on. I soon had a copy of the score marked up like a highway map, trying to trace the tone rows."

(Like his Violin Concerto, Berg's *Lyric Suite* alternates between twelve-tone and more conventional styles, taking advantage of musical procedures of themes and developments, instrumental colors and sonorities to "narrate" quite detailed dramas. Berg had specified the "meaning" of the Concerto, a portrait of and requiem for Manon Gropius, the daughter of Alma Mahler and Walter Gropius, who had died at the age of eighteen. But it would be decades before Perle would discover the "secret program" of the *Lyric Suite*, an impassioned love letter from Berg to the wife of a Czech industrialist. These scores do in fact suggest ciphers: Erickson was right to sense their "highways," which ultimately involve more than tone rows.)

In addition to the music of Berg, Erickson and Perle managed to hear some of their own music for string quartet through the efforts of Irving Ilmer and the cellist Seymour Barab. And, with Ben Weber, they also produced a concert series called the New Music Group of Chicago. They intended to present all of Schoenberg's quartets, on programs also including the late Beethoven quartets, but they actually achieved only one concert: a pairing of Schoenberg's String Quartet no. 1 with Beethoven's F Major Quartet, op. 135.

In 1938, too, Erickson, Perle, and Weber attended a lecture at the School of Design, recently opened in Chicago by the emigré artist and educator Laszlo Moholy-Nagy, a Hungarian refugee who had been at the celebrated Bauhaus in Weimar before settling in Berlin. The lecturer was the Austrian composer Ernst Krenek, like Berg and Webern a native of Vienna. Krenek was noted, even notorious, throughout German-speaking Europe, for his music, including the "jazz opera" *Jonny spielt auf* (Johnny Plays On), which had had a considerable vogue in the late 1920s, and for his hundreds of reviews and essays in the cultural press of Germany and Austria. His commitments were outspoken: to progressive music, to conservative liberal politics, and to the ironic and skeptical manner of his literary hero, the intellectualist-journalist Karl Kraus.

Krenek was a prolific composer who had worked through a number of styles. His first music, written in his early twenties, was expressionistic and clangorous, in a post-Mahler vein; subsequently, influenced by Darius Milhaud, he returned to more conventional tonal harmony in order to assimilate popular music (what Europe thought of as "jazz"). His passionate Austrian patriotism had led him to study and defend the music of Franz Schubert, which was still, in 1928, being attacked as incompetent by academic musicologists in Vienna, and for the next four years Krenek composed in a sort of updated Schubertian romanticism. But by 1932 he had abandoned this tonal-romantic approach to composition, taking up instead the twelve-tone technique.

Krenek had just arrived in the United States, a refugee from the Nazis, and was making a lecture tour while waiting for the fall semester to begin at Vassar College, where he had found a teaching position. Erickson was impressed by Krenek's urbane, sometimes ironic, articulate lecture on atonal and twelve-tone music, and by his performance (on an unsatisfactory piano) of his *Twelve Short Piano Pieces*, which the Erickson circle had carefully studied before the lecture.

In 1939 Krenek published *Music Here and Now*, a layman's guide to "music of lasting importance" (meaning, always, "progressive" music) and an attempt to overcome the "inertia which increasingly affected the mentality of the middle classes" in the musical developments of the nineteenth century. Erickson wrote him enthusiastically and at length about the book and quickly received a reply: Krenek was an indefatigable letter-writer. Before long Erickson was sending his music to Krenek for criticism, and seeking advice concerning a scheme Erickson was developing for a record society devoted to new music. This led to another concert project, an all-Krenek concert on which the Austrian composer played his *Two Suites*, op. 26, and *Twelve Variations in Three Movements*, op. 79, for piano. Erickson produced the concert on his monthly salary of $75 from the Gamble Hinged Music Company, with the help of friends who designed the program and sold tickets. The recital hall was filled, and a large group remained to discuss the music into the night.

The Krenek-Erickson correspondence continued, setting an informal but particularly helpful style Erickson would later follow in corresponding with his own students. In the summer of the following year, 1940, Erickson spent his two-week vacation studying at the University of Michigan, where Krenek taught a summer session. During these daily composition lessons Krenek discussed Erickson's music, commented on the favorable passages, occasionally pointed out something interesting in other music he happened to be analyzing (or, when asked, in his own), and never assigned tasks.

In these matters and many others Krenek was to serve the young Erickson as a model. As a teacher Erickson was remarkably indulgent, letting students find their own voices, preferring to bring interesting new music to their attention rather than focus on specific flaws of their own, and sharing his enthusiasms as a fellow student rather than imposing them as a master. Erickson continued his own correspondence with Krenek for decades (Krenek died at ninety-one on Dec. 22, 1991), and encouraged similar correspondences from his own students.

The Nazi conquest of France during those weeks was a recurring topic of conversation between the two men. So were Krenek's operas, anti-Fascist in tone, and so was the music of Schoenberg, Berg, and Webern, which had been banned in Austria and Germany. Krenek had known Berg, who had died in 1935, and had been close to Webern, then still living in Austria, his music all but unknown, where he would be killed by an American GI in the nervous weeks following the European armistice. (Schoenberg, who had maintained characteristic aloofness from Krenek, had emigrated to the United States in 1933, settling in Boston for a year, then moving on to Hollywood; he died in Los Angeles in 1951, having taught for a year at the University of Southern California and then for eight years at the University of California at Los Angeles.)

In 1940 the Ericksons lived in a fourth-floor apartment on Fullerton Avenue in Chicago. A German refugee dentist across the hall introduced Erickson to a violinist friend of his, Francis Aranyi, who taught at Michigan State University in Ypsilanti, near Detroit, and, part-time, at the Chicago

Conservatory. Aranyi invited Erickson to accompany him to Michigan State later in 1940 to hear a lecture by Arnold Schoenberg. On the drive to Ypsilanti—140 miles across southern Michigan and hair-raising, "allegro molto all the way," Erickson recalls—Aranyi recounted a number of Schoenberg stories: he had been concertmaster of the orchestra at the premiere of *Gurrelieder*, and had witnessed an argument between Schoenberg and the first horn player that almost came to blows.

At Ypsilanti Erickson checked in at the YMCA, then went to the crowded lecture hall to hear Schoenberg speak on "Brahms, the Progressive." Between Schoenberg's quiet voice and his thick accent very little was comprehensible, except for the musical illustrations. Afterward, though, at a reception, Erickson talked to Schoenberg for a few minutes, first asking about tempi in the First Quartet (then being prepared for the New Music Group concert), then asking Schoenberg whether he might look over Erickson's own music the next day.

On the following day Erickson spent an hour with Schoenberg, showing him a little suite of three movements, hardly more than three or four minutes long. Schoenberg silently turned the pages back and forth. It was quiet: Erickson heard robins on the lawn outside.

> *I wondered what he was looking for—the pieces weren't that difficult. Perhaps he was looking for rows, or more likely some sort of musical sense. For tone rows he would have had to search all day. Those pieces were, as I remember, violently atonal, athematic and without much rhythmic profile. I was a long way from thinking about organization. Anyway, like any beginner I wanted to know only if he liked them, if he thought there was any hope, if he thought I should give it all up or continue. Big questions, to be settled by no more than a hundred little black notes. Not much evidence on which to pronounce. There must have been some sort of communication because I left the meeting encouraged, buoyant....*

The War Years, 1940–1946

After the summer of 1940 the Ericksons packed up and left Chicago. War was on the horizon; the country was only slowly pulling out of the darkest days of the Depression. Money was short and employment was scarce, but idealism— of a sort that now seems naïve or romantic—was still possible. The Ericksons headed for Saugatuck, on the east shore of Lake Michigan at the mouth of the Kalamazoo River, about halfway between Chicago and Lenore's home town, Cadillac. Today Saugatuck is a popular and fairly expensive resort community, but during the Depression it was a fishing village and the port serving the local fruit orchards. As the economy worsened it had also developed into an artists' colony.

There, inspired by a recently published book praising the pleasures of subsistence farming and private enterprise,[1] the couple planned to support themselves making pottery. Erickson's lessons had taken well; his wife recalls him as having been a good man at the wheel. They settled in Douglas, a town of fewer than three hundred people across a small lake from Saugatuck. The town's peach-basket factory had burned to the ground in 1927, and over a decade later the village was still full of empty houses. The couple rented a coach house from a suave, friendly, boozy entrepreneur who had prospered in the tax-counseling business during the Depression. Lenore landed a job making ice-cream sodas and selling magazines in the country store, earning ten cents an hour, and Erickson wrote music.

A few months later they moved into a house at an old peach-boat landing a few blocks downhill on Lake Saugatuck, a house with a garage big enough for a proper ceramics studio. The days were placid. Abandoned farms yielded fruit, wild grapes and blackberries were plentiful, wild watercress and dock furnished salads. The beach supplied pebbles and driftwood, constant visual stimulation to a potter; and the sounds of lake and meadow recalled Erickson's childhood, returning his developing musical ideas to a real-life context.

At first the sojourn may have seemed idyllic, though hard: traveling by bicycle, the couple dug their own clay from roadside deposits. They built a wood-fired kiln with the help of Mike and Helen Czaja, a couple they had met and befriended at Park House. Czaja combined a builder's approach with an artist's in a manner that appealed to Erickson. (While observing and helping Czaja rebuild a house ten years later, in California, Erickson further developed the "hands-on" attitude that would contribute greatly to his musical experimentation for the rest of his career.) The days were spent in building, revising, and rebuilding; only in the evening was the day's work reduced to plans and drawings. "There is nothing wrong with plans: they are wonderful, in their place; and that place is after the construction has been done."

It *was* in many ways an idyllic interlude. Erickson's inbred love for tinkering and speculation had found its ideal place. When their sources of cheap firewood ran out, he adapted the kiln to fuel oil. There was the thrill of digging their own clay, firing it in their own kiln, transforming it into finished pots. They made lots of pots, but not much money. Production was understandably limited and glazes were hard to get. People seemed to want cheap, mass-produced souvenirs. There was little interest in their more artistic work, even in Chicago, where they traveled with their pots, transporting them eighty miles or so, with some difficulty, on the Greyhound bus. Erickson ultimately wound up working in an electroplating factory, putting copper and chromium on plumbing fixtures for forty-five cents an hour. Teaching looked like a better solution to the problem of earning a living.

By the fall of 1942 they gave up this artist-craftsman life and moved to St. Paul, Minnesota, working at the YMCA—Erickson as a coat-room attendant, Lenore at the soda counter. The move was inspired by Ernst Krenek, who had just joined the music faculty at Hamline University, a small Methodist liberal-arts college occupying shabby quarters in a nineteenth-century residential neighborhood a mile or so west of the state capitol in St. Paul. Krenek had arranged a scholarship there for Erickson. The school was then less grand than its name implied: a "somnolent collection of ancient, decaying buildings, surrounded by high untended grass … [whose] ambience of poverty and neglect extended throughout the four-block-square campus, and the interiors of the buildings.… "

Krenek taught harmony, counterpoint, music history, composition, and piano in a tiny classroom in the men's dormitory, which apparently also functioned as housing for married students: its hallway was obstructed by children's outdoor toys, and its atmosphere was permeated with the odors of cooking. In this classroom Erickson met significant future friends and colleagues: Glenn Glasow and Wilbur Ogdon—composers who, like Erickson, would travel to California, serve their turns as music director at the Berkeley radio station, KPFA, and then turn to academic careers—and Tom Nee, the conductor who would champion Erickson's music throughout his own career and ultimately join him on the San Diego faculty.

At first Krenek gave private composition lessons to individual students, developing graduate composition seminars only later, when Hamline added its graduate department. Krenek's undergraduate classes were in music history. They were particularly stimulating and focused sessions, often concentrating on the teacher's own enthusiasm: the complex but sensuous polyphonic music of Josquin des Prés, Johannes Ockeghem, and Jacob Obrecht. The music of these Renaissance composers, still largely unknown to concert audiences, appealed to many instincts of modernist composers. It is intellectually complex, highly personal in its expression, and powerfully direct, and it relies on melodic contour and rhythm, rather than orchestral color and force, for its effect.

Krenek's classes studied more conventional concert fare, too, and gave particular attention to opera, from Monteverdi to the twentieth century. Like the Renaissance music—this was before the rise of historical performance practice—the operatic literature was read through at the piano, Krenek at the keyboard and singing all the roles, traversing even Wagner's entire *Ring* cycle. Krenek was devoted to stage music: he was to compose twenty operas in the course of his long life. Unfortunately, the opera medium never attracted Erickson: he always composed for specific performances, and opera producers in the United States were notoriously negligent toward contemporary (and especially native) composers for many years.

Krenek's was not the only enthusiasm for new music at Hamline University. There was a fine chorus led by Robert Holliday, who developed its expertise in contemporary repertoire, over the years performing most of Krenek's considerable output for unaccompanied chorus. This reverberated with the music of Erickson's childhood, much of which was sung by community choirs and choruses; and it encouraged his experimentation with choral composition. In fact, his earliest extant compositions date from his Hamline days, and are written for chorus.

Holliday and Krenek also worked with Dmitri Mitropoulos, the music director of the Minneapolis Symphony Orchestra from 1937 to 1949. Prosperous and industrious Minneapolis, across the Mississippi River, was a more progressive city than St. Paul, the state capital; and Mitropoulos's progressive tastes in music managed to find some support there (though there would always be problems with the conservatives). Mitropoulos lent his authority to Krenek's case for new music at Hamline. The conductor introduced Krenek to St. Paul in a lecture-recital at the St. Paul Gallery and School of Art, for example, where Krenek played recordings of music by the fourteenth-century French composer Guillaume de Machaut to prove that dissonance was not a newfangled invention. Mitropoulos and Krenek performed together in Stravinsky's *Concerto for Two Solo Pianos*. And when Krenek accompanied Hamline students Shirley Hammergren and June Peterson in songs by Berg and Schoenberg, Mitropoulos was in the audience. Later, he hired Hammergren to sing the "Lied der Lulu" when he scheduled the excerpts from Berg's opera with the Minneapolis Symphony.

In September 1943, seven months past his twenty-sixth birthday, Erickson was drafted into the army. For most of his service he was stationed at Fort Snelling, just five miles south of the Hamline campus, so his participation in St. Paul musical life was little interrupted. Before reporting to basic training he was assigned to the band, which needed a recruit to carry its brand-new bell lyre, a sort of portable glockenspiel. Since he was able not only to carry it but actually to play it, adapting piccolo parts at sight, Erickson became a member of the band.

This band was not an officially recognized military unit, so he was assigned to personnel as a sort of cover. Here he interviewed recruits, transferring their personal histories to the forms that were to follow them through their army careers. Erickson found this work an engaging and interesting respite from his somewhat frustrating band activities, which left some musical accomplishment to be desired: the conductor was competent in marches, less successful with overtures and dance-medleys. When Erickson ultimately did report to basic training, at Camp Dodge, Iowa, he drew, because of his nearsightedness, the relatively light version tailored to limited-service recruits. Returned to Fort Snelling, he continued to live off base with Lenore, near the cathedral in St. Paul, commuting to the army by streetcar.

This pleasant life ended in June 1944 when he was sent to Camp Claiborne, Louisiana, for a second round of basic training. The camp was intended to turn out specialists in heavy construction, mechanics, demolition, and diving but was filling up with a disproportionate number of malingerers, complainers, college students, and intellectuals. Erickson's skills with personnel forms were badly needed. With Aaron Dorsky, a New Yorker who became a very close friend, Erickson studied the camp personnel-assignment systems:

> *Largely through Aaron I developed an interest in organizations: how they really worked as against how they were supposed to work, what sorts were bound to fail, where the failures occurred, the nature of those informal networks of human beings who could occasionally make things go smoothly for a time.*

Among their other duties, Dorsky and Erickson were to assign soldiers to various schools, some of which sounded interesting. Dorsky conceived the plan of their assigning themselves to Adjutant General School, near San Antonio, Texas, and they drove there in November, meeting their wives (and Dorsky's son Nick) en route at Port Arthur, on the Gulf coast. They spent Thanksgiving, Christmas, and New Year's Eve in a motel in San Antonio, where Lenore, ever resourceful, had found a job at an army air field. Erickson studied for officer's school by day, marched in parades, admired the elegant bearing of the commanding officer, and learned to type. He spent his spare time discussing cultural philosophy with Dorsky: C. K. Ogden's *The Meaning of Meaning* was a favorite topic.

After the six weeks they returned to Camp Claiborne, where they were directed to take furloughs, get shots, and prepare for overseas duty. But by early 1945 the war was slowly winding down, and Erickson was sent back to Fort Snelling, now being converted to a separation center. He was assigned to a personnel officer, an easy assignment leaving plenty of time for composing, and he remained until his discharge in March 1946, when he was just over twenty-nine years old.

He would not realize it until five years later or so, but his army career, apparently dull and bureaucratic, had taught him how to take advantage of postwar American society, supporting himself and his wife while still leaving time for study, research, and composition. And the absurdity of much of his wartime experience was not lost on him, or on his music.

There is always a danger that progressive serious music might become excessively dry or academic, particularly as it is pursued in the classroom. Erickson's music, though, took on a playful quality in this period, an irony softening its technical experimentation. During his last year at Fort Snelling he composed his first major work, *The 1945 Variations*, a set of three pieces for solo piano. In the first, marked simply "Fast," the left hand follows a measure behind the right, turning its note-patterns upside-down in the technique called inversion—aptly taking advantage of the mirror relationship of the two hands. The third piece, composed first, is headed "Fast Boogie-Woogie," and incorporates the sardonic interpolation of the first two words of the "Miserere"—"have pity on us"—sung by a carefully concealed baritone in a parody of Gregorian chant. Only the central movement, finished last, on January 17, 1946, is in fact a normal set of variations.

The title, playful and allusive as would be typical of the composer's titles later, may refer to the diverse influences and experiences he had encountered during the previous five years—idealistic craftsman, attentive student, bored clerk, ingenious improvisor of his own opportunities.

Compositions, 1940–1946:

1940	*Three Rilke Songs* for soprano and piano
1943	Motet, *Song of Songs* for unaccompanied chorus
1944	*Two Christmas Choruses* for unaccompanied chorus
	The Star Song for women's chorus (SSA)
1945	*Be Still My Soul* for unaccompanied chorus
	Three Contralto Songs for contralto and piano
1945–46	*The 1945 Variations* for solo piano (and offstage baritone)
1946	*Five Job Choruses* for unaccompanied chorus

---

1. M. G. Kains: *Five Acres and Independence* (New York: Greenberg Publishers, 1935). The book went through many printings in the following ten years.

Interlude, 1946–1953

Erickson immediately returned to student life at Hamline, continuing his studies with Krenek, whose influence continued to be strong. Krenek was a prolific composer, a serious scholar of music, and a constant proselytizer for music in general and contemporary music in particular. All three roles appealed to Erickson, who had already developed similar enthusiasms. By 1948 he had published an article, "Krenek's Later Music," in the British periodical *The Music Review*. He was enthusiastic about the complexity of Krenek's music, its intellectual component—but also impressed by its immediacy and expressive quality. During the war Erickson had found two performances especially powerful: Krenek's collaboration with Mitropoulos, as producer and artistic director, on Stravinsky's *A Soldier's Tale*, and Krenek's own *Cantata for War Time*, which Mitropoulos performed with the Minneapolis Symphony and the Hamline University Women's Choir.

Though immensely sophisticated and intellectually motivated, Krenek was fond of turning to unlikely but everyday sources of inspiration. Since childhood he had been fascinated by trains and the American Southwest, and in 1947 the Hamline chamber chorus presented his *Santa Fe Timetable*, whose libretto simply recites the place-names and scheduled times of the Santa Fe timetable between Albuquerque and Los Angeles. It was an exciting piece and a popular success, and must have made a considerable contrast with another work on the program, Erik Satie's quietly moving cantata *Socrate*, a setting of Plato's account of the death of the Greek philosopher, with Krenek accompanying the soprano Shirley Hammergren.

The farewell of Socrates and the train to California may have been anticipatory. Krenek, who had become a naturalized American citizen in 1945, was Dean of Fine Arts at Hamline, but was not making much money. Furthermore, he loathed the Minnesota climate. The American composer George Antheil encouraged Krenek to try his luck in Los Angeles. (Antheil, like Krenek, had achieved considerable notoriety in the 1920s only to fall out of fashion within the music establishment. Unlike Krenek, however, Antheil had prospered in Hollywood by writing film scores.)

And Krenek's second marriage was in trouble. His first had been bad enough: at twenty-two he had fallen in love with Anna Mahler, the vivacious, seventeen-year-old daughter of Gustav Mahler, although she was already married to a rich, older (and considerably less fascinating) German industrialist. Krenek finally married Anna in 1924, but that marriage lasted hardly a year, and in 1928 he married the German actress Berta Haas, fifteen years older than he. Now, nearly twenty years later, at forty-seven, Krenek had fallen in love with a young, gifted, vivacious Hamline student, Gladys Nordenstrom.

Torn by a number of conflicting demands—romantic, domestic, artistic, and professional—Krenek asked for a leave of absence from Hamline's fall 1947 semester in order to complete his Fourth Symphony, which Mitropoulos premiered that November with the New York Philharmonic. He had secured a summertime lectureship at the University of New Mexico in his beloved Southwest. And in June of 1947, quite precipitously, he completely cleaned out his desk, even to the badminton shuttlecocks he kept in one drawer.

Erickson was severely affected by Krenek's departure: he had composed a symphony as his master's degree thesis, and Mitropoulos had intended to program it. Knowing that his board of directors, scandalized by Krenek's departure, would refuse permission to program a work by his student, Mitropoulos canceled the piece. (Later, however, he performed Erickson's first mature orchestral piece, *Introduction and Allegro for Orchestra*.) Krenek's students had further reason to be dismayed and bewildered by his defection, not formally announced by the college administration until December, when Krenek formally resigned his position. Many had only partly completed their own graduate work under him and were unsure of obtaining further courses needed for their degrees. Erickson, however, had already taken his own master's degree and had himself begun teaching, at St. Catherine's College in St. Paul, where he continued on the faculty until 1953.

At St. Catherine's Erickson learned to teach. He soon realized that more is involved than transferring information from teacher to student. The essentially social, even conversational habits that Erickson had developed, from childhood games to the late-night discussions at Park House to the seminars with Krenek and his fellow students at Hamline, had begun to consolidate into a mature concept of thinking and talking about music. Musical understanding, he realized, is nonverbal, and no two people understand a piece of music in the same way. Certain basic musical processes could be described simply, and Erickson was already working out methods of explaining them to the average nonspecialist student. Krenek's book, *Music Here and Now*, had undoubtedly served as a model, though Erickson was soon to find simpler, more direct ways of explaining the rudiments of music in his own first book, *The Structure of Music*.

But if the basic procedures of music are relatively fixed, the individuality of personal responses to music, which are the real substance of music as it is perceived, is mercurial and kaleidoscopic. Yet, as Erickson had found in his discussions over the years at Park House, in the army, and at Hamline, the individualities of each listener's musical experiences can be retained while they are exchanged in discussion.

In the process, the music itself can be illuminated. Erickson found that it was not a question of explaining the music, or revealing what it means, but of exploring its own processes as they are heard by each listener, as listeners bring their own intelligence and experience to the music. This was no more than what he, Ben Weber, and George Perle had brought to their gradual understanding of Alban Berg in their excited discussions in Chicago ten years earlier; but it is not every teacher—certainly *was* not, in the 1940s—who takes such a collaborative approach to discussions with students. This approach would pay dividends ten years later in Erickson's composition seminars at the San Francisco Conservatory of Music, when teacher and students worked and learned together, sharing enthusiasms, pooling ideas, mutually developing imaginative new solutions to problems as they occurred—theoretical problems in composition seminars, practical problems in the workshop and studio. And ten years later yet, this essentially egalitarian concept of teaching would result in the establishment of a new, innovative music department at the University of California at San Diego.

In 1948, though, the Ericksons were content with the security offered by their first postwar full-time employment. With his teaching assignment safely in hand, they now found the summers free for travel. They spent the summer of 1948 camping. They loaded Erickson's portable harmonium and Lenore's painting supplies, along with camping supplies, into a yellow Jeep station wagon that had been fitted out as a homemade mobile home, and they drifted west, through South Dakota's Badlands (rain-drenched that summer), through Yellowstone Park, south through the Grand Tetons to Salt Lake City to revisit old Park House friends, and into Nevada. Painter and composer found new inspiration in nature: the dampened colors of the Badlands, bubbling mud-pools and geysers, the grandeur of the Sierra Nevada peaks—the "Range of Light."

Helen and Mike Czaja awaited the Ericksons a few miles south of San Francisco, in Redwood City. While visiting them, Lenore arranged shows of her paintings at Stanford University and in Santa Barbara, but Erickson made no efforts to see musicians on the trip. Two years later, however, in the summer of 1950, they spent the entire vacation in the vicinity of San Francisco, where Erickson met a number of musicians in the composition seminar he took with Roger Sessions at the University of California at Berkeley. (Sessions was to spend the 1951–52 year on sabbatical leave and tried, unsuccessfully, to get Krenek hired as his replacement.) Erickson considered staying on at Berkeley to work toward a further degree, but couldn't bring himself to spare the time from composing, and returned for another year's teaching at St. Catherine's in St. Paul. One's time could be divided two ways, but not three; and it was necessary to work for a living in order either to study or to compose.

Composing wasn't easy. Apart from *The 1945 Variations* for piano, until now his only successful compositions—those he would retain in his mature catalogue—had been two sets of songs with piano accompaniment and six pieces for chorus, the latter written for the Hamline chorus. On finishing graduate school and beginning teaching at St. Catherine's, Erickson undertook his first really ambitious works: his first orchestra piece, *Introduction and Allegro*; a full-scale piano sonata; and a string quartet—the first and, with two exceptions soon to come, the last pieces he would complete in the historically conventional forms. These compositions cost Erickson considerable thought and labor, and their completion left him both tired and a bit unsure of the next step. This exhausting rhythm—periods of intense mental activity alternating with discouraging stretches of comparative idleness—would characterize much of his creative life.

Erickson had had plenty of opportunities to hear his own music. Mitropoulos led the Minneapolis Symphony Orchestra in *Introduction and Allegro for Orchestra* in March, 1949. The Piano Sonata was played by five different pianists, in Minnesota, Texas, and New York, by 1951. The String Quartet was given in 1951 in St. Paul, to good reviews. Still, there was more to learn, and in the summer of 1951 Erickson enrolled in another summer institute, this time in Colorado Springs, where he began, but soon dropped, a composition course—the teacher being what Erickson called a "Hindemith boy with righteous ideas," hardly Erickson's ideal of an inspiring, supportive guide to enterprising composition. He completed a course on the teaching of musical theory with the same instructor, whose example taught him what not to do, and he studied conducting as well. He was working at the time on a chamber symphony, but the problems it posed did not find ready solutions. He visited Krenek in Albuquerque earlier in the summer and showed him the first movement, completed in a piano version (the orchestration not yet begun); Krenek was impressed, apparently finding no trace of the drift toward "classicism" he had noted in earlier projects of Erickson's. The second movement and finale, however, resisted Erickson, who wrote to his friend Wilbur Ogdon that the "[m]ain trouble is that the lines are so long and looping.... So far I like it but it is incredibly difficult to write."[1]

The "lines" were the bones of this chamber symphony, which was planned to fall into sections set off by successive entries of recognizable melodies. This kind of organization was, to "progressive" composers of the first half of the twentieth century, the favored solution to the problem of organizing big musical structures without resorting to conventional chord-expressed harmony, which was considered the bankrupt solution of the preceding century.

Such contrapuntal organization was not new: Mozart found a particularly brilliant example for the finale of his "Jupiter" Symphony. (Of course that finale rests equally on a harmonic organization.) Schoenberg's method of "composing with the twelve tones related only to one another," as he referred to what would become better known as the twelve-tone technique, was the most influential twentieth-century approach to the idea, and Krenek was a master of it, having published his own textbook on the subject in 1940. Krenek, like his friend Webern, looked to such Renaissance masters as Heinrich Isaac, Ockeghem, and Giovanni Palestrina as pioneering predecessors in the art of contrapuntal organization, and Erickson had studied their scores eagerly as they arrived in microfilm to join the library Krenek was greatly expanding at Hamline.

By 1951, for his own further clarification as well as for use by his students, Erickson was contemplating his own textbook on the subject. Having codified his approach to explaining the basic principles of music to his students, and impressed with Krenek's example, Erickson had begun the full-length manuscript of *The Structure of Music: A Listener's Guide*. Again like Krenek, Erickson was idealistically hoping to popularize his enthusiasm for the progressive music of his own time. He was also aware of commercial possibilities (as well as the enhancement of his academic reputation). Characteristically, *The Structure of Music* would not analyze the music of past masters for their own further explanation: it would survey the subject for its possible use in mid-century America. He described the project in a letter to Ogdon:

> Instead of teaching in either Bach style or Palestrina style, I propose to teach the contrapuntal techniques ... across the styles.... I shall use illustrations from classic and romantic times, but the thing will not be rooted there. Student will write in the style which is most appealing to her—or several styles if she wishes. Basic idea is that the bright students will write in contemporary idioms, and book will constantly show affinities between contemporary and older practices. [Letter to Wilbur Ogdon of September 1, 1951, *Erickson Celebration*, p. 49.]

To gain a year's respite from teaching to work on the book, Erickson applied for a Ford Foundation fellowship, and while studying that summer in Colorado he received word that he had won it. That September the Ericksons paid their first visit to New York City, driving by way of Michigan's Upper Peninsula to visit his parents. The Ericksons settled on Third Street in a quiet working-class East Side neighborhood, and Lenore, who had found room for a studio, eagerly resumed painting. Erickson found his manuscript stubborn at first, its organization and expression giving him considerable trouble. His Camp Claiborne army friend, Aaron Dorsky, lived nearby, and they had many discussions about the problem. Dorsky, who characteristically suspected psychological causes for all such difficulties, recommended a psychiatrist friend of his who listened sympathetically, administered a test or two, and concluded that Erickson would probably get over his New York anxiety soon enough.

This proved true: Erickson's mental and emotional stability, in spite of his tiring creative rhythm, were rarely a matter for concern. His childhood upbringing, like his experiences during the Depression and in the army, had encouraged him to find straightforward solutions to the practical problems of everyday life. His wide-ranging reading had acquainted him with deep and complex issues in philosophy and psychology, but the Ericksons had never developed a taste for cultivating abstruse or complex emotional and psychological problems of their own—perhaps simply because such immediate issues as making a living and finding new households left little time and energy for such luxuries.

In spite of his own psychological complexity, however, Dorsky remained a close and lifelong friend. The two had little opportunity for conversation after leaving Camp Claiborne, but their companionship had never depended on verbal communication. It had the depth unique to substantially divergent but mutually reinforcing outlooks on closely held common interests and values. From Erickson's perspective the friendship had deepened and advanced through his introducing Dorsky to Zen Buddhist concepts, which did much to alleviate Dorsky's own postwar anxieties. Dorsky's premature death, of diabetes, in 1965, was to affect Erickson deeply; their friendship, and Dorsky's complexities, had perhaps provided a surrogate family for the childless and parentless Ericksons. Dorsky's son Nick, who had been a toddler at Camp Claiborne, was later to join the Ericksons in Berkeley.

Compositions, 1947–1952:

1948   *Introduction and Allegro for Orchestra*
        Piano Sonata
1950   String Quartet No. 1

---

1.   Letter of September 2, 1951, to Wilbur Ogdon, reproduced in *Erickson Celebration* (San Diego: Univ. of California, 1987, program booklet), p. 48.

San Francisco: KPFA, 1953–1956

The New York stay was successful: Erickson finished *The Structure of Music*, Lenore's painting evolved considerably, social life was rewarding, and there were many concerts to hear and musical contacts to make. Memories of the camaraderie of Park House were probably revived by the Erickson's idyllic but productive residence at the Yaddo artists' colony in upstate Saratoga Springs in the summer of 1952, where *The Structure of Music* was completed. There, too, he worked on a new composition that turned out to mark a turn away from counterpoint, toward more conventional tonal harmony. (Perhaps this was the "classicism" whose advent had concerned Krenek.)

But the Ericksons were confirmed in their preference for California. They returned to St. Paul for a final academic year at St. Catherine's, where a burst of creative confidence gave them the assurance needed for the move. Erickson quickly wrote a *Pastorale* for soprano, tenor, chorus, and string quartet, setting a poem written to order by his friend Jane Mayhall. The subject, which merges love and the passing of summer into autumn, recalls (though more optimistically) the subject of Schoenberg's early sextet *Transfigured Night*, and the harmonies, organized by fourths rather than the conventional thirds or fifths, may also reflect Erickson's study of Schoenberg, whose early "atonal" music often proceeds by fourths.

Two pieces followed quickly: a trio for violin, viola, and piano, composed for the faculty at St. Catherine's; and a "sort of divertimento or serenade" for flute, clarinet, and string orchestra, written for his Hamline classmate, Tom Nee, who had organized a chamber orchestra. Erickson described the genesis of the Divertimento, as he ultimately decided to call it, in a letter to Ogdon:

> This is the piece which originally started out to be a chamber symphony. I gave it several good hard looks during the past three years (yes it was begun that long ago) and finally threw out the old first movement, wrote a new second and finale. The finale was done at

> Yaddo last summer, and was my first tonal piece, a rondo, very simple, very classical. NOT NEO-CLASSICAL. This piece looks like a winner....

In the same letter he announced the impending move to California

> to make a new life. We have no jobs there and we expect a couple of very hard years but we are confident that we'll find a niche to fit into somewhere out there. We have gone as far as possible in St. Paul and now seemed the psychological moment to move. We are both confident, sure of our powers and willing to gamble.
>
> My book will be published in the fall and the money from that will help us to get some kind of a start. We don't have much to move on, but what the hell, we came to St. Paul with thirty dollars and if you never take a chance you just rot. [Letter of May 20, 1953, to Wilbur Ogdon, *Erickson Celebration*, p. 49.]

By October 1953 they were in San Francisco for good, staying with friends and looking for work. Lenore landed a job on a survey team, canvassing San Francisco's attitudes to Hamm's beer, which quickly helped her learn the terrain. Erickson fell into a one-fifth-time teaching job at San Francisco State College. In a few weeks another faculty member left for a job in the Rochester Symphony, and Erickson was teaching three-fifths time. By the following quarter three more classes had fallen his way.

San Francisco State College was a small teacher's college in those days, and its music department was dominated by its concert band. Subsequently it has become one of the biggest campuses of the state university system, set in the windy, foggy southwest corner of the city, but in 1953 it was located in the heart of town, on the Powell Street cable-car line. Here its liveliest teacher, Wendell Otey, was leading a Composers' Workshop, encouraging young composers and helping them get their music performed. Pauline Oliveros and Loren Rush, later to become influential composers themselves, were among the students; before long they began studying privately with Erickson.

Concerts of contemporary music were being given by the Composers Forum in the San Francisco Museum of Art, and Erickson quickly became a participant in their production, whether stuffing envelopes or serving on programming committees. In the early 1950s, established cultural institutions (excepting opera companies) promoted regional and local activity as a matter of policy, as they had done since the Depression. Establishment insistence on nationally or internationally promoted figures, validated by an international press, would not begin to submerge native artists until the 1970s. The City, as San Francisco was then known throughout California, was still "provincial," but its own creative life and heritage, vital since the Gold Rush, continued to be indulged if not encouraged. (And though provincial, the Bay Area had long maintained an interest in whatever window might be opened onto the rest of the world. Arnold Schoenberg, for example, had conducted his *Gurrelieder* with the Oakland WPA Orchestra during the Depression, and in 1939 Krenek had participated in that orchestra's performance of his Concertino, op. 27.)

But Erickson found the local concerts more conservative than those Krenek had led in St. Paul, and he argued strenuously for the inclusion of a larger proportion of music by Bay Area composers, as well as a work by an internationally known master of contemporary music, on each program. The 1950s were a conservative decade, however, and while a considerable number of composers and musicians in the Bay Area were devoted to music of their own time in those years, the political intrigue and horse-trading was often heated.

After two semesters of temporary teaching at San Francisco State, a permanent faculty position failed to materialize, and Erickson took the job of music director at KPFA, the noncommercial FM radio station in Berkeley. This was a pioneering station, conceived during World War II by a Quaker conscientious objector, Lewis Hill, and established immediately after the war, experimentally in 1946, finally to lasting success in 1948. (Erickson had been impressed with some early programs while he was visiting the Bay Area in the summer of 1948.)

The radio station operated from second-floor offices on University Avenue, with a paid staff consisting of a station manager, a program director, directors for each program area (music, public affairs, drama and literature), a subscription clerk, and a station engineer. A number of volunteers helped out in every department. The model was the British Broadcasting Corporation's Third Programme, with its mix of news and public affairs, drama and literature, children's programming, and music.

The administration was largely liberal and pacifist—the foundation operating KPFA (and, since 1963, its sister stations, first in Los Angeles, then in New York, Houston, and Washington) is called the Pacifica Foundation. But even through the turbulent 1960s the station's programming was relentlessly nonaligned, attempting to avoid any kind of overt political or social advocacy. Political commentators spoke for views ranging from anarchy to conservative Catholicism, mainstream Republican to Socialist labor.

The cultural programming was not quite so carefully balanced. It was committed to an intellectual stance, in general, but also toward emphasizing the contemporary, even the avant-garde. The attempt was clearly to put the local listener-subscriber in touch with a wide range of cultural issues, and this appealed to Erickson's own experience. He had been fortunate in moving beyond the tranquil backwater of Marquette to the cosmopolitan intellectual and artistic life of Chicago, fifteen years earlier; here was an opportunity to provide similar growth to the radio listeners of the San Francisco Bay Area.

No commercials were broadcast on KPFA, and in those days no foundation grants, corporate underwriting, or government subsidies were sought or collected: the station's independence from outside commitments was jealously guarded. All the station's funds came from subscriptions: Hill's original thesis was that a radio station could succeed if only five percent of its listeners were willing to pay a modest annual fee, and KPFA did succeed on this basis well into the 1960s.

Part of this success was due to ruthless self-exploitation on the part of the staff. Salaries were low: Erickson earned $72 a week on his appointment, in 1954, and a successor ten years later made only three dollars more. (Lenore contributed to the household: in the spring of 1955 she was teaching art at Dominican College in San Rafael, across the bay in Marin County.) The music director was responsible for live and recorded concerts, lectures and panel discussions, reviews and historical overviews. Music programming occupied up to thirty-two hours a week, and although the music director was expected to recruit and supervise volunteer assistants, he was the only paid music staff member. The workweek regularly ran to sixty hours, and vacations and holidays were rare. These conditions were offset by the total freedom given the staff to program as they saw fit—but that had its penalty in endless discussions among the staff (and the small board of directors) as to just what station policies should be.

"My experience at KPFA was intensely sociological and political," Erickson has recalled—"the politics of small groups." His baptism was sudden: the day after his appointment, coincidentally, a large group resigned from staff and board. Erickson was fascinated with the power struggles, factionalism, and ideological controversy that seemed inseparable from life at Pacifica (as from American life in general), and in the following year, 1955, he was elected to the small board of directors. The next eight years, critical for Pacifica and absorbing for Erickson, were marked by constant controversy within the board, whose members included political scientists, pacifists, lawyers, the station's program director, and a dentistry professor. The controversies reached tragic proportions when Lewis Hill committed suicide a few months after an attempt to impeach him from the board. Ultimately Harold Winkler succeeded him, presiding over the creation of new stations in Los Angeles and New York and stabilizing the entire operation. But when he, too, lost support and resigned in 1963, Erickson had had enough. Shortly after, he resigned from both the board and his position as secretary of the foundation.

Though active for nearly a decade at Pacifica, Erickson had long since resigned from the music directorship at KPFA. But first he had taken care to build the foundation for an impressive operation that would last into the 1970s. As soon as he could he had added a second person to the music department: Alan Rich, a graduate student at UC Berkeley whose later, influential career in music criticism would take him to the New York *Herald Tribune*, the magazines *New York* and *Newsweek*, and journalism in print and broadcasting in Los Angeles. Erickson presided over station politics, live concerts, panel discussions, and interviews, and left the extensive recorded-concert programming to his assistant.

In addition to planning coherent record-concert programs and relentlessly seeking free records for the growing KPFA library, Rich produced historical programs. "The Romantic Art Song," which ran to many hours, introduced a delighted listenership to the pleasures of Schubert and the Lied. The programming on other radio stations, conventional in the extreme, avoided not only contemporary music but also chamber and vocal music.

Meanwhile Erickson expanded KPFA's already active program of live-broadcast concerts. Under his aegis, carefully extended for a decade beyond his own tenure as music director, these activities became ever more important. At first, for technical and economic reasons, all live concerts had to originate in the KPFA studios. Local performers, including pianists Bernhard Abramowitsch and Maro Ajemian; her sister, the violinist, Anahid Ajemian; and the Griller and California String Quartets, played contemporary American music as well as the classics. Young pianists appeared from the area: Dwight Peltzer, Stephen Bishop-Kovacevich, David Del Tredici. Concerts by the Composers Forum and the San Francisco Chamber Music Society were tape-recorded for subsequent rebroadcast. Later, when technology (and station finances) had sufficiently improved, the station provided remote live broadcasts, relaying the signal over rented telephone lines, beginning with the weekly noon concerts at UC Berkeley's Hertz Hall. Soon annual summertime concerts were added from the Carmel Bach Festival, one hundred miles to the south—the Mission's bells and the Carmel Beach surf becoming familiar sonic signatures to the programming. Later, in the mid-1960s, the Oakland Symphony subscription concerts and the annual Cabrillo Festival, both directed by conductor Gerhard Samuel, were added to the station's programming.

KPFA's commitment to contemporary music extended to co-sponsorship of concerts and, for two years, even a competition for new scores. Erickson's *Chamber Concerto* was performed on a San Francisco concert in 1963, and his *Concerto for Piano and Seven Instruments* was premiered on one of three concerts by "Performers' Choice," a series programmed by the performing musicians—among whom were also some of the participating composers and performers, led by Dwight Peltzer and Loren Rush. These programs also included Anton Webern's *Concerto for Nine Instruments*, a worthy and complementary companion to Erickson's, and Loren Rush's *Mandala Music*, a collective-improvisation schema of unusual coherence and lyricism.

While all this was going on, contemporary music from abroad had also become an important part of KPFA's music programming. The station featured tape recordings of significant European festivals, Warsaw, Donaueschingen, and Darmstadt among them. Transcriptions were obtained from the BBC, as well as from Swedish, French, Italian, and Japanese radio systems, and the burgeoning music of the postwar international avant-garde was common currency within KPFA's signal area—then a circle of perhaps seventy-five miles in diameter centering (somewhat lopsidedly, to favor San Francisco) on the hills behind Berkeley.

Listeners did not have to endure this new music unprepared. Lectures and musical demonstrations were provided by a number of sources, including the UC Berkeley faculty and, often, the historical and analytical skills of Pacifica music directors themselves. One series, Gunther Schuller's *Contemporary Music in Evolution*, which traced the development of twentieth-century music year by year to the time of its own broadcast, was virtually a complete musical education to a number of lucky young composers listening.

All this admirable music programming was Erickson's legacy; but, as we have seen, he was KPFA's music director for less than a year, the draining administrative chores leaving him no time to compose. After his 1953 Trio for Violin, Viola, and Piano, largely completed before he left St. Paul, Erickson did not finish another work until the String Quartet No. 2, hurriedly (but masterfully) composed in 1956. On leaving KPFA in 1954, Erickson returned to teaching, first combining part-time jobs at San Francisco State and the San Francisco Conservatory, then for a short time joining the faculty full-time at UC Berkeley. But he took considerable care with his successors at KPFA, choosing them single-handedly or discreetly guiding their choice by others. Loren Rush was one of the earliest, hired as Alan Rich's assistant. Later came Glenn Glasow and Will Ogdon, Erickson's younger colleagues in Krenek seminars at Hamline, and the present author. Erickson's influence thus continued at KPFA until 1967, by which time he had left not only Pacifica but also the San Francisco Bay Area.

In the meantime Erickson had extended the musical interests of many, himself included. As the decade of the 1960s gathered its enormous cultural energy, vernacular music infused serious music with new vitality, much as tribal art had energized post–Impressionist painting in the age of cubism, sixty years earlier. KPFA's music programming ran to small-audience tastes, but found airspace for other views. Anthony Boucher's enthusiasm for "Golden Voices"—dim recordings, often from cylinders, of great performers from the past—was infectious, as was Philip Elwood's enthusiasm for "mouldy fig" jazz.

Henry Jacobs presented a program on "Music and Folklore" for years, considerably helping the development of Folkways Records. In the 1960s, folk music gained adherents through weekly live sessions run by Gertrude Chiarito, whose ex-husband Amerigo had been KPFA's first music director, and through carefully researched and engagingly presented recorded programs by Chris Strachwitz, the founder of Arhoolie Records. Finally, in the late 1960s, these parallel musical cultures began to merge in late-night programs of "mixes" produced by UC Berkeley students, including Jonathan Cott, who would later write a book on the German avant-gardist Karlheinz Stockhausen while contributing to the rock periodical *Rolling Stone*, and John Rockwell, who went on to become an influential music critic on *The New York Times*.

Compositions, 1953–1955:

1953   *Pastorale* for chorus, soprano, tenor, and string quartet
Divertimento for flute, clarinet, and string orchestra
Trio for violin, viola, and piano
Fantasy for cello and orchestra

San Francisco: UC Berkeley, 1956–1958

Conditions at KPFA contrasted with those at the University of California at Berkeley, where Erickson found himself next. In the 1950s Berkeley still seemed small and sleepy, a typical university town of the period. The student population, about fourteen thousand young adults, lived in dormitories, fraternity and sorority houses, furnished rooms, and apartments within a few blocks of the campus. The four blocks of Telegraph Avenue leading south from campus, which would become notorious for demonstrations in the 1960s, then lapse into squalor in the 1970s, were still furnished with small grocery stores, pharmacies, and department stores. There were no espresso bars and only one record store—Art Music, with an impressive collection of imported discs, often lent to KPFA.

Berkeley's business section centered on Shattuck Avenue, a block from the western edge of campus, and it was steeped in complacent tradition: Hink's, the local department store, was yet to integrate its sales staff racially. (A prolonged boycott, which forced the issue in 1963, was perhaps the first of the many Berkeley social protests.) The flatlands adjacent to the campus were middle-class and white; the hills just north of campus housed faculty and white-collar families; a farther-flung area, nearer San Francisco Bay and in the southwest corner of town, was largely black. The city government had been comfortably Republican and genteel for a generation, under the benign stewardship of Mayor Laurence Cross, a Congregationalist minister. College boys wore neatly ironed white shirts, corduroy trousers, and crew sweaters; the coeds dressed in pullovers, pleated skirts, bobby sox, and loafers.

An aura of gentility permeated the university's music department, housed in a brown-shingle building on the shady bank of Strawberry Creek, just a few blocks from KPFA. And the department's origin was genteel enough: in 1905 the state legislature—lobbied by a San Francisco women's club, the California Club—appropriated $6,000 "to provide for two years the salary of a Professor of Music."[1] But Charles Seeger, who succeeded John Wolle in the position in

1912 (at the age of twenty-six), was a confirmed modernist and pluralist. His own compositions apparently gave considerable evidence of these interests; unfortunately nearly all were lost in the Berkeley Fire of 1923. By 1919, though, his academic influence had ebbed and the music department continued along more conventional lines.

The Seeger years had a profound but sadly curtailed impact on American music through their influence on Henry Cowell, a bold and precocious composer and pianist born in Menlo Park, a few miles south of San Francisco, in 1897. Cowell made his debut as composer and pianist in 1912, then studied with Seeger from 1914 to 1918. During that time Cowell wrote his pioneering book *New Musical Resources*, completing it in 1919 but not publishing it until 1930. After touring Europe as a pianist-composer in the early 1920s, Cowell settled in Los Angeles, where he founded the New Music Society, moving with it back to San Francisco the following year. In 1927 he began his quarterly journal *New Music*, which published forward-looking music by European and North and South American composers, doing much to confirm and encourage innovative concert music internationally. It was within the characteristic brightly colored wrappers of *New Music Quarterly* that many composers first saw scores by such European avant-gardists as Webern and Schoenberg and such Americans as Charles Ives and Carl Ruggles. Later, New Music Quarterly Records issued the first recording of Ives's orchestral music, conducted by Nicholas Slonimsky; Ives's Fourth Violin Sonata, with Joseph Szigeti and Andor Foldes; and his *Psalm 67*, with Robert Holliday conducting the Hamline University A Cappella Choir. (This last recording also included music by Ernst Krenek.)

During the Depression years Cowell taught at the New School for Social Research in New York City, where he greatly impressed the young Los Angeles-born composer John Cage. Cowell also taught occasionally on the opposite coast: at San Francisco State College he had influenced Lou Harrison, that other pillar of the California avant-garde, teaching him what is now called "world music," helping him with his compositions, and encouraging his correspondence with Charles Ives. Cage and Harrison helped consolidate the twin columns of progressive American music: innovation (the invention of new techniques and sounds) and import (the research, mastery, and assimilation of techniques and sounds previously foreign to the European-derived concert-music tradition).

Unfortunately, from Erickson's point of view, the heady American (even Californian) music of Seeger and Cowell, and of the younger Cage and Harrison, members of his own generation, was not a part of UC Berkeley in the 1950s. An eclectic international modernism had set in at the department, strongly anchored in the somewhat conservative, profoundly worked influence of the Swiss-born composer Ernest Bloch, who had headed the San Francisco Conservatory from 1925 to 1930, returned to Switzerland until 1939, and taught summer courses at Berkeley from the early 1940s until his retirement in 1952. While Erickson was at Berkeley in the late 1950s, the music department was in transition, with the older, West Coast-born faculty giving way to a younger, more East Coast-oriented generation. Albert Elkus, born in Sacramento in 1884, had run the department from 1937 to 1951. Already with him on the faculty before World War II were the courtly but at times irascible francophile Charles Cushing, born in Oakland in 1905 and himself a product of Berkeley's school; Seattle-born William Denny, whose music was in a neoclassical style and who had studied in Paris with Paul Dukas (best known for *The Sorcerer's Apprentice*); and Joaquín Nin-Culmell (son of the Spanish composer Joaquín Nin, an enthusiast of French and Spanish music, and Anaïs Nin's brother), who had been Denny's classmate in Paris.

Later to arrive were Edward Lawton, who had studied with the Italian composer Gian Francesco Malipiero, and two younger, New York-born composers, Seymour Shifrin and Andrew Imbrie. Both of the latter wrote music in an expressive, linear style not incompatible with that of the older members of the faculty, but more aligned with the Germanically dense and heavy (though claimed admirably lucid by some) style of Roger Sessions, who had taught at Berkeley from 1944 to 1953. Erickson felt that their music was neither innovative nor open to fresh influences from outside the prevailing Eurocentric tradition.

Not even the notable festivities celebrating new facilities (including the acoustically superb Hertz Hall and the impressive music library) in 1958 could do much to dislodge what Erickson saw as a prevailingly academic and intro-verted mood. All composers then or formerly present on the Berkeley faculty were represented, including Bloch, Arthur Bliss, and Sessions. Erickson's String Quartet No. 2 was included on one chamber program: it had been requested by the California Quartet, four musicians from the San Francisco Symphony Orchestra. Other composers, internationally famous, were also included, such as Darius Milhaud and Paul Hindemith. But nothing of the Viennese school was presented: no Berg, no Webern, no Krenek, not even anything of Schoenberg, who had taught at the university's Los Angeles campus. "The power of the academy to dig in its feet is awesome," Erickson reflected later on recalling the event.

Further, Erickson felt that the Berkeley music department was becoming polarized between composers and musicologists, and that the latter were gaining in influence. A similar division obtained among the visual arts: Lenore had found a part-time teaching position on the decorative-art faculty, in those days a subsidiary of the school of architecture; the art department was largely dedicated to art history. Erickson's promise was evident but not seen as compatible with the Berkeley department, and he remained on the music faculty only two years, leaving in 1957.

Until the present day the department has approached radical music rather tentatively. Arnold Elston, a New Yorker who joined the faculty in 1958 and who had studied with Webern, mounted an impressive concert of the Austrian serialist early in the 1960s. But in general innovative music was tolerated, not encouraged. La Monte Young and Terry Riley, radical composers of the generation after Erickson's and continuers of the Seeger-Cowell-Cage-Harrison tradition of innovation and import, had to give their concerts al fresco in the courtyard of the architecture building. When Young's *Poem* (scored for furniture, including a piano bench, which was dragged across the floor, and punctuated by the release of butterflies into the room) was presented in Hertz Hall at a free lunchtime student concert, Karl Aschenbrenner, the influential philosophy professor who headed the esthetics curriculum, stalked noisily out of the audience.

Still, the two years on the Berkeley faculty had reawakened Erickson's drive to compose. For three years after arriving in San Francisco in 1953, he had been in a slump, first while scratching together a living out of various part-time positions, then while dealing with the administrative and political turmoil of KPFA. This proved to be the longest, most painful dry period of his mature career as a composer. When it finally broke, with a string quartet whose idiom was a departure from his earlier style, with greater emphasis on color and texture, Erickson felt his "scattered parts had somehow knitted together, but differently, and beyond my notice." Perhaps he'd been aroused by his reaction to the conservatism he'd heard in the music of his colleagues; perhaps he'd simply been animated by resumed contact with students—always his most invigorating inspiration.

For whatever reason, three significant pieces represented the harvest of this transitional period: the newly assured, expressive String Quartet No. 2; the sinewy but lyrical Duo for Violin and Piano; and the rich, colorful *Variations for Orchestra*. They would be followed by another long lull while he found a new teaching position and prepared for the next major step in the evolution of his music: the shift of emphasis from construction (the interior processes at the composer's desk) to performance (the collaborative interplay between composer and performer). But although another lull was in the immediate future, and although there would be frequent "dry periods" after the completion of major pieces, Erickson's confidence would never again be shaken. New York, KPFA, and UC Berkeley had finished the lesson begun in the army. Henceforth he would finesse political situations, taking advantage of their complexities to assure himself intellectual stimulation, academic resources, a reasonably assured income—and time to compose.

Compositions, 1956–1957:

1956   String Quartet No. 2
1957   Duo for violin and piano
1957   *Variations for Orchestra*

1.   This information comes from David Boyden's history of the UC Berkeley music department, prepared for the university's centennial celebration in 1968. The California Club's contribution is revealed in Gertrude Atherton, *My San Francisco* (Indianapolis: The Bobbs-Merrill Co., 1946, p. 186). Boyden's account is at variance with the entry on the University of California in *The New Grove Dictionary of American Music*, ed. H. Wiley Hitchcock and Stanley Sadie (London: The Macmillan Company, 1986, vol. 1, p. 344).

San Francisco: The Conservatory, 1957–1966

Ironically, while the university music department was growing staid in Berkeley, a town now generally thought of as radical, the San Francisco Conservatory, even under a conservative director, was soon to develop one of the most innovative music schools of the 1960s. This would be almost entirely Erickson's work. The Conservatory had an impressive though conventional history: Ernest Bloch had directed it in the late 1920s, and Yehudi Menuhin, Ruggiero Ricci, and Isaac Stern had been students. When Erickson arrived in 1957, Albert Elkus was finishing his seven-year tenure as director (nearing his mid-seventies, he was eking out his retirement from UC Berkeley). He had developed the Conservatory's educational standing, seeing it accredited for the bachelor of music degree; and he had managed a successful fund-raising campaign for the purchase of a new campus: a rambling, vaguely Mission-style building in a foggy, middle-class, single-storey residential section far from the center of town.

After settling the school in its new building, Elkus retired. His successor, Robin Laufer, was a European, a graduate of the Vienna Conservatory who had earned his doctorate at a German university just as the Nazis began their attacks on progressive music. Laufer had fought in the French army, been captured by the Germans, escaped from a prison camp in eastern Poland to Russia, and returned to France to become part of the underground in the Pyrenees. Erickson recalled him as natty, proud, diplomatic when that quality was advantageous, but a tough opponent in negotiations. He was handsome and masterly in his appearance, a great success in society and no doubt with his board of directors. There was always a rumor that he was somehow in a secret service.

In any case he was tenacious, keeping the Conservatory alive on a budget much tighter than those at the state-run college music departments. Erickson taught a number of classes, up to sixteen class-hours a week (the more usual figure is six to nine, to which counseling, research, and committee work must be added) for a small salary. The family income was augmented by Lenore's teaching at Dominican College in San Rafael and the California College of Arts and Crafts in Oakland, and the Ericksons were finally able to move from rented homes, most recently in a cottage in the Berkeley hills, to a purchased house in San Francisco.

At the Conservatory Erickson taught a wide range of classes: history; practical courses in sight-singing, ear training and dictation; and theoretical classes in composition and analysis. For a year or two he prepared the groundwork for what would later be seen as a unique moment, when theory and practice, convention and innovation, discipline and imaginativeness would combine to usher in the 1960s. At the same time, from 1957 to 1960, Erickson's own music was moving into a new dimension. Still soundly reasoned and intelligently constructed, its theoretical grounding was becoming more responsive to external influences. His *Chamber Concerto*, completed in the pivotal year 1960, still recalled the dramatic gestures and complex textures of Alban Berg, but it permitted in its final movement a certain amount of improvisation by one or two instruments while the rest of the ensemble continued with conventionally determined material. One can see this as a composer's expression of the influence of such practical and collaborative processes as classroom seminars and ear-training on such conventionally individual intellectual or scholarly work as theoretical analysis. (It is tempting, too, to see the newly emerging polyphony of improvised melodies, reacting to one another while steadfastly developing their own profiles, as analogous to the freewheeling negotiations and the opportune evasions Erickson had always enjoyed in turning organizational structures to the advantage of his own agendas, whether in the army or as a faculty member.)

Many particularly gifted students in their middle to late twenties were attracted to Erickson during this period. Texas-born Pauline Oliveros had graduated from San Francisco State University in 1957 and immediately began working with group improvisation. Spanish-born, New York-reared Ramon Sender was a Conservatory student from 1959 to 1962. Californians Loren Rush and Terry Riley had studied with Erickson at San Francisco State before going on to graduate school at UC Berkeley; Rush joined the music department at KPFA from 1957 to 1960 and then moved to the Conservatory faculty, where he was to develop a significant performing ensemble in the later 1960s.

All these musicians, first as students and then as young professionals, shared a common interest in hands-on collaborative performance. Until their generation, composition had generally been an individual, studio-cloistered affair, whether the composer was loyal to the radical Viennese twelve-tone school gathered around Schoenberg or to the neoclassical style dominated by Nadia Boulanger, who had taught three generations of composers (among them Aaron Copland and Philip Glass) at Fontainebleau outside of Paris. With this new generation, the creation of music turned toward the group-performance orientation that had already been pioneered in San Francisco and Oakland in the 1930s by John Cage and Lou Harrison.

While the younger generation of composers was turning its attention from private scholarship to collective innovation and performance, in the world at large new tools and techniques were being found and developed. The electronics industry had produced the transistor and the tape recorder. Easier travel, together with more widespread recording and broadcast, had opened up the world's ethnic musics. And a new cult of political, sensual, and spiritual liberation was soon to break down a generation's accumulation of constraints. San Francisco, with its tradition of individualism, regionalism, insouciance, and enterprise, would inescapably be a center of whatever new cultural forms might emerge from this ferment.

At the Conservatory, this innovative musical activity first attracted public attention in 1960, when a week of open rehearsals and evening concerts offered premieres of Oliveros's *Variations for Sextet* and music by Kenneth Gaburo, Richard Swift, and others. The Minnesota-California connection already established by Erickson, Will Ogdon, and Glenn Glasow had been reinforced the previous year when Gerhard Samuel, Mitropoulos' assistant in Minneapolis from 1949 to 1959, was appointed music director of the Oakland Symphony. Samuel led Ben Weber's *Composition for Violin and Chamber Orchestra*; and another Minnesota conductor, Tom Nee, conducted Krenek's *Marginal Sounds*, Charles Ives's *Set of Pieces* (which had been published in San

Francisco thirty years before, by Henry Cowell's *New Music Quarterly*), and a chamber-orchestra work by Richard Hoffmann, who later served a year as composer-instructor at UC Berkeley. (Hoffmann was born in Vienna in 1925, emigrated to New Zealand with his parents in 1935, and studied in Los Angeles with Schoenberg in the late 1940s.) The Parrenin Quartet participated in Donald Martino's Quintet for Clarinet and Strings; Elliott Carter's Sonata for Flute, Oboe, Cello, and Harpsichord; and quartets by Pierre Boulez and Gunther Schuller.

These performances were successful enough to prompt a second "Composers Workshop" the following year. This time the new musical resources were fully evident, with music for tape and electronic instruments and, as a climax, one of the first San Francisco performances of what later came to be called a "theater piece." Los Angeles-born Morton Subotnick, then a graduate student at Mills College in Oakland, presented his Three Preludes for piano, whose third movement included taped sounds. Milton Babbitt's Composition for Synthesizer was heard. Gerhard Samuel returned to lead Ramon Sender's *Four Sanskrit Hymns* for four sopranos, instrumental ensemble, and two tape recorders. Terry Riley ended the concert by performing Richard Maxfield's Piano Concerto. Critic Alfred Frankenstein, always receptive to new developments, described the performance in the next day's paper:

> During the course of this work, Terry Riley, dressed in a tuxedo and wearing a stocking cap and dark glasses, poured marbles into the piano, set its strings vibrating with a child's gyroscope, and dropped all manner of objects onto some sheets of foil over the strings.
>
> During part of this, an assistant lay on the floor under the piano pummeling it with a timpani stick, while a half-masked lady assistant sat near the instrument and handed Riley his equipment with jerky motions. All we needed was the fur-lined teacup and the piece of porcelain plumbing signed "A. Mutt" [sic] and we'd have been right back in the Twenties, when such things were the rage. [*San Francisco Chronicle*, June 15, 1961.]

Richard Maxfield had just come from New York, where he had taken over John Cage's classes at the New School for Social Research for two years. He was an American pioneer in *musique concrète*, the postwar French music composed of natural and altered sounds collaged on tape, and he was already famous among the underground for such pieces as *Cough Music* and *Fermentation Music*, tape pieces manipulating natural sounds with great imagination. These pieces, like La Monte Young's *Poem* first heard a year earlier at UC Berkeley, inescapably recalled Dada experiments in both collage and theater, especially to such critics as Frankenstein, who was equally versed in the history of the visual arts and music.

Frankenstein's intuitions were right to juxtapose Meret Oppenheim's 1936 *Object*, the famed fur-lined teacup that triumphed in the London Surrealist Exhibition, and Marcel Duchamp's very different 1917 *Fountain*, the Dada "readymade" rejected by the Society of Independent Artists' New York exhibition of that year as plagiarism. The young composers in San Francisco were neither simply neo-surrealist nor dedicated to neo-Dada. To the historic resonance of Dada, born in protest of what seemed the bourgeois idiocy of World War I and the sociopolitical events that led to it, and the poetic revelations of the subconscious of surrealism, they were adding a new cultural resonance.

Partly through the example of John Cage, partly through their own awareness, young Bay Area composers were finding ways of expressing values growing out of an appreciation (though perhaps not fully informed) of Asian philosophical principles—an acceptance of external events, even a collaboration with them, as well as an expression of internally developed material. Cage had already proclaimed that a good piece of modern music won't be hurt by the imposition of random sounds from outside the concert hall, any more than the composition of a good modern painting is injured by a chance shadow falling across its surface. The "meaning" of music—the possible concepts its sounds and procedures could relate to, whether "seriously" or humorously, "accidentally" or premeditatedly—was being extended beyond the traditional musical processes and material as conventionally conceived.

Pleased of course with the success of their work to date, Riley, Oliveros, Sender, and Subotnick returned to the Conservatory to give a number of concerts in the fall and winter of 1961. Erickson participated in a piece featuring dancers John Graham and Lynn Palmer, who paraded through the

Conservatory halls accompanied by a Maytag washing machine on a long extension cord, its interior, awash with pebbles, adding a soft seawash of sound to the taped music playing back from near and distant rooms.

Already, though, further research into the new technology of magnetic tape, stimulated by Richard Maxfield's early work, was preparing these young composers for a new direction. During the summer break, Sender had built a modest electronic studio in the Conservatory attic, with a small grant from the school, oscillators and other equipment donated by manufacturers, and a considerable amount of army-surplus material. At about the same time, Subotnick had been putting together a backyard studio of his own. In 1962, he and Sender joined forces to start the San Francisco Tape Music Center in an empty Victorian house downtown. The following year they moved once again, to a third-floor loft at 321 Divisadero Street, where Anna Halprin's San Francisco Dancers Workshop had its studio and KPFA ran a concert hall on the second floor. Until 1966, when the Tape Music Center moved to Mills College, this was the site of a number of epochal concerts of new music. Live and prerecorded electronic music, theater-pieces, and new pieces for more or less traditional instruments and ensembles, by composers from the Bay Area and elsewhere throughout the world, attracted overflow audiences to the 250-seat hall; many concerts were recorded or broadcast live.

Throughout this period Erickson's own music kept abreast of his younger colleagues. Any traditional teacher-student relationship had long since been replaced, almost entirely, by an atmosphere of convivial joint research and development. His own interest in practical applications of scholarly research had not been dormant: in the late 1950s he had already built a lyre-like *kithara* to prove the practicability of ancient Greek tuning systems that interested him. In the middle 1960s he renewed this practical curiosity. He was, in a sense, rejuvenated by the creative energy around him and took to building instruments himself—partly in the spirit of the 1960s' search for new sounds, partly in continuation of the instincts that must have gone back through his pottery-making days to the dimly remembered scene of his uncle Gus building violins at the kitchen table.

One impetus for this tinkering was pure curiosity. Early in 1965, in a conversation with Lenore's friend and associate Bob Holbrook, a maker of faceted glass windows, the talk turned to ancient Chinese stone-chimes and speculation as to how they may actually have sounded. Holbrook cut some flat pieces of marble into various sizes. He and Erickson improvised a suspension out of rubber bands, "and I heard for the first time the sound that the ancient Chinese valued so highly, a rich, ringing sound with many partial tones, like a bell, yet not quite, somewhat softer, less clangorous, and with fewer obvious beats." ("Beats" is used here in a technical sense, to refer to the repeated "warble" heard when two sustained tones are nearly, but not quite, in tune with one another—a common phenomenon in such complex sustained tones as those of struck gongs.)

At about the same time Erickson strung together metal rods, small bells, glass strips, and chunks of metal in a construction that expanded throughout the kitchen and dining space. A push or two on this homemade indoor wind-chime would result in five or six minutes of tinkling, rattling, thumping, and clicking.

This construction was joined by another, formed by lashing together two toy pianos bought from a local import store. The hammers of toy pianos strike steel rods, not strings; Erickson "damped" one set of rods, stifling their tendency to resonate and altering their sound quality. He recorded the sounds of the wind-chime on a professional portable tape recorder and mixed the results at the Tape Music Center to make a final tape that accompanied music composed for live performance on the toy pianos. The resulting *Piece for Bells and Toy Pianos* was soon filmed, using experimental montages and other visual effects (but in black and white), for broadcast on San Francisco's educational television station, KQED.

Erickson next turned to a real piano, using C-clamps to attach lengths of welding and brazing rods from ten inches to three feet long to the resonating soundboard of a grand piano. With the lid removed, there was room for several players: Erickson enlisted Rush and trombonist (and, later, composer) Stuart Dempster, who also taught at the Conservatory, and two students, Alan Johnson and George Duke. In a single lengthy session he got them to record the source material for a stand-alone tape piece, *Roddy*. The sounds are quite varied. Deep bell sounds result from struck rods; rich, stringlike sounds result from playing the rods with a cello or contrabass bow; clearly tuned squeaks result from rubbing the strings; and percussive clacking sounds are produced by wooden dowels. Rods, dowels, glass, and metal slabs accumulated over the months, filling the Ericksons' garage; they would soon form a considerable impediment to the next major household move.

Roddy was first programmed on a concert in the fall of 1966 at Mills College—not in the capacious 1929 Concert Hall, a Walter Ratcliff-designed building with early-modern symbolist murals by Ray Boynton, but in the more domestic though equally beautiful wood-paneled student union, designed earlier by the great California architect Julia Morgan. Here a large audience of students and new-music aficionados heard the piece on a concert exploring various aspects of electronic music. In addition to the austerely beautiful *Roddy*, for tape only, there was Robert Ashley's threatening, ear-splitting, yet fascinating *Wolfman*, performed by the composer wearing gangster-style dark glasses and screaming at top volume into a closely held microphone; and Douglas Leedy's very different and modest *Usable Music 2* for amplified mouth organs (harmonicas), quietly and devotionally played by a number of musicians seated, gamelan-style, on cushions on the floor. Fascination characterized all this music: lyrical in the case of *Roddy*, repellent in *Wolfman*, microscopic in *Usable Music*.

Along with electronics, Erickson was pursuing his experiments with improvisation as a performance technique, not merely for the production of sounds to be used as source material in electronically manipulated tape recordings. As we have seen, he first used improvisation in the 1960 *Chamber Concerto*. He pursued it more intently in the 1963 *Concerto for Piano and Seven Instruments*, inspired partly by Dwight Peltzer's technical command of the piano, partly by the equally artistic sensibilities of the hand-picked ensemble accompanying Peltzer in this graceful, witty piece.

A similar inspiration came next from Dempster, who was principal trombonist in the Oakland Symphony as well as Erickson's colleague at the Conservatory. Needing a solo piece for the 1966 season at the Tape Music Center, Dempster worked closely with Erickson on what would ultimately become *Ricercare à 5*—the ricercar being a kind of contrapuntal music, popular in the baroque period, involving a good deal of imitation among the various voices. The two met for three hours twice a week for several months,

Dempster demonstrating the new sounds he was finding in his tenor, alto, and contrabass trombones, Erickson absorbing them completely, considering the uses he could put them to. When he had determined the scope and nature of the various families of sounds available, Erickson began to mock up a final piece, writing out rough directions for each part, recording Dempster's performances of them, then playing them back in varying relationships and superimpositions, using four borrowed tape recorders. The results were further refined and developed, again collaboratively, and finally four of the five trombone parts were recorded in Lenore's high-ceilinged studio. The time would come, later, when five sufficiently virtuosic trombonists could be found to play *Ricercare* live; for the present, it was completely owned by Stuart Dempster.

An entirely different kind of improvisation is at the heart of *Scapes*, a "contest" for two groups of instruments (five or more in each) "with the format of tic-tac-toe." Here Erickson made the structural process of the composition an integral part of its performance. Instead of working out charts and tables of possible sounds or procedures for his own use, consulting them while making decisions as to how his sounds would proceed in order to write down a score of instructions for the performers, Erickson gave the charts to the musicians for them to consult during performance. Arranged in two "teams," each with its own conductor, they were guided loosely (but specifically) through their charts, which resembled such game-boards as Monopoly, by their conductors, who chose their process through the score by playing a game of tic-tac-toe.

Scapes was first heard at the Conservatory in 1966 on a concert with Pauline Oliveros's music-theater piece *George Washington Slept Here Too* and a revival of Terry Riley's *In C*. Oliveros, playing her accordion, took the title role in *George Washington*, and it was a big hit, especially when Stuart Dempster strode purposefully into the audience, whirling a garden hose around his head, lasso-style, while playing drones on it. *In C*, with its insistent percussive "pulse," ended the concert on a mesmerizing, joyous upbeat. But *Scapes* seemed hardly to start before it was over, its ten musicians falling all over themselves in a game of tic-tac-toe which reached too quick a conclusion. Here—as had been the case, ironically, in the complex but very different twelve-tone and serial music it was in complete reaction to—both the amount of musical material and the method of its organization were too dense, too quick, for the audience to comprehend. *In C* would usher in an era of "minimal" music, music whose point is very soon understood by even an untrained audience. *Scapes* was closer to "maximal" music.

At the time all this music was seen as "experimental," music being produced in a continuing mood of exploration: of sounds, of techniques, and of esthetics. The composers and performers were co-participants, sharing discoveries that enlarged the dimensions of new music. Many of these discoveries were to be developed further by one composer than another. Oliveros was fascinated by collective meditative participatory improvisation; Subotnick by the mutual inflection of electronic and live instrumental techniques; Steve Reich, then a graduate student at Mills, by the fascinating drifts into and out of phase of almost identical tape loops. There was no center to all this activity, but the foci were clearly at the Tape Music Center and at Mills College, where Luciano Berio's appointment (as successor to Darius Milhaud) had combined with the already active Mills Chamber Players to spark a new interest in the performance of avant-garde music. There was no center, but Robert Erickson's students and colleagues were everywhere present.

Meanwhile, Erickson's earlier music, by now more conventional, was also being heard. In 1963 *Variations for Orchestra* was played by the Oakland Symphony, with Gerhard Samuel on the podium. This was not Erickson's first orchestral piece: we have seen that Dmitri Mitropoulos conducted his 1948 *Introduction and Allegro* in Minnesota, and Enrique Jorda had led the San Francisco Symphony in the 1953 *Fantasy* for cello and orchestra. (Samuel, unimpressed by Jorda's performance, scheduled it with his Oakland Symphony immediately afterward.) But for almost twenty years *Variations* would stand as Erickson's most persuasive music for orchestra, easily demonstrating the composer's practical mastery of the big scale and of the technical demands of writing for orchestra.

The work also took advantage of the resourcefulness of the Oakland Symphony, which had a long history of commitment to new music. Originating as a community orchestra, the Oakland Symphony proudly played Bay Area music on each concert program in the 1920s and 1930s; even after converting to a professional orchestra in 1958 it continued to play new music, reaching a peak of enterprise under Samuel's leadership. Samuel introduced music by Karlheinz Stockhausen and Luciano Berio, commissioned an elegy on the Kennedy assassination from Darius Milhaud (who was then resident at Mills College in Oakland), and even opened one concert with Terry Riley's then-notorious *In C*.

After the *Variations* Erickson wrestled hard with the problem of incorporating the new-found sounds and techniques of the 1960s into the recalcitrant medium of the conventional orchestra, settling finally on *Sirens and Other Flyers III*, finished in 1965 after nearly three years' work. But *Sirens* still awaits its second performance, fascinating and well-conceived though its score reveals it to be. It was composed at the end of a period of progress and expansion, and it fell victim to the subsequent period of contraction and conservatism.

On the public, social level, musical progress had peaked during the Tape Music Center years, the first half of the decade of the 1960s. In 1966, unsuccessful in quests for independent grants, Oliveros, Sender, and Subotnick negotiated the Center's move to Mills College, where Oliveros became its director. Subotnick went to New York University, Riley to the State University of New York at Buffalo. Reich formed his own performing ensemble in New York City. Rush, succeeding Erickson, took on the chairmanship of the composition department at the Conservatory. Sender joined a commune in northern California. Samuel, his position with the board of directors weakened by his intransigent support of contemporary music, resigned the directorship of the Oakland Symphony. And the rock scene had simplified, focused, and ultimately commercialized much of the inventiveness of the music of the first half of the decade.

In 1966 Erickson was awarded a Guggenheim Fellowship and spent part of the year in Europe with Lenore. They attended the Darmstadt Festival in Germany, where *Scapes* was performed, and the Warsaw Autumn Festival, where it was scheduled but canceled. They did, however, hear some oddly non-American sounding jazz performed by Polish musicians. In Sweden they visited the composer Folke Rabe, who had earlier visited the San Francisco Tape Music Center. They also visited every museum they could find whose collection boasted a Greek vase, for Erickson continued to be fascinated with the problem of reconstructing ancient Greek methods of tuning. (Once again, the confluence of musical tone and ceramic vessel represented a merging of the Ericksons' artistic curiosity and inspiration.)

On their return, they headed for a new job in southern California. Much of the musical energy seemed to flow from the Bay Area with them. But during that heady half-decade, while so much experiment around him seemed to produce so much fruit, in a burst of energy signaling a new-found enthusiasm and inventiveness Erickson had composed ten pieces that contain within them virtually all the directions he would later follow—and through which he moved from being a composer of European-influenced mainstream twentieth-century music to a restless innovator, gamely and delightedly seeking new ways of playing with instrumental virtuosity and new sources of sensuously beautiful sounds.

Compositions, 1960–1966:

1960	*Chamber Concerto*
1962	Toccata for Piano, "Ramus"
1963	*Concerto for Piano and Seven Instruments*
1963	*The End of the Mime of Mick, Nick and the Maggies* for SATB chorus
1963–65	*Sirens and Other Flyers III* for orchestra
1965	*Piece for Bells and Toy Pianos*
1966	*Ricercare à 5* for solo trombone with four self-prepared tapes; or five trombones
1966	*Scapes* for two groups of instruments, five or more in each ("a 'contest' with the format of tic-tac-toe") *Roddy* for two-channel magnetic tape

San Diego: Building a Department, 1967–1975

Outsiders tend to think of universities as ivory towers, protected places for absent-minded professors, but to me they seem more like places where problems are concentrated into hard, indigestible pills. Angers are hotter, notions are crazier, ineptness more profound. But this is exactly what we should want and expect in a university, for arguments are sometimes more lucid, and notions more original, too. Certainly it is no refuge from the world, it is continuous with all the rest of our industrial civilization. It is a unique place, not a heaven, but not a hell, either. Within its rigid structure one can sometimes learn to think about things slightly differently, and for that reason, of all the ways I have tried, I like this kind of moonlighting best.

Erickson had been sought out in 1965 by John Stewart, provost of the newly formed San Diego campus of the University of California. Stewart was looking for a chairman for the new music department. He was interested in new music, was aware of international avant-garde developments, and had met Krenek in Los Angeles in 1948. (In 1991 Stewart was to publish a full-length biography of Krenek.) Stewart had already turned for advice to Joseph Kerman, the eminent musicologist-critic at the University of California at Berkeley, who had recommended Erickson. Quite independently, Krenek made the same recommendation.

Erickson, however, had learned to distrust administration and recommended his friend Will Ogdon, who had also been recommended by Krenek. Ogdon was hired, but he insisted on recruiting Erickson for the department as his first move. When tenure as a full professor was added to the San Diego package, Erickson could no longer resist its attractions: "It was a once-in-a-lifetime opportunity to start a music department, to do it right, no waiting for dead wood to rot away, no factions to appease."

Ogdon had been his classmate at Hamline University. They had kept in touch and had worked together in Berkeley, where Ogdon had followed Glenn Glasow in the succession of KPFA music directors after Erickson. (By the time Erickson was hired by San Diego, though, Ogdon had joined the University of Illinois as the coordinator of audio-visual programs.) In a series of discussions the two friends envisioned a new kind of music department, one that would bring the serious study of music into the twentieth century—quickly, before the century was over. It would rest on a truly egalitarian relationship among teachers and students. Composers and performers would work together to perform music of all periods. Research and theory would reflect contemporary concerns, not merely historical ones. And administration and the apparatus of higher education—"degrees, units, grades and other trivia"—would recede into the distance or, preferably, vanish altogether.

The department took shape in a former Marine Corps base whose mess hall had been converted into a small auditorium. In Erickson's view, class schedules and formal curricula were happily vague and often improvised; time and money were treated casually. In fact, Ogdon, as chairman—and virtually alone, since Erickson was still on his Guggenheim for the first two quarters—pursued an aggressive campaign for funds and faculty appointments. Stewart's first vision was of a department dedicated to undergraduate instruction, and Ogdon was joined by two instrumentalists: the violinist-conductor Daniel Lewis, who later went to the University of Southern California, and the pianist Rosalyn Tureck, the "high priestess of Bach," recalled with little affection by Ogdon and Erickson because of her scorn for contemporary music.

The department could compete viably with others among the university only if it had sufficient enrollment, and it had to enlist students from every source. Undergraduates in the college of sciences provided a particularly fruitful one—but only for courses of general interest. This inevitably led Erickson to faculty meetings of the scientific disciplines, and they confirmed his belief that the arts and sciences had drifted too far apart in the conventional twentieth-century university:

We need a music theory that can apply to all the music of the world. This theory is likely to be developed by musicians, but musicians who have been exposed to developments in many scientific and humanistic disciplines; and the American university, where occasional conversations across the fences of the disciplines can take place, is a likely breeding ground for that new theory.

From the beginning, in 1967, Erickson and Ogdon intended the department to grow slowly, avoiding large classes. By 1969, though, the faculty had attracted six more full-time and a number of part-time and associate members. Kenneth Gaburo joined the graduate division, having left the University of Illinois; Pauline Oliveros arrived from San Francisco; the composer-conductor-pianist Keith Humble moved from Australia; and John Silber came from Wesleyan University, where he had been a colleague of Ogdon's (and where Erickson had been a guest composer earlier in the decade). Even so, more classes were required by the state of California—complete with course numbers, credits, and the rest of the academic apparatus—than could comfortably be managed.

Still, a collegial atmosphere (if not a collegiate one) managed to prevail. Everyone performed, students and faculty together, for it was believed, reasonably enough, that composers learned most by hearing their music played, and that performers learned most about contemporary music by playing it. The concerts were well attended by gratifyingly enthusiastic audiences—but there was dissent from a few music-loving members of other faculties, some of whom tried to pressure the university to change the shape of the emerging music department. Behind the scenes John Stewart resisted their pressure. He protected the visionary but unconventional, even innocent, policies that Ogdon and Erickson were elaborating—some of them naïve, from the point of view of entrenched academics who disliked hiring "trombonists" and who felt that undergraduates, while they might profitably compose symphonies, needn't take piano lessons.

Their goal was a kind of research-and-development center parallel to the music department, with facilities for research and experiment in new music, for performance and recording, and for film and television archiving as well as production. In 1973, with an initiating grant from the Rockefeller Foundation (which earlier had financed Mills College's adoption of the San Francisco Tape Music Center), the Center for Music Experiment was installed in a former bowling alley at Camp Matthews. Pauline Oliveros had helped establish the Tape Music Center at Mills College and had been instrumental in transforming it into a Center for Contemporary Music. The supervision of the Center for Music Experiment fell to her.

Erickson was one of the first composers to benefit from the new center. He had been pondering a number of theoretical questions about timbre—the relationships among the dozens of individual pure tones, all sounding simultaneously though at widely different loudnesses, that combine to produce a single complex "tone-color." Many of his abstract questions remained unresolved for the moment, but a number of compositions, especially *Rainbow Rising* and *White Lady*, grew out of the research.

It may be that his experiments were not controlled as precisely as possible, for Erickson's investigations have tended always to pursue immediate, hands-on results. More music, not more complete intellectual knowledge and understanding of more music, has been his primary immediate goal. This is not to say that Erickson's intellectual interests and achievements have been negligible. The 1974 research provided significant material for his book *Sound Structure in Music*, published the following year by the University of California Press. In this book, as we will see later, Erickson rambles easily among theoretical and practical concepts whose sources range from the electronic laboratory to the gamelan orchestras of Bali, from scholarly articles perused in the university library to collaborations with performers of his own music, from established music of the standard "classical" repertoire to an extended discussion of the transformation of speech sounds into ritual music, from pre-Christian Egypt to twentieth-century New Guinea.

Such scholarship drew on many sources: wide reading, observant travel, hands-on studio work, collaboration with other researchers, composers, performers, and students. In its early years, the music department at UC San Diego reflected such conjunction of interest. Although Erickson was spending more than forty hours a week teaching individual students and classes, planning curricula and organization, reading and appraising work by students and by colleagues, and attending endless numbers of meetings, he was helping to build a community within which he could do his own work, too. As he had composed at work in the army, in the otherwise boring hours of administrative duties at Fort Snelling, so he attempted to compose at the meetings, sometimes in an effort to stay awake. It was occasionally possible to compose mentally, writing the music down later, but composition, he noted, was a solitary pursuit, demanding large chunks of time.

It also demanded large quantities of space. The Ericksons arrived in San Diego with fifteen hundred pounds of glass, wood, metal, and stone accumulated in the course of his San Francisco researches—sound sources he just couldn't bring himself to leave behind. Before long this material was joined by marble and travertine slabs found in the scrap pile of a San Diego marble yard: these stone "chimes," resonated with tubes made from empty tin cans, became a principal source for the sounds in *Cardenitas 68*, a one-act monodrama for Will Ogdon's wife, the soprano Beverly Ogdon. (Though suggested by Stuart Dempster, the title is typical Ericksonian wordplay: he began the work while living in Cardiff, completed it after moving to Encinitas, another San Diego suburb, and composed the whole during the year 1968.)

Marble slabs, their delicate sounds amplified by resonating tubes made by soldering together bottomless tin cans, are, after all, only a variation on such familiar instruments as the vibraphone and marimba. But the tubes led Erickson to other ideas: tube drums—some of them huge carpet tubes, struck with timpani sticks, prominent in the 1968 *Drum Studies* and in the more "finished" *Cradle* and *Cradle II* composed four years later—and, more experimental, a "noise organ" made by installing loudspeakers at the end of tubes. Since the tubes were of different sizes, they favored and therefore reinforced certain pitches of the sounds that were played back through the loudspeakers. Prerecorded sounds were distributed among these tubes, the speakers selected by a keyboard salvaged from one of the toy pianos. This was used to provide taped sounds for *Summer Music*, composed in 1974.

(A further precedent for these instruments may have been the Chamberlain Organ, a Rube Goldberg contraption that had awed early visitors to the San Francisco Tape Music Center back in the early 1960s. Each of its keys actuated an individual tape-loop, originally intended to play a single organ note, but soon replaced with endlessly repeating loops of barking dogs, slamming doors, or whatever else might inspire the musician of the moment.)

In spite of the demands of the new department at UC San Diego and the distractions of instrument building, Erickson completed an unprecedented number of scores in the eight years following his move to San Diego. *Birdland*, his second (and last) piece for magnetic tape alone, reflected a new enthusiasm, the whistling, warbling effects produced most familiarly by birdsong (but almost equally familiarly, though more distractingly, by radio interference).

The *Ricercare à 5*, composed in 1966 for Stuart Dempster, was followed in 1967 by another, in only three voices this time, for the equally virtuosic contrabassist Bertram Turetzky, who soon joined Erickson on the San Diego faculty. *Cardenitas 68* inspired further investigation of the voice as musical source in the next two works, *Do It* and *Down at Piraeus* for chorus. (These marked Erickson's first return to choral music since 1952, with the single exception of the 1963 *The End of The Mime of Mick, Nick and the Maggies* for unaccompanied chorus.) *Do It*, as the title suggests, was written in the heady days of the 1968 liberation of social and political restraints, using words quoted by the composer from presidential campaign speeches; radio, television and magazine advertising of the period; and a poem by Donald Peterson. *General Speech*, another solo piece for Dempster, continued this political acknowledgment in its theatrical parody of an icon of American conservatism, Douglas MacArthur. (For the premiere—and what proved to be numerous subsequent performances—Lenore designed lighting and costume. In his dark glasses, snappy uniform and correct, elegant bearing, Dempster evolved into the very model of a modern stagy general.)

High Flyer, another virtuoso solo piece and (through a pun) another expression of Erickson's fascination with birdsong, was followed by three pieces expressing another kind of collage of environmental and composed sounds reflecting his meditations on the modern collision of natural and industrial sounds and values. For these sounds Erickson made a number of collecting expeditions with portable tape-recording equipment, recording the sounds of superhighways, oil refineries, and other industrial settings, as well as the surf of the Pacific Ocean. It is not hard to see in this enthusiasm a recollection of the streams and sawmills of the composer's youth; but a sinister note was added: Erickson manifested disquieting symptoms of allergic reactions and had to wear protective clothing to minimize skin and eye irritations at many sites.

The last of the three pieces resulting from this work, *Oceans*, for solo trumpet and four-channel tape, propels this environmental (and uniquely Southern California environmental) attentiveness forward into what would become the haunting, hypnotic sound-world of such music as *Night Music* and *East of the Beach*. But these latter works were also prepared by the three major, pivotal pieces of 1974 and 1975. In *Rainbow Rising* and *White Lady* Erickson translated his researches among electronically processed sounds into a new, masterly manipulation of standard concert-hall instruments (aided, in the percussion section of the former piece, by his reliable metal rods), investigating the very different sonorities of two familiar ensembles: the standard symphony orchestra and the wind band. (Surprisingly, given Erickson's youthful experience and the marvelous timbres available from the concert band, this was to be his only composition for that ensemble.)

In *Summer Music* Erickson produced his final piece for magnetic tape, combining it with a meditative, lyrical, fanciful solo violin part perhaps recalling sounds of Erickson's youth. This was the first time he had written prominently and soloistically for violin since the 1956 String Quartet No. 2. *Summer Music* seems, at least in retrospect, to inaugurate a late, valedictory, nostalgic, but unsentimental mood, the tape's droning accompaniment of a quiet brook, its gurgle focused on certain specific pitches, supporting the serene meditation of the solo violin. It was written while Erickson was feeling the first discomforts of what turned out to be the onset of an alarming physical condition. He was only fifty-eight years old.

Compositions, 1967–1975:

1967   *Birdland* for two-channel magnetic tape
        Ricercar à 3 for solo contrabass
1967–68 *Cardenitas 68* for singer, five musicians, and tape
1968   *Do It* for solo speaker, two choral groups, gongs, contrabasses, and bassoons
        Down at Piraeus for chorus, soloists, and tape
        Drum Studies for tubular drums
        General Speech for solo trombone
1969   *High Flyer* for solo flute
        Pacific Sirens for instrumental ensemble and two-channel tape
1970   *Nine and a Half for Henry (and Wilbur and Orville)* for instruments and tape (with film)
        Oceans for solo trumpet and four-channel tape
1971   *Cradle* for three sets of tuned tube drums and instrumental ensemble
1972   *Cradle II* for four sets of tube drums and instrumental ensemble
1972–73 *Loops for Instruments* for clarinet, trumpet, alto saxophone, bassoon, marimba, and flute with instrumental ensemble
        Percussion Loops, for solo multiple percussion
1974   *Rainbow Rising* for orchestra
        Summer Music for violin and tape
1975   *White Lady* for wind ensemble

Teaching, Travel, and Retirement, 1976–1990

For years Erickson had investigated the tuning systems and instruments of cultures other than his own, and had transferred that research into practical application, building instruments for his own music. He had also had considerable involvement in collaborative social organization: studying and performing with friends and classmates; working in the collective politico-cultural context at KPFA; building, with his friend Will Ogdon, a music department at a new campus of a great university.

In the summer of 1974 the Ericksons traveled to Indonesia. In Bali he found what seemed to be an unspoiled application of both of these drives. He was taken to a gamelan rehearsal in a small village in South Bali:

> *Twenty men, from about fifteen to fifty-five or sixty years of age, played the large hanging gongs, horizontal button gongs, drums, cymbals and keyed metallophones of a typical Balinese orchestra. Their music was a delight, especially a composition called* Flower of Cambodia. *This was a composed piece in the brilliant North Bali style, an overture really, which could be played as a prelude to a traditional dance drama. It was full of striking effects: passages that threw into relief the playing of the various sections of the ensemble, feats of precision, sudden silences, elaborate figurations—a virtuoso showpiece demanding a high level of musical proficiency and a disciplined, professional approach.*
>
> *Not one of the musicians was a professional player. They were rice farmers, woodcutters and tile makers who came together to make music for pleasure, to provide music for ceremonies and festivals, and to give their village a good name. Siladen is not very different from hundreds of other Balinese villages. Music is built into the religious and social life of the community.*

It is easy to see the appeal this event would have had for a composer whose first musical experiences had been in a similar (though far less sophisticated) community, where music had been a normal part of daily life; and a composer whose early career had evolved in community-house entertainments, playing homemade percussion instruments to accompany dancers.

Bali appealed to him for the richness of its musical life: every village had its gamelan orchestra, whose players came from every profession and class. The complexity of the music appealed to him, too. Balinese music is played in an apparently simpler tuning system than that familiar to Western concert audiences, but its rhythmic life is richer. Traditional Western concert music builds big, often noisy and dramatic forms out of individual elements that are often imperfectly designed, like the instruments of the orchestra, or even unsoundly conceived, like the very notes of the common diatonic scale. The best compositions succeed by overcoming these obstacles, even by distracting the audience's attention from them. In Bali this is reversed: the instruments have evolved into a sonorous unit, and the individual sounds they make are in tune within themselves as well as among one another.

The social and political implications in this striking opposition of musics would not have escaped Erickson. He has noted the difference between the Balinese music, whose performers can play any instrument of their (gamelan) orchestra and who play for communal enjoyment (and meaning), and the professional Western orchestra, whose performers specialize and who are paid for their work. "Our musical organizations are part and parcel of our industrial way of life, and no doubt their cooperative musical organizations are a reflection of methods that work so well in their agricultural techniques, water rights organizations, village governance and religious observances," Erickson noted. Similar village communities in the twentieth-century American experience obtain in very few cases. The rural hippie collectives that grew up in the late 1960s are not the only example, however. Tightly knit academic think-tank atmospheres of research-and-development teams of scientists or, rarely, workers in the humanities have recurred from time to time. This was the atmosphere Erickson found at Park House, in Chicago; at KPFA; and, through his own efforts, at San Diego.

Such an atmosphere has built-in tensions, though, and continues only at great expense of individual effort and collective compromise. The mood at San Diego began to change in the mid-1970s—necessarily, as the campus itself grew and matured. The extent of the change struck Erickson fully only in 1983, when he discovered that composition students were being subjected to a style-rule: they must not compose repetitive music—music that proceeded by the repetition of short "cells" of melodic material, gradually spinning them out into big-scale structures. (Such music, typified by the work of Steve Reich and Philip Glass, drew its immediate inspiration from Terry Riley's *In C* but had perfectly honorable precedents in Sibelius, Bruckner, Schubert, and, ultimately, the finale of Beethoven's "Waldstein" Sonata.) It was even more shocking to Erickson that when he brought this to the attention of the faculty "there was no sense of alarm, only nodding heads and a murmured 'of course.' Seed, root, and branch of academicism, all in a phrase and a nod."[1]

Erickson found a sad reversal of social posture here. In 1961 Ramon Sender's vision of the Tape Music Center was "a community-sponsored composers guild, which would offer the young composer a place to work, to perform, to come into contact with others in his field, all away from an institutional environment."[2] In fact the Center shared its audience, in the middle 1960s, with the emerging rock scene at the Avalon and Fillmore auditoriums. Fifteen years later, in the once progressive music department he had hopefully co-founded in San Diego, Erickson was to brood over "evidence of hardening of the musical arteries":

> *Music in the idioms of composers from the early and mid-20th century are* [sic] *acceptable; roughly speaking, everything through what I think of as "fifties music." Developments since then, particularly explorations that have gone on in contemporary American music, especially music by composers working in repetitive idioms and idioms that seem to appeal to wider audiences, are viewed with disdain or contempt by most of our composers. Wagons are drawn into a circle, guns are loaded for elaborate and tenacious defenses of hard-won artistic territory. The music of the evil barbarians must be kept at bay.*

Erickson saw this academicism related to the "manufacture of Ph.D.'s and M.A.'s" and "intimately related to the esthetic loyalties of a group of aging composers." That development, together with his need to conserve energy in the face of deteriorating health, may at least partly account for the growing distance between Erickson and the other faculty members toward the close of the 1970s. Furthermore, while younger composers on the faculty continued to explore new developments in computer technology, Erickson's study of the mutual implications of social and musical issues, and the renewed interest that study had developed in the phenomenon of the traditional Western symphony orchestra, brought him to a new consideration of the standard repertoire and specifically the music of Richard Strauss and Gustav Mahler.

Ironically, while these studies made him an even more accessible and relevant teacher from the students' point of view, the application of these orchestral studies in his own composition resulted in work that became increasingly introspective and even mystical—as in fact had Mahler's in his final decade. The surfaces of this orchestral music may appeal to the late-twentieth-century taste for rippling, bright-colored facades with relatively simple structures behind them, but the focus of such music as *Night Music* (1978) and *East of the Beach* (1980) is both beyond and more basic than that of most "minimalist" repetitive music.

Erickson's domestic life, as well as his professional and artistic ones, was in a period of consolidation in the middle 1970s. The Ericksons built a new house, a simple A-frame with a loft above for Lenore's watercolor studio, on a high bluff in Encinitas, north of San Diego, facing east—"east of the beach"—out over a desert landscape toward distant mountains. It was not wilderness: the house had near neighbors, and the view now includes housing developments. But neither is it depressingly inner-city. In a sense it represents a balance between the best aspects of contemporary technology, demographics, and commercial distribution, on the one hand, and, on the other, the reas-suringly recurrent truths and beauties of the natural environment. This is, of course, a cliché view of California's promise, particularly of that of southern California. It is not irrelevant to a consideration of Erickson's life and music, however; in fact, it is central to Erickson's own view of his role as a composer in American society.

> The real America is California. You know what New York magazines
> and newspapers say about California, and you may not understand that
> the reason they say that is that they too know that the wind is blowing
> from California towards the East. They may not like it, but that's what
> it is. So you are the center of the USA. California is one of the places
> where you can be an outsider still.... It is possible not to be a coopera-
> tive member of the group if you can stand the isolation. I'm going to
> follow my whim, I really don't need to be bound.... I just don't want to
> be bound ... I don't advise anybody to do this.... You need to be
> immune to loneliness, and very few people are. Because you're going to
> be lonely.*

Apart from such metaphorical implications, the new Encinitas outlook directly
inspired *Rainbow Rising*:

> *Late one afternoon in 1973 we saw a double rainbow to the east, very
> close; so close that one end went to ground only a few hundred yards
> from our front window.*
>
> *The colors moved and shifted as we watched. I could not maintain
> a stable image of any single color. Colors melted into their bordering
> colors in a baffling way, yet when I looked at the rainbow as a whole
> the color scheme seemed to be fixed.*
>
> *Flocks of gulls were returning to the ocean after a day inland, and,
> as they flew past to the east of the rainbow, their white bodies changed
> color according to the sequence of the rainbow's hues.*
>
> *My composition owes something to this experience, but it is not
> about rainbows or gulls or anything pictorial, and it has no plot or
> story.*

Program notes of this sort were of intense concern to Erickson, who was after
all a professional writer as well as teacher and composer. His second book,
Sound Structure in Music, was nearly finished in 1974; in the meantime, he had

---

*Erickson Celebration program (San Diego: Music Dept., Univ. of California, 1987), p. 12.
While his remarks celebrate California, they confirm a connection between the West and New
England, for the word "whim" figures prominently in Ralph Waldo Emerson's essay "Self-
Reliance": "I shun father and mother and wife and brother when my genius calls me. I would
write on the lintels of the door-post, *Whim*." (italics in original)

begun writing up some memoirs, at first to amuse an old friend hospitalized in 1973, soon because he realized the values of communicating with himself.

In general his writing was especially concerned with clarification—with clear accounts of even recalcitrantly complex or speculative issues. He was aware of the danger of unknowingly misleading the reader. The title *East of the Beach*, for example, was chosen as a relatively neutral reference to his location in Southern California, a sort of "here I stand": but at the premiere, at the New Hampshire Festival, it turned out to imply some watery context in mid-Atlantic, and Erickson was chagrined by a comment from one listener that "all the fishy noises and gurgles" were clearly heard in the music.

Like most composers, Erickson wants his music to make its own sense—*musical* sense (and sensation), not verbal sense. But the American public is intensely verbal, bombarded with words, either in print or (increasingly) in the air, throughout the day. As a professional scholar in a major university, Erickson was affected (though not unduly) by the notorious "publish-or-perish" syndrome; his bibliography includes a number of articles in scholarly journals in addition to his two books. And as a composer he was expected to provide the program notes contemporary concerts require, on the assumption that lay audiences will thereby somehow gain otherwise un-available access to the new music confronting them.

His study of late-romantic orchestral music inevitably led Erickson to confront the often elaborate programs attached to that repertoire, beginning in comparative antiquity (and relatively innocently) with Beethoven's "Pastoral" Symphony, extending then to Berlioz's famously programmatic *Symphonie fantastique*, climaxing in Richard Strauss's *Sinfonia domestica*, "a triumph in art of bourgeois life and manners," in Erickson's words, "the humdrum enshrined." At this time, too, Erickson's former classmate George Perle made the sensational discovery of the "secret program" to Alban Berg's *Lyric Suite*, revealing that this string quartet was, in fact, an elaborate tissue of interwoven tunes, numerical symbolisms, and melodic allusions recounting, or at least alluding to, an extramarital love affair.

Erickson's matter-of-fact response to all this is that the worlds of music and words are incommensurable; that each world has its place; that, being both ubiquitous and insinuating, words not surprisingly even get mixed up with music, and may even seem to help in the understanding of musical experiences; but that "the understanding of music is fundamentally non-verbal, its materials are sounds, not concepts, and words usually make more darkness than light."

These are significant musings to a consideration of Erickson's mature music, for while it can be approached as intellectually as any mainstream twentieth-century music, it is composed through *sounds*, not through either a verbal armature like Berlioz's program or an intellectually conceived structure like Schoenberg's "method of composing with the twelve tones related only to one another." In other words, Erickson *thinks sounds*, rather than thinking *about* sounds. (This is true of Erickson the composer, of course; Erickson the teacher and writer is another matter.) Through the writing of his memoirs—"communicating with himself"—he clarified this:

> ... *the sounds that interest me are constantly brought to consciousness, listened to, compared with other sounds in memory, put into groups of sounds and combined with other sounds into textures.... I find myself doing this even when I have no composition under way. In fact I seem to do it for the fun of it.... The sounds are material to be thought about, yes, but they are also, and probably more importantly, material to be thought with. I believe that when I am imagining, combining, categorizing and comparing sounds I am mentally doing something very like thinking. When engaged in this work and play with sounds I use words very sparingly, though I do end up with conclusions of a sort.*

In the summer of 1978 the Ericksons traveled for four weeks in Japan, in company with Glenn Glasow, who speaks fluent Japanese, and his companion Yoshiko Kakudo, then Curator of Japanese Art at the Asian Art Museum in San Francisco. In Japan Erickson was characteristically most interested in the everyday, vernacular culture: "the workman's food, the non-stylish eating.... "

> One of the best things I heard, overheard, was from a farmer's banquet in the room next to where we were eating at a Japanese inn. Each man stood up and sang an unaccompanied song. And what songs! They sounded old, old, full of the most detailed ornamentation, very wide in

range, slow, heavily encrusted, and marvelous. I could find out very little about them. The snobbish Japanese scholars will apparently pay no attention to this tradition, concentrating only on the official traditional art music. [Erickson: letter to the author, October 13, 1978.]

As we have seen, Erickson gathered his sounds from a wide range of sources—but always real, physical sounds, sounds that come through the ear. After the rich and sumptuous but relatively conventional sonorities of *Rainbow Rising* and *White Lady*, composed following his ruminations on the sonorities of the late-nineteenth-century orchestra, he returned to the more intimate collaboration with a single instrumentalist that had been so productive with trombonist Stuart Dempster. This time Erickson's collaborator was the trumpeter Edwin Harkins, a colleague at the university. *General Speech*, the MacArthur parody Erickson had composed for Dempster in 1968, had set Erickson to thinking about the relationships of speech and music— relationships of vowel sounds, rhythms, and accents. Harkins was already fluent in the incorporation of vocal sounds in his playing, and the two refined these further. Erickson was also aware of the slight inflections of pitches so basic to speech and so studiously ignored by European concert music (but not by the music of other cultures, including jazz), and the piece under way, *Kryl*, turned out to be among other things a study in the use of microtones—pitches "within the cracks," between the keys of a piano, outside the normal European chromatic scale.

Kryl led directly to what is perhaps Erickson's best-known major work, *Night Music*, another in his catalogue of pieces for solo instrument and chamber ensemble. (Previous examples had been the *Concerto for Piano and Seven Instruments*; *Cardenitas 68*, for voice, six instruments and tape; and *Garden*, for violin and small orchestra. It is tempting to see these pieces, like Berlioz's *Harold in Italy*, as musical metaphors of the position of the artist in society, or of man in nature. This reading is confirmed by the valedictory nature of what is apparently Erickson's farewell to composition, the 1990 *Music for Trumpet, Strings, and Timpani*.)

Night Music combined the microtonal world of *Kryl*, the nearly motionless sonorities of *White Lady*, and the reiterations of *Loops for Instruments* to a newly contemplative effect. Erickson was particularly pleased with it: "Just completed a 20 minute piece for 10 insts with some lovely microtonal writing and a nice hypnotic flavor that will cure all human ills."[3]

This success seemed to spur Erickson to a burst of activity, for he composed sixteen works, most of them major pieces, in the next eight years—in spite of worsening health on top of heavy teaching assignments. In the spring of 1979, for example, he taught two graduate seminars and an undergraduate course in advanced theory. "Keeps me humping," he wrote, "with little time left over for dreaming pieces, tho I am in the finger exercise stage of something. I'm not quite sure of what it will be, but I do know that it will have a harp in it."[4]

Erickson continued to write for solo instruments: flute, in *Quoq* (1978); violin, in *The Pleiades* (1981); and timpani, in *Dunbar's Delight* (1985), a piece that also relates to the *Cradles* composed for tube drums in 1971 and 1972. But much of the music of this late period reflects a fascination with the speculative, still, hypnotic sound-world of *Night Music*. This is particularly clear in its near neighbors, *East of the Beach* and *The Idea of Order at Key West*, a 1979 work whose literary source—the poem by Wallace Stevens—suggests a community of esthetics that bears examination.

Except for the first work in his catalogue, the 1940 *Three Rilke Songs* for soprano and piano, Erickson—though an appreciator of literary poetry—had never been particularly interested in setting noted poems as songs. Three other early vocal works, all written for Hamline College's chorus, were settings of Biblical texts. The 1952 *Pastorale*, like the *Three Contralto Songs* written seven years earlier, set poems written by friends. Twenty years later an unaccompanied chorus work, *The End of the Mime of Mick, Nick and the Maggies*, did set an excerpt of James Joyce's *Finnegans Wake*, but thereafter Erickson provided his own texts.

So it was a departure when Erickson turned to the poetry of Wallace Stevens—doubly surprising, because any close correspondence between Erickson and Stevens would be hard to draw. Stevens was wealthy, an epicure, a francophile, reclusive, a fantasist; Erickson was middle-class, contentedly uncritical at table, suspicious of foreign intrusions on the American sensibility, collaborative even in his creative work, and intensely practical. But there are hidden similarities that, considered, may reveal more of the inner meaning of

Erickson's life and music—and thereby demonstrate more clearly both its attractiveness and its usefulness to the contemporary American experience.

In a letter to Ronald Lane Latimer, Stevens discusses his poem "The Idea of Order at Key West":

> In "The Comedian as the Letter C," Crispin was regarded as a "profitless philosopher." Life, for him, was not a straight course; it was picking his way in a haphazard manner through a mass of irrelevancies. Under such circumstances, life would mean nothing to him, however pleasant it might be. In "The Idea of Order at Key West" life has ceased to be a matter of chance. It may be that every man introduces his own order into the life about him and that the idea of order in general is simply what Bishop Berkeley might have called a fortuitous concourse of personal orders. But still there is order. [*Letters of Wallace Stevens*, selected and edited by Holly Stevens (New York: Alfred A. Knopf, 1966), p. 293.]

Beginning with *Rainbow Rising* in 1974—that orchestral translation of the experience of seeing the double rainbow in the desert just outside his window—Erickson's music had been "about" a similar ordering of the life about him. As in *The Idea of Order at Key West*, the images inspiring this order—revealing it, rather, for the order is implicit in the natural world, whether of rainbows, waves, or sonorities—are directly and personally observed in intersections of human experiences and the natural world. The *Collected Poems* of Wallace Stevens had occupied a favored place on Erickson's bookshelf, near *Finnegans Wake*, for years; and he had read "The Idea of Order at Key West" as long ago as 1953, when he composed incidental music for a series of KPFA programs on American poetry. (That music has been dropped from the composer's catalogue.) But the uniquely autumnal mood of much of "The Idea of Order at Key West" was undoubtedly beginning to assume greater relevance to the composer's own situation. It would be hard in any case for a composer in San Diego, casting about for a text for a rich-voiced soprano, to resist a poem that opens

She sang beyond the genius of the sea....

and subsequent lines are even more resonant of concepts Erickson had considered over the years:

> The song and water were not medleyed sound
> Even if what she sang was what she heard,
> Since what she sang was uttered word by word . . .
> For she was the maker of the song she sang. . . .
> It was her voice that made
> The sky acutest at its vanishing.
> She measured to the hour its solitude.

And the poem ends, poignantly, ironically, observantly, even critically:

> Oh! Blessed rage for order, pale Ramon,
> The maker's rage to order words of the sea,
> Words of the fragrant portals, dimly-starred,
> And of ourselves and of our origins,
> In ghostlier demarcations, keener sounds.

> [*The Collected Poems of Wallace Stevens*
> (New York: Alfred A. Knopf, 1980), pp. 128–130.]

"Music *is* about something," Erickson wrote in 1980, a year after composing *The Idea of Order at Key West*, "it is always about human experience, human emotion when you get to the essentials." And there has always been something private about Erickson, as blandly forthcoming as he is about social, political, even esthetic matters. His memoirs are conversational, but, in his own admission, "mute about the deepest, most important experiences of [his] life." It's likely that his upbringing made it difficult for him to be casually informative about those experiences. It's equally likely that when (and indeed even if) he considered them at any length he thought about them in sounds, not in words. It's certain that in some regards his manipulations of events, even of people—and they seemed always benign manipulations—were matters he kept slyly to himself: arrangements for a succession of music directors at KPFA, for the nurture of experimental music at the San Francisco Conservatory, for the development of the San Diego department.

He was not one to take public credit for such matters, though he didn't deny it, on the rare occasion when it was forthcoming. Equally: when plans—or, more often, hopes—for a nearly idealistic arrangement went awry, or (more discouragingly) when the success of a visionary plan went to seed, Erickson had a way of shrugging it off: that was the way of the world: one hasn't failed for lack of trying. There is something fastidious, almost in the sense of Wallace Stevens's fastidiousness, in the objectivity of such an attitude, an objectivity curiously blended with practicing advocacy.

The summer of 1979 was devoted to study: Erickson returned to a "recurrent obsession—Greek music, ancient music, all of that." He had been giving considerably thought also to ancient Chinese music, and had concluded that

> there is no primitive music—never has been.... We probably have to take another look at our western conception of history—it is fatally Darwinistic. We can't seem to get free of the notion that everything that happened before us was inferior to what we now have, and that, at most, it was the "forerunner" to the marvelous music we now enjoy. I think that view is self serving baloney. [Letter to the author, December 21, 1979.]

By the close of 1979 Erickson's health had deteriorated alarmingly. The diagnosis, after five months of examinations and analysis, was myositis, a disorder causing the immune system to attack muscle cells. He was treated with Prednisone, which depresses the immune system to bring the production of antibodies within normal ranges.

> At the high initial dose it also makes one quite mad. I was sky high for several months—at one point I went for several weeks without sleeping, enjoying every minute! And I became very very talkative—babbling all the time, on any provocation, to the point where I sometimes felt I was holding nothing back. A very strange time. Naturally, I floated down to earth—even below, and have been suffering a mild chronic depression which is more like my usual unoptimistic outlook. The drug works as it should, however ... I spent a week in New Hampshire this summer with no problems, and I expect some inconvenience from my muscles but no super difficulty. I will have to take that drug forever, however, and I don't know too much about its long term effects. [Letter to the author, September 18, 1980.]

Erickson was to become increasingly confined by his advancing illness, however. In July 1981 he underwent a cataract operation, which went well, but a planned trip to San Francisco to hear *Night Music* had to be canceled when his right hip failed, consigning him to a wheelchair. By that winter he was worse:

> I walk with a cane, climb no steps, and travel not too much—to school and back. The bones in my hips are breaking down for lack of blood supply. The Prednisone I took to control my polymyositis did the damage. It is not likely to improve. [Letter to Patricia Smith, January 12, 1982.]

Erickson had never been drawn to physical activity for its own sake, and he accepted advancing physical infirmity wryly, commenting that since he was forced to use a wheelchair, as Darius Milhaud had been by his chronic arthritis, he was becoming as prolific as Milhaud, though he preferred his own music. He continued to teach full-time, giving seminars at home when he could no longer manage the trip to campus. Finally, in December 1982, both hips were replaced, and the Erickson house was remodeled against the inevitable day when he would be confined to the wheelchair.

Throughout this period Erickson worked on a third book, *Hearing Things*, a collection of memoirs, unpublished articles on tuning and homemade instruments, and travel notes. And he had begun a serious study of late-romantic music, primarily in order to analyze the orchestral sounds favored by such composers as Mahler and Debussy. He also began to distance himself from the university, although he hoped to continue teaching until mandatory retirement at seventy, in 1987:

> We are changing at UC San Diego into a hi tech wonderland, flooded with students who are good at math and terrible at reading thinking or hearing music. Computer types (wrong sort) obsessed with typing in the perfect algorithm for the ultimate intellectual construction. They are not much concerned with how the result sounds—it is sort of accident, tho all is well if the algorithm is [s]ound. A new kind of program music. So—a certain distance is developing between me an[d] my colleagues. I won't, can't, show these budding composers—deafer than Beethoven—how to write a moderne, up-to-date piece of music. Worse, I want to teach only the ones I think have talent! In the modern

university, in the modern world, this is heresy. Everything, absolutely EVERYTHING is supposed to be teachable and learnable. This is a very modern point of view, in tune with our media civilization, where nothing is presumed to be new, and where talent is equated with re-makes of movies, tv shows, even the news.... [Letter to the author, March 22, 1983.]

Still, Erickson was not overly depressed. The recording of *Night Music, The Idea of Order at Key West*, and *Pacific Sirens* (1969), released by Composers Recordings in 1984, brought him a new audience. And that year, too, he entered into a contract with Smith Publications: ultimately all his music would be available on paper, facilitating its further study and performance. Throughout the 1970s Erickson's music had begun to be heard beyond the university, largely through special festivals rather than the emerging contemporary-music industry. He was not likely to be named composer-in-residence to a major orchestra: his age, his precarious health, and his repu-tation as an eccentric on the American musical scene would weigh against him in the increasingly bland and conformist national arena. But Tom Nee, conductor of the La Jolla Civic Orchestra, also directed an annual summer festival in New Hampshire, and faithfully performed Erickson's music there. UC San Diego collaborated with the Las Vegas campus of the University of Nevada and with the private California Institute of the Arts in an annual festival for a number of years, and Erickson's music was heard on some of those programs. And twice the Cabrillo Festival in Santa Cruz broke the Northern California silence that had largely greeted Erickson since his move south in 1967, programming *White Lady* in 1983 and *Auroras* in 1989.

In 1983 Nee led the American Composers Orchestra of New York in the premiere of *Auroras*, to impressive reviews; two years later Joel Sachs led the new-music ensemble Continuum in music by Erickson and Lou Harrison, again precipitating considerable press activity in New York. These performances, and the loyal support of Alan Rich, brought him and his music to the attention of the art and music patron Betty Freeman. She com-missioned Erickson's first string quartet since 1957, *Solstice*, which was completed in 1985 and won the Friedheim Award for chamber music that year (sharing first prize with a string quartet by Donald Martino). This success prompted Freeman to offer two more commissions: for *Corfu*, a sequel to *Solstice*, and for *Corona*, for string orchestra. (Freeman also supported the CRI recording cited earlier.)

In the meantime two other commissions had come in for small mixed-instrument ensembles. The San Francisco Contemporary Music Players applied to the National Endowment for the Arts for a "consortium commission," shared with the New York group Speculum Musicae and SONOR at UCSD; the resulting Quintet for flute, clarinet, trumpet, viola, and cello was premiered in San Francisco in 1985. And Continuum, pleased with the success of their 1985 performance of *Night Music*, requested a new work for their 1987 tour to Germany. This resulted in *Recent Impressions*, Erickson's final "orchestral" piece—really scored for chamber orchestra: one player on each instrument, with solo piano.

Then, in 1987, the University of California at San Diego celebrated a triple Erickson event: his seventieth birthday, his retirement, and the twentieth anniversary of the founding of the music department. The fifty-six-page program was full of encomiums and anecdotes; Glenn Glasow and Alan Rich gave seminars on the music; a roundtable gathered Erickson's colleagues and protégés from the KPFA days; a screening offered two documentary films on his researches and the music that resulted; and five concerts presented no fewer than twenty-two compositions. For a week the department seemed to revert to the one Erickson had so enjoyed twenty years before, with generous tables of fruit and cheese, animated and friendly gatherings of students and colleagues, and a series of performances whose energy and dedication overcame pressures of time and space. Regrettably, Erickson was absent, flat on his back on a hospital bed, fighting off a severe reaction, either to a scratch from his cat Skitters or to the medication he'd been given in its wake. His health, already precarious for the preceding two decades, declined alarmingly. Two of his most transcendent compositions were still to come: *Fives*, a dark piece for English horn, bass clarinet, viola, cello, and piano, composed in 1988; and the enigmatic *Music for Trumpet, Strings, and Timpani*, slowly and painfully written out in 1990.

Compositions since 1976:

1976–77	*Garden* for violin and small orchestra
1977	*Kryl* for solo trumpet
1978	*Night Music* for trumpet and ten instruments
	Quoq for solo flute
1979	*The Idea of Order at Key West* for soprano, flute, clarinet, trumpet, viola, and cello
1980	*East of the Beach* for orchestra
	Postcards for mezzo-soprano and lute
1981	*The Pleiades* for solo violin
1981–82	*Three Songs for the Five Centuries Ensemble* for two voices, harpsichord, and viola da gamba (contains: "Night Sky"; "Birds at Dusk"; "Before Dawn")
1982	*Auroras* for orchestra (rev. 1985)
1983	*Mountain* for soprano, small women's chorus, and chamber orchestra
	Taffytime for chamber orchestra
1984	*Sierra* for tenor and chamber orchestra
1984–85	*Solstice* for string quartet
1985	*Dunbar's Delight* for solo timpani
	Quintet for flute, clarinet, trumpet, violin, and cello
1986	*Corfu* for string quartet
	Corona for orchestra
	Two Songs for soprano, clarinet, viola, and piano ("Days and Nights"; "Seasonal")
	Trio for clarinet, harp, and violoncello
1987	*Recent Impressions* for flute, oboe, bassoon, horn, trumpet, percussion, two pianos, and strings
1988	*Fives* for English horn, bass clarinet, viola, cello, and piano
1990	*Music for Trumpet, Strings, and Timpani*

1. *Hearing Things.*
2. Ramon Sender: prospectus for the San Francisco Tape Music Center, 1964.
3. Erickson: letter to the author, April 9, 1978.
4. Letter to the author, February 9, 1979.

Lenore Alt-Erickson and Robert Erickson in Douglas, Michigan, early 1940s. Family photograph.

Erickson as personnel clerk, U.S. Army, ca. 1945. Family photograph.

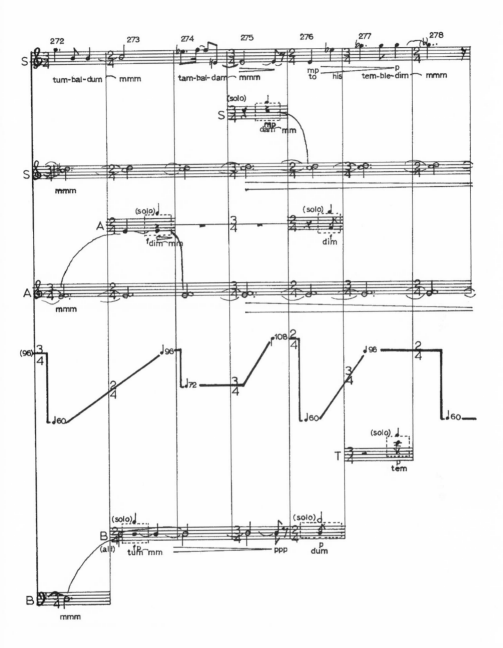

A page from *The End of the Mime of Mick, Nick and the Maggies* (1963) for eight-part chorus. (One tenor part is silent on this page.) Note the angular line through the middle of the page, indicating changes of tempo between 60 (bottom) and 108 (top) quarter-note beats per minute. Courtesy Smith Publications.

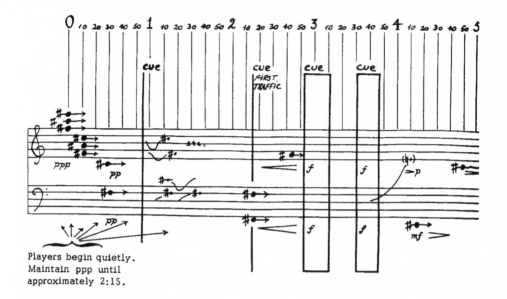

Players begin quietly.
Maintain ppp until
approximately 2:15.

PERFORMANCE NOTES

Score in C.

Instrumentation:

      Recommended: 2 wind - flute, piccolo, clarinet
                  2 brass - trumpet, trombone (no tuba)
                  2 percussion (no mallet instruments or timpani)
                  1 contra bass (no high string instruments)

Other instruments may be added, such as oboe, bassoon, French horn.
Doubling of instruments is encouraged.

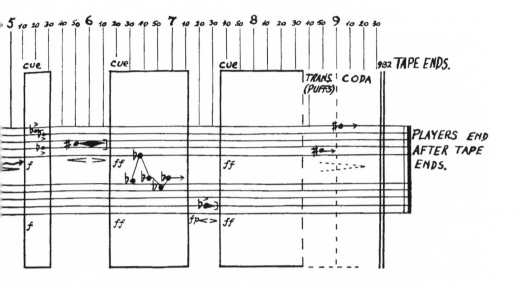

1. Musicians should relate to the timbre of the tape sounds (abrupt).

2. No half or whole-step pitch changes. No tunes.

3. Bend pitches with descretion.

4. Air sounds are OK.

5. Relate to auto, airplane, jet, etc. without direct simulation of sounds.

6. Tune carefully to tape pitches and other players. Percussion should tune skin instruments to chief pitches of tape and/or octaves of those pitches. Wild pitches should ornament the structural pitches in significant ways.

October, 1970

The score of *Pacific Sirens* (1970). All performers play from this score, responding to a prerecorded tape. Courtesy Smith Publications.

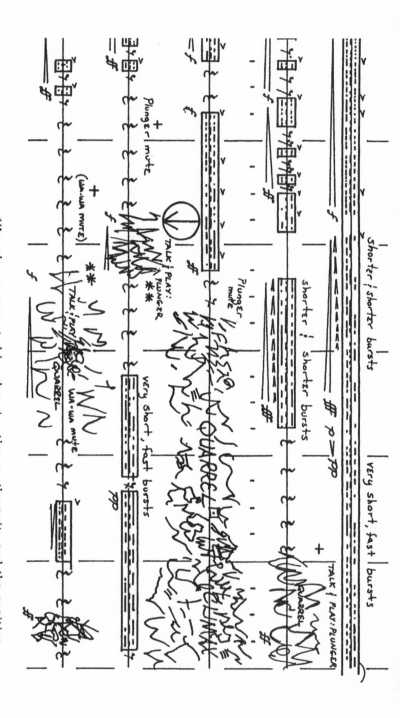

Excerpt from *Ricercare à 5*, for five trombones or solo trombone and four self-prepared tapes, commissioned by and dedicated to Stuart Dempster (1966). Excerpt edited and annotated by Dempster. ©1993 assigned to Smith Publications.

*Vowels are executed by changing the mouth cavity and the position of the tongue within the mouth while otherwise playing normally.

Stuart Dempster performing Robert Erickson's *General Speech*,
April 1995, University of Arizona, Tucson. Photograph by Russ
Widener; used with permission.

PART TWO: THE WORKS

A composer's idiom is his own manner of speaking as creative thinker, original as the sound of his own voice. His content is his esthetic consistency, saying what he has to say. A composer is not uniformly aware of the forces which make him what he is; they are a part of him. The consistency he must achieve if he is to become a composer, instead of [merely] a practitioner of his art, will be under his control exactly to the degree that he is able to direct his intuitive conditioning to its creative purpose.... The consistency, as it is achieved, matures within the composer as his content, what he has to say. The subject, not yet married to content, grows within the composer as an irritant, putting him to work; his manner of disposing of it will be his style for that work or that period.... Style follows content, the outward sign of the composer's growing inner consistency; the achieved consistency of the artist extrudes the idiomatic consistency of his style. Together they evolve.

—PETER YATES: *TWENTIETH CENTURY MUSIC*
(Pantheon Books, 1967), pp. 40–41

I. THE EARLY WORK: MUSIC AND THE MIND,
   COMPOSITIONS THROUGH 1957

Early Vocal Music and *The 1945 Variations*

Three Rilke Songs (1940); Motet, "Song of Songs" (1943); *Two Christmas Choruses* (1944); *The Star Song* (1944); *Be Still My Soul* (1945); *Three Contralto Songs* (1945); *The 1945 Variations* (1945–46)

The line between apprentice and fully mature work is hard to draw in any composer's output. In the twentieth century, however, it has become customary to render this difficulty moot, for many composers conceal the line. Some simply make no attempt to keep early pieces available to performance. Others stop discussing them, or go so far as to destroy early work altogether. An industry has grown up centered on the discovery and publication of early scores: student works by Anton Webern, interesting for those tracing his stylistic evolution, but not particularly helpful in filling out the standard repertoire, have taken their place in his catalogue alongside undisputed masterpieces. The early work of Edgard Varèse, on the other hand, was all destroyed during the First World War—all but one orchestral score, which he destroyed himself to make the historic disaster complete. (Even here, though, a musicologist would prove capable of thwarting the composer: Robert P. Morgan exhumed, annotated, and republished an early song—definitely a student assignment—in *Musical Newsletter* [III, 2], with the ironic title "Not Even Varèse Can Be an Orphan.")

Robert Erickson's music does not fall easily into stylistic periods in any case. There does seem to be a break of sorts in 1960, when the *Chamber Concerto* records his first tentative approaches toward granting permission to the performer to improvise. Otherwise, as might be expected from a composer already keen on producing music that develops organically from constantly extended ideas, one piece suggests the next, as each phrase or section has responded to the one preceding.

That said, there are ways of focusing our attention to his music. John Mac-Kay, in his study of Erickson's music, has sketched out four general groupings: the early pieces through the String Quartet No. 2; the music from 1957 through 1963; that composed during the rest of the 1970s, typified by "new and ancient means: collaboration, extended virtuosity, collage, and 'communal' music"; and the later music, considered as exemplifying "refinement, introspection, and 'tonal narrative.'"[1] Like any, this schema profits from certain local adjustments that illuminate the terrain at the cost of simplicity and fixity.

The earliest Erickson music we know of seems no longer to exist—pieces like the dance score composed at Park House in 1936, the movement for string quartet apparently tried out in Chicago in 1938, even the symphony Mitropoulos had wanted to play in Minneapolis in 1947. The earliest scores available for inspection, composed during World War II, are all vocal compositions: choral settings (*The Star Song*, for women's voices; *Be Still My Soul* and *Five Job Choruses*, for mixed chorus) and *Three Contralto Songs*, for voice and piano. These were preceded by another set of songs, the earliest music acknowledged by the composer: *Three Rilke Songs*, dating from 1940. (The poems chosen are "This Is My Strife," "Thou My Sacred Solitude," and "You Come Too," in M. D. Herter's translations, published by Norton.) MacKay finds (as may have been expected) traces of Schoenberg and, especially, Berg in these songs. (For many years Berg's own catalogue began with the work he himself called *Seven Early Songs*, echoing Gustav Mahler's *Youth's Magic Horn*.)

While these early pieces are soundly constructed and effectively phrased, they are relatively unimaginative in their treatment of either texts or performance resources. The words are characteristically set one note to each syllable; the accompaniment (where present, in the songs) is melodic rather than sonorous. The two wartime sacred choruses, Motet "Song of Songs" and *Two Christmas Choruses*, undoubtedly influenced by Krenek's example, look back to the polyphony of the Renaissance—while observing practical limitations of immediate performance (though by a chorus, at Hamline University, whose director was undoubtedly a master at realizing difficult music with not necessarily exceptional singers). Interestingly, with these pieces Erickson all but closed the vocal pages of his catalogue for over twenty years: only the 1952 *Pastorale* and another "leftover" request, not to be realized until 1963 with *The End of the Mime of Mick, Nick and the Maggies*, would intervene before his return to chorus in 1967–68 with *Do It, Down at Piraeus*, and *Cardenitas 68*.

(He did not disown the early vocal music, however. In fact, he dusted off the 1940 *Three Rilke Songs* for a 1957 Composers' Forum concert in San Francisco: according to Erickson's own catalogue, this was their first public hearing.)

The vocal element literally faded into invisibility. Late in January 1945, Erickson drew the final double bar on a "Fast Boogie-Woogie" for solo piano—a minute of raucous, eccentric barrelhouse music suddenly interrupted by slow chords punctuating what sounds like another minute of Gregorian chant, the *Miserere*, intoned by an offstage baritone. No sooner does his plaint dwindle away than the piano resumes, only to get stuck in a groove, lose its left-hand boogie, and fade out to a quiet, inconclusive ending.

It's hard to tell where any of this came from. Erickson datelined it "25 Jan., 1945/St. Paul, Minn.," but it must have been sketched, at least, while he was still in San Antonio; perhaps he heard boogie-woogie there. The offstage performer had a precedent in the *Concord Sonata* of Charles Ives, which calls for (optional) flute and viola, both offstage, in its transcendent final movement (the music is meant to be expressive of Henry David Thoreau at Walden Pond). And the sacred text, though undoubtedly meant ironically—this is the first instance of the irony that would frequent his later music, occasionally turning sarcastic—must nevertheless represent a farewell to the choral writing that had marked his apprenticeship with Krenek at Hamline.

In any case the movement demanded an explanation, or at least a setup, and Erickson immediately began another fast movement, a minute and a half long or so, in fairly strict counterpoint, the left hand imitating the right, though lagging a beat behind and inverting its notes (as the two hands invert the relationship of thumb to fingers). Here the motor energy and the simple two-step rhythm of the boogie-woogie are retained, but the notes tend not to spell out conventional tonal relationships. Too, the rhythm is sprung, not only by syncopations but also by occasionally intruding measures of odd beats.

The result is an interesting pair of fast movements, the first a sort of high-art commentary on the second—a commentary that slyly keeps a second vernacular reference in its vest pocket: early twentieth-century piano ragtime, whose syncopations distinguish it from the more obsessive boogie-woogie of the 1940s. Traditional concert purposes, however, demanded a third movement, a slow one separating these two fast ones. This took Erickson another year to produce, for it turned out to be both elusive and the prelude to the first technique of his mature style, the sort of emerging organic thematic evolution that would reach its highest point in the *Variations for Orchestra* and the *Concerto for Piano and Seven Instruments*, fifteen and eighteen years later.

This central movement also suggested the title for the resulting collection, in which three disparate movements are convincingly welded into a single musical event: *The 1945 Variations*. The Adagio opens slowly, in calm, measured chords, rather like a pianist experimenting, for nearly two minutes, with successions of minor and major chords. The music builds to an unhurried loud climax, then hesitates on an isolated low bass note, repeated with increasing speed but decreasing loudness to usher in a fast, rhythmic, rocking bass figure supporting a new, angular music taking the right hand well above the treble staff. From here the music returns to earlier contemplations, alternating the chordal and the rhythmic ideas, ultimately concluding in a lyrical line (marked "free, expressive") in the baritone register over a counterpointed deep bass.

The center of this big middle movement refers to both the opening movement and the chorale-like interruption of the *Miserere* in the finale. Erickson is clearly motivated by the traditional arch-shape of the conventional three-part form, yet he is also working toward the continuously progressive kind of form that Schoenberg and others had developed to displace such more classical forms. (Schoenberg found the idea in Brahms.) The result is a convincing piece, solidly reasoned in its structure; offering both challenge and display to the performer; imaginative in its juxtapositions of speed, loudness, texture, and range; and—most impressively—commuting easily between lyricism and irony, sentiment and wit.

Yet the piece remained unknown for many years. It does not appear in the catalogue maintained by the composer through the late 1970s. It may have received its first public performance in 1987, at the San Diego festival celebrating the composer's seventieth birthday, when it was a surprise addition to an afternoon seminar on the composer's early music presented by Glenn Glasow. It was finally copyrighted in 1988, when it was belatedly published.

1.   John MacKay: *Music of Many Means: Sketches and Essays on the Music of Robert Erickson* (Metuchen, NJ: Scarecrow Press, 1995).

Postwar Transitional Work, 1948–1950

Introduction and Allegro for Orchestra (1948); Piano Sonata (1948); String Quartet No. 1 (1950)

Two orchestral pieces occupied Erickson in the years immediately after World War II, while he was working on his graduate degree at Hamline University: a symphony, submitted to Dmitri Mitropoulos through Ernst Krenek and scheduled for performance (but, as we have seen, withdrawn when Krenek left Minnesota for California), and an *Introduction and Allegro*. The symphony was dropped from the composer's catalogue; parts of it may have been recycled into subsequent pieces, but Erickson is characteristically silent about compositions he no longer recognizes.

The earliest extant orchestral piece of Erickson's, then, is the *Introduction and Allegro for Orchestra* completed in 1948—a rhythmic, focused, and clearly structured piece. Significantly, Erickson continued to work on a basic structural idea that preoccupied him for the next fifteen years: building a piece of music that unfolds out of its opening sounds, like a house whose sequence of rooms is suggested in the layout of the details in its entrance hall.

In part *Introduction and Allegro* responds to Erickson's dedication to counterpoint as a clarifying device—a preoccupation whose scholarly climax came five years later with the writing of his first book, *The Structure of Music*. But counterpoint—the juxtaposition and combination of various melodic statements relating harmonically to a single underlying concept—was not the only means by which the material of *Introduction and Allegro* was articulated. The structural form also profits from an early exploration of the device of "continuing variation," as Schoenberg had developed it: a way of generating new twists on familiar themes; its most frequent analogy is the continual un-folding of a branching structure from a single bud. (The most familiar Brahms example is perhaps the *Variations on a Theme of Haydn*; another is the finale of the Fourth Symphony, cast in the baroque variation form of passacaglia.)

Erickson returned to the device more masterfully in the *Variations for Orchestra* of 1957 and subsequently explored a completely new use of the technique in the *Concerto for Piano and Seven Instruments* of 1963.

Like *Introduction and Allegro*, the Sonata for Piano (as the composer calls the work in his final copy) has the neoclassical stamp suggested by its title. Its dimensions are small: a five-minute fast movement, a slow intermezzo running a little under two minutes, and a finale not quite four minutes long. But the piece is concise, not small, and manages to convey a considerable homage to Schoenberg, whose piano pieces in opus 11 are hinted at in the opening movement, while developing through gestures that are by now recognizable thumbprints of Erickson's growing maturity of style. As in *The 1945 Variations*, much of the music resembles a two-part invention for keyboard, each hand playing a single note at a time. Chords appear infrequently in the first movement, notably in a slow, sepulchral passage near the middle, reminiscent of the interruption preceding the baritone's appearance in *The 1945 Variations*. Chords are absent entirely from the middle-movement Adagio until its close, when they contribute to a sense of repose; and they are found in only one moment of the third movement, where they function more as quick complex splashes of single sounds than as harmonic support.

The outer two movements are fast and rhythmic, a nervous kind of energy expressed through short, deft gestures, often quickly turning into the compulsively repeated short motives appropriately termed *ostinati*—"obstinate." In the first movement these motives give way to the oddly brooding, often languorously downward-curving phrases that recall the opening gesture of Schoenberg's fin-de-siècle opus 11 piano pieces—a sort of musical equivalent of the decadent lyricism of Art Nouveau. Erickson's sense of playful irony pulls him out of this mood, at the beginning of the second half of the first movement, by repeating a dark and complex chord, on each repetition omitting the lowest notes, one by one, until only a single repeated pitch remains to return to the opening theme, ushering in the recapitulation required of a formally correct sonata-allegro movement.

The Adagio, unusually for Erickson in this period, is free of metrical regularity—indeed, innocent of the bar lines that impose such regularity on the performer. Marked "Sostenuto e espressivo," it proceeds through ten or so supple phrases, each six or eight seconds long. The movement is generally quiet, though it rises rather quickly to a loud climax just past the center, where chords are finally introduced into the sonata's texture. The piece is poised, direct, spare, and warm. It has the air of an improvisation; one can readily imagine Erickson working it out at a single sitting, probably at the piano. Its character is utterly unlike the quick, nervous movements flanking it, yet it is logically connected to them: the two hands move in opposite ("contrary") direction most of the time, joining (one after the other) in upward motion only to introduce the climax in a slower, more sustained version of the quick three-note upward gestures that animate the opening piece.

One might think a piece like this formally integrated three-movement sonata was the product of an intense, relatively short period of work. But the end of the first movement is dated November 28, 1947; the Adagio December 22, 1947; and the finale October 26, 1950. This is a revision: the piece as a whole is dated at its head "1948," and it was premiered (by Marjorie Winslow Briggs) in 1949 in Minneapolis. In any case the revised finale, while linked to the earlier movements in terms of its spare texture and its clearly articulated phrases, leads toward a new direction in its shifting, irregular accents, and the overlapping nature of the phrases played by its two hands. The latter characteristic was hinted at in the intermezzo, but there it led to sustained, ambiguous lines; in the finale it tends toward more ragged, animated sentences, in which the regular rhythm breaks down, not simply through occasional dropped beats—a characteristic of the first movement—but through displaced accents recalling the effects of a classical fugue *stretto*, when the familiar fugue theme, by being begun in one voice before it is finished in another, takes on a new sense of urgency, sometimes to a dramatic purpose, sometimes to a playful one.

We have considered the Sonata at some length, as it is typical of Erickson's music of the late 1940s. With the First String Quartet and *Introduction and Allegro*, it typifies above all a formal, almost a neoclassical preoccupation. The composer had acquired his art in an orderly, natural progression. Beginning in childhood he learned music as a performing instrumentalist; next, in youth, he began to learn the literature, both as it was available from the radio and occasional concerts, and, later, as it became available through the printed page.

Finally he had learned, particularly through studies with Krenek, the history of the actual composition of music.

As the adept begins transition to mastery, he is concerned above all with formal matters: with structure, clarity, and technique. The ultimate instrumental musical forms at the mid-twentieth century, as at the end of the nineteenth, were the variation form and the sonata; and their highest expressions were in the media of the symphony orchestra, the solo piano, and the string quartet.

In four years Erickson had come to terms with those forms and media. The results may have been mixed, to his own way of thinking: he made no subsequent attempt at securing performances of the First String Quartet, and *Introduction and Allegro* has been largely ignored since its premiere. (The quartet, though, had been played three times, apparently by three different ensembles, and to good reviews from John Harvey in the St. Paul *Pioneer Press* and Peggy Glanville-Hicks in the New York *Herald Tribune*. Its disappearance from the Erickson catalogue is a disappointment.)

To a degree these early successes may have been the cause of their own disappearance: Erickson may simply have solved his own apprentice problems with them—satisfied their challenges sufficiently to lose interest in them for further activity as a composer. They prove, though, that he could occupy a part of his attention, over a fairly long period of time, with the development of a fairly big musical structure, restricting the number and variety of sounds he needed to fill it without letting the energy flag—either his own energy or that of his music.

The consistency described by Peter Yates, in the memorable divagation in his book *Twentieth Century Music* quoted at the head of this section, has evolved in Erickson's work. When it evolves so far as to become the composer's mature "style"—his manner of disposing of the content of his music, within a specific piece, or a specific period—it ceases to be an object of study or technique, as far as the composer himself is concerned. Erickson didn't simply abandon this line of stylistic evolution: he tried to pursue the contrapuntal complexities, held firmly in check in the relatively modest confines of the Sonata and the First Quartet, in a chamber symphony on which he worked throughout 1951. But he found that piece, still in the shadow of Schoenberg's contrapuntal precedent, "incredibly difficult to write," as he confessed in a letter to Wilbur Ogdon.[1] He reworked it, as we shall see, into the 1953 Divertimento. (The revisions were so radical as to constitute a total abandonment of the original.) The composer's attention was by then transferred to something else. That new object was, typically, not a matter from the period of his teachers; it was a part of the artist's own, contemporary, immediate world. Before he began to address that new object, though, Erickson was distracted from composition by another matter entirely: the writing of his first book, *The Structure of Music.*

As we have seen, the book was the product of a number of influences and motivations—perhaps too many, contributing to too tense and dynamic an undertaking. Ernst Krenek's *Music Here and Now* was the first impetus: a defense of new music, written by the master for the layman. Erickson's own students undoubtedly provided the second impetus: the need for a straight-forward, untechnical discussion of the internal, structural workings of "classical" music—in terms understandable by the average American college student of the 1940s, considerably less prepared for intellectual challenges than the European student of a generation or two before.

A third motivation was very likely the artist's need to work out on paper some of the procedures he had been evolving in his own study and his own composition. And not only procedures, but *values*, too: the relative positions, in terms of importance in esthetic and intellectual terms, of the processes, events, and goals of musical organization. There is no doubt that the art of music consists in the arrangement of sounds in contexts that make sense: but according to what kind of awareness do they make sense? The history of esthetics—the study of that ineffable satisfaction that results from the contemplation of the various kinds of art—is fraught with poignant approaches to theories of art-awareness, approaches that were tremendously significant in their time, only to become dated, then quaint, then ludicrous, finally incomprehensible. Beauty has been associated with Justice, Truth, the (moral) Good, the Sublime. Even Krenek's view, which tended to equate artistic (especially musical) value with the socially useful, must have begun to seem occasionally dubious to Erickson as he dealt with the issue of writing music in a society that relegates contemporary music to the back room of an already infrequently visited edifice.

The reader will be disappointed who looks in *The Structure of Music* for a direct discussion of these matters. Plain-spoken and straightforward, the book discusses the nuts and bolts of music, exactly as its subtitle promises: "A study of music in terms of melody and counterpoint." But Erickson does occasionally reveal the standards by which he judges the ultimate goal of musical expression. He describes J. S. Bach's *The Musical Offering* as "full of curious and beautiful things.... But they are musical, not merely technical marvels.... Playfulness, technical mastery ... is only the outward sign of the profound inner unity and purity of the music.... The deeper meaning of canon and its validity as a procedure is involved with the whole matter of unity and variety in music."[2] As he had explained traditional harmony—tonality—in terms of the familiar metaphor of "these simple ideas: (1) a home base; (2) harmonic movement to areas within a key or even to new keys, in order to express harmonic tension, which (3) is finally resolved by a return to the home base,"[3] so Erickson discussed his chief subject, counterpoint, in terms of a single kind of tension: that between unity and variety. That tension was already becoming a chief concern, artistically and socially, in mid-twentieth century America, where World War II had laid to rest, permanently, the idea of a homogenous society of monolithic values. Erickson found the contrapuntal tension throughout the history of art, from such Renaissance composers as Ockeghem and Josquin to such modernist masters as James Joyce and Anton Webern. And he traced for his American undergraduates, with admirable efficiency and clarity, the methods by which contrapuntal composers throughout history had related various processes to achieve a unified work of art.

Direct and simple as the book seems today, in its time it represented a revolutionary revision of the academic approach to teaching counterpoint. The traditional approach was through analysis and imitation of the style of a historic master—J. S. Bach or Palestrina. Instead, Erickson proposed to focus on the techniques themselves: spinning long melodic lines out of short motives, imitating melodic shapes in different voices, and so on. Instead of hopelessly attempting to apprehend the style of a master long dead, through a complete understanding of masterpieces from the past—masterpieces whose full implications and detailed workings probably eluded even the geniuses who created them—the reader, the young woman in Erickson's classes at St. Catherine's, would be introduced to the relatively simple methods used to make not only those masterpieces but others closer to her own time and place. The "[b]asic idea is that the bright students will write in contemporary idioms, and [the] book will constantly show affinities between contemporary and older practices."[4]

But he closed the book with what he called "A last word," typically Erickson's in its pragmatic tone and its almost ironic detachment:

> The procedures we have discussed are to be found everywhere in music. They are a part of the equipment of every composer. Every performer needs a thorough understanding of them in order to interpret contrapuntal music properly. Listener and amateur may profit from an acquaintance with them. But it is so easy to point them out, to compare them and to relate them to each other, that one can easily mistake them for counterpoint itself.
>
> The procedures are not the music. They are ways of working, and the composer, not the procedure, makes the music. A canon may be perfectly strict and still be worthless. A fugue may be packed with countersubjects, interchangeable counterpoint, cunning strettos and other devices, yet sound dull as dishwater.
>
> Conversely, a composition may use no "standard" procedures at all, nothing we can abstract and attach a label to, yet be truly contrapuntal—because in the balance of the lines, at once independent and dependent, forming a larger whole, yet each contributing its perfect wholeness, is the essence of counterpoint.
>
> Analysis and discussion may help us to understand the procedures, at least in an intellectual way, but to feel these relations only the ear is of use.[5]

1. September 2, 1951, in *Erickson Celebration*, p. 48.
2. *The Structure of Music*, p. 150.
3. *Structure*, p. 83.
4. Letter to Wilbur Ogdon, September 1, 1951, in *Erickson Celebration*, p. 49.
5. *Structure*, p. 201.

Breakthrough: Early Mature Work, 1952–1954

> *Pastorale* (1952) for chorus, soprano, tenor, and string quartet; Divertimento (1953) for flute, clarinet, and string orchestra; Trio (1953) for violin, viola, and piano; *Fantasy* (1953) for cello and orchestra

Before Erickson began to compose the kind of music that would reveal, through the mastery of his technique, the unique relevance of his view of the world as he conceived and expressed it through sounds, he passed through yet another transition.

This one was characterized not by approaching and achieving a perfection of form through counterpoint, in the almost neoclassical style of *Introduction and Allegro for Orchestra*, the Piano Sonata, and the String Quartet No. 1, but by relinquishing that goal. Erickson was setting aside classicism in favor of expression. Not expressionism, the achievement of heightened emotional content through exaggerations of volume, instrumental sound, or discord: he was familiar enough with that, having long been fascinated with the music of Berg. Instead he toyed with an almost opposite kind of musical discourse—a romantic, even pastoral lyricism, revealed by the very titles of three of the next four compositions: *Pastorale* (1952) for chorus, soprano, tenor, and string quartet; Divertimento (1953) for flute, clarinet, and string orchestra; *Fantasy* (1954) for cello and orchestra.

These pieces have another aspect in common: they represent Erickson's first approach to the differentiation of soloists, or groups of soloists, from the musical contexts in which they are set. In the Sonata, Quartet, and *Introduction and Allegro*, the maturing composer was honing his skill with musical rhetoric, the art of developing themes and laying out structure. Now he was adding another item to the "content" of his work: the distribution of the music, among instruments and voices, to a dramatic or expressive effect. Only the 1953 Trio for violin, viola, and piano was to revert, in its title and its performing medium, to the "abstract" quality of the period that had preceded the writing of *The Structure of Music.*

The first of these compositions was the *Pastorale*, a setting, for soprano, tenor, chorus, and string quartet, of a lyric written for the purpose by Erickson's friend Jane Mayhall. The subject is appropriate to a composer undergoing stylistic transition: a couple whose love, as it reaches its climax and then passes into transcendence, is likened to the natural progress of the season from summer into autumn. The poem is bucolic, in almost a Hellenistic vein, its lines divided between a chorus (onlookers, gods, or nymphs, perhaps) and the amorous couple. There are three parts. A four-minute introduction sets the pastoral summertime scene, with the chorus, supported by the string quartet, singing primarily chordal, relatively harmonic music. This section ends with the chorus commanding the couple to speak for themselves, and a middle section, not quite three minutes long, follows. Soprano, then tenor sing of their love, culminating in an instrumental passage, playfully militant in tone, meant to describe the climax of their love. (Erickson cannot resist poking a bit of fun at similar moments in the music of Richard Strauss.) The chorus then reappears: "Now the center has been taken. Let no word be spoken." A four-minute conclusion has begun, in which a downward mood-curve, developed alternately by chorus and string quartet, describes the ebbing energy as the couple's love ripens and subsides to its inevitable repose.

It is interesting to contemplate a possible source for this subject in Arnold Schoenberg's *Transfigured Night* (1899) for string sextet—a purely instrumental meditation on a similar though more complex lyric. It is not irrelevant that the Ericksons themselves were spending the summer of 1952 in the artists' colony at Yaddo in New York and had spent their previous summer in the relatively idyllic setting of Colorado Springs—though in their mid-thirties they were no longer youthful. In fact, they were approaching the age at which climax and continuance become familiar comforts measuring the larger progress of domestic life, not dramatic events marking its most immediate meaning. In any case poet and composer alike approach the subject directly, rather than impressionistically. The perfumed, languorous world of Debussy's *Prelude to the Afternoon of a Faun*, not to mention the orgiastic events of Ravel's *Daphnis and Chloe*, are far away from Mayhall and Erickson's couple, who seem more like college students than shepherds. Yet the juxtaposition of a certain playful irony, in the music describing the couple, with the lyricism of the choral writing, which at times approaches hymn-tune sentiment, suggests a certain detachment on Erickson's part. He manages easily enough to propel Mayhall's lyric with his musical energy, and to express it through his melodic fragments and his harmonic coloration. Beyond this, though, chiefly through negative means, he expresses a realistic view of his subject, a view that is essentially postwar and American, not prewar and European. The scene is set, the story told, the conclusion drawn economically though not tersely. The chorus of elders is matter-of-fact, not wondrous or probing; the couple is youthfully exuberant, but neither innocent nor fated.

In April 1953 Erickson completed the next two scores, the Divertimento for flute, clarinet, and string orchestra, and the Trio for violin, viola (the more usual instrument would have been cello), and piano. Structurally, both pieces recall the Piano Sonata, laid out as two fast movements, the second prefaced by a slow intermezzo-like introduction. The unusual instrumentation of the Trio was determined by its intended ensemble, faculty performers at St. Catherine's. Only seven minutes long, and a "fairly easy piece to perform," as Erickson noted in a May 1953 letter to Wilbur Ogdon, it was written quickly: the first movement is dated March 20, the second, April 8. Both quick movements are integrated, through the use of short, repeated motives, almost to the point of monotony, and the short second movement breaks off before achieving a fully stated purpose of its own. (This happens twice in succession in this short piece.)

The Trio appeared simultaneously with the Divertimento, the first of a number of orchestral pieces to be written for the conductor Thomas Nee, always an enthusiastic supporter. The Divertimento had a much longer gestation than the Trio: it was "the piece which originally started out to be a chamber symphony," Erickson continued in the same letter to Ogdon:

> I gave it several good hard looks during the past three years (yes it was begun that long ago) and finally threw out the old first movement, [and] wrote a new second [movement] and finale. The finale was done at Yaddo last summer, and was my first tonal piece, a rondo, very

simple, very classical. NOT NEO-CLASSICAL. [May 20, 1953, in *Erickson Celebration*, p. 49.]

In an ebullient mood, Erickson went on to describe projects for further work: an a cappella piece for Robert Holliday's chorus; a trio for the traditional violin-cello-piano instrumentation; a string orchestra piece suitable to amateur community organizations. "What fun, Will; the music is just pouring out of me.... I drop everything just to get at it."

Yet these new pieces did not materialize. Perhaps Erickson recalled an observation he had made a year and a half earlier, when he had written to Ogdon of Krenek's recent work: "I heard a lot of his new music, and some of it is pretty good—6th [piano] sonata—but I still believe he is writing too much. Somehow, the music seems a little too thin, a little on the surface."[1]

Instead, Erickson undertook an unanticipated work, the *Fantasy* for solo cello and orchestra. This was precipitated by the death of Frank Kearney, the vivacious, intellectual, complex personality who had led Erickson to the music of Berg fifteen years earlier at Park House in Chicago. In the *Fantasy* Erickson makes his closest approach to old-fashioned romantic expressionism of a programmatic kind, the solo cellist clearly a protagonist in a musical drama. Erickson begins the piece in a slow-paced, declamatory, plaintive mood, the unaccompanied soloist rising through the bass range in a series of fourths—expressionist intervals of pitches recalling Schoenberg. (The fourth is a difficult interval to sing twice in succession, let alone five times: a rare example is found in the first three notes of the popular song "When I Fall In Love.") The cello is answered by the woodwinds, then by the strings, which build to the first loud climax of the piece, two and a half minutes in. This is answered by the soloist, then the strings, subsiding to near-inaudibility to end the four-minute introductory movement.

The main part of the *Fantasy* follows without a break, "fast and intense," in the composer's instruction, propelled by nervous, repeated sixteenth notes in the strings. After only a minute or so the music turns more lyrical with the entrance of the solo cello, but in the next minute the solo declamation becomes increasingly intense, leading to an almost Mahler-like outburst, the timpani mimicking the four notes that end the cello's original rising theme. This two-part structure is then repeated in a varied form, leading to the final third of the work. For four minutes or so the music is calmer and more expressive, the orchestra treated more like a collection of chamber ensembles that enter into alternating dialogues with the soloist. A suddenly urgent phrase from the cello is met by full-voiced replies from brass and timpani; the cellos in the orchestra twice take up the short introductory theme; the soloist repeats it, and the piece ends quietly.

The *Fantasy* requires what had by then become the minimum instrumentation of the standard symphony orchestra: pairs of flutes, oboes, clarinets, bassoons, and trumpets; four French horns, three trombones and tuba; and the five string sections (first and second violins, violas, cellos, and contrabasses). Erickson requests a third clarinetist, who also plays bass clarinet; and requests also piccolo and English horn, but without requiring the third flutist or oboist to take those instruments. Four timpani are needed, the normal number; and two percussionists are called on to play a relatively modest array of instruments: xylophone, small and large snare drums, tambourine, bass drum, cymbals, glockenspiel, and large gong.

The solo cello is given challenging material, but nothing the average competent soloist couldn't be expected to accomplish, and the orchestral parts are relatively easy but rewarding. No instrument is neglected; even the contrabasses have their solo moments. The composer's fair copy of the score was completed in San Francisco, June 21, 1954, and performances followed shortly in Hamburg (with Ernst Krenek conducting), Chicago, and San Francisco.

---

1.   September 1, 1951, in *Erickson Celebration*, p. 49.

Second Wind: The Early Masterpieces, 1956–1957

String Quartet No. 2 (1956) ; *Variations for Orchestra* (1957); Duo (1957) for violin and piano

Erickson completed the *Fantasy* shortly after moving to the San Francisco Bay Area. After his fairly settled life in St. Paul, where he had taught at St. Catherine's since the end of his own student days, he found this relocation unsettling. As we have seen, the family income depended on a succession of part-time appointments for both Robert and Lenore. Royalties from *The Structure of Music* contributed little. A hiatus of nearly three years followed the *Fantasy* for cello and orchestra: a "dry" period that he found disturbing, but during which, to judge from his next three compositions, he made yet another stylistic advance.

In these three pieces Erickson went back to the classic forms he had visited in the First Quartet, the Piano Sonata, and *Introduction and Allegro*. In so doing, he also returned to the contrapuntal values those pieces had expressed. In fact, he had never really dropped them, though the harmonic and melodic language of the more recent pieces had temporarily overshadowed them. But in his work of the late 1950s he retained the dramatic contours and colorful sonority he had more recently developed. In these three new works—the Second String Quartet, the Duo, and above all *Variations for Orchestra*—he wrote what were effectively masterpieces, the first scores that expressed his fully mature style. As Peter Yates expressed it, the forces that had made Erickson what he was as he approached forty—his inner consistency of artistic and social values, of domestic routines of work and study—were now being directed to their creative purpose. His idiom—his own manner of speaking, even more significantly of thinking, musically—had matured. In these three pieces it became the content of his music, became what he had to say. It may be that this is a function of "dry" periods: they are the visible part of a subterranean process through which an artist's creative labor is applied, not to the production of works of art, but to the maintenance and evolution of the tools that produce them.

The first of these pieces was the Second String Quartet,* requested by the California Quartet, an ensemble that specialized not only in the performance of contemporary scores but of music of their own area as well. Its members, violinists Felix Khuner and David Schneider, violist Detlev Olshausen, and cellist Detlev Anders, were prominent members of the San Francisco Symphony. Erickson must have known, certainly must have hoped, that its premiere would be a part of the festivities opening the new concert hall at the University of California in Berkeley: a great deal of scholarly and critical attention would be focused on the event. The result makes no concessions, for this was an opportunity to pull out all the stops: no need to worry about ease of performance or ingratiating the audience. Instead, Erickson could concentrate on exploring to the utmost what is in any case both a challenging and a rewarding medium: the string quartet.

The challenge is both immediate and historical. Immediate, because the composer of a string quartet must produce music that gives each of the four musicians an equal role: no part is relegated to the background for more than a few moments; interplay among the ensemble can be quick, playful, and brilliant. (A memorable description of the potential of the medium was made almost accidentally by the critic who complained that hearing a quartet of Schoenberg's was like being beat up by four immensely clever and witty thugs.) Even more, the challenge is historical: the string quartet offers perhaps the most highly evolved musical literature of its scope, for it was virtually created, a mere 250 years ago, by Franz Joseph Haydn, and explored throughout the succeeding years by such masters as Mozart, Beethoven, Schubert, Schumann, Brahms, Dvořák, Schoenberg, Bartók, Shostakovich, and Elliott Carter—to cite only those who contributed *series* of quartets to the ongoing exploration. In addition to them, of course, brilliant single or dual examples of the medium were composed by Ives, Stravinsky, Janáček, Berg, Webern, and John Cage,

---

*The work is unnumbered on the title page, which reads simply "Quartet for Strings/[signed] Robert Erickson 1956." This indicates the low regard the composer has for the First Quartet of six years earlier—unless, as is possible, he had simply forgotten about that work.

to cite only twentieth-century masters. (A more fascinating list would be made of the masters who refused to write for quartet, including Bruckner, Mahler, Varèse, and Satie—all matters of regret, for the listener and the musician.)

Erickson's Second String Quartet is his densest piece of chamber music and among the most complex music he was ever to compose. Its opening moment is one of the few making a clear gesture toward a precedent, for it irresistibly recalls the opening of Berg's String Quartet—not the *Lyric Suite*, which Erickson had met through Frank Kearney's enthusiasm, but the early Quartet op. 3, which Berg wrote as his first independent piece after leaving Schoenberg's tutelage. Berg, however, curves the six notes of his opening gesture downward, answering it with three two-note "chords," themselves proceeding downward and stated once, then twice, and finally three times. And Berg then immediately protracts and repeats the opening idea, developing a sinuous, continuous line of sound, a sonic equivalent of the characteristically Art Nouveau tendril-inspired lines of much of the graphic art of Berg's day. Erickson, on the other hand, curves the six notes of *his* opening gesture upward, answering it with two five-note chords, each stated only once, almost like the "amen" cadence of a hymn-tune or a march. And then, after hesitating for a beat of silence, Erickson thinks of two other little musical sentences, with similar chords accompanying quite different melodic shapes. The mood is not 1900 Vienna but 1950 America; not moody and sinuous but cheerful and jaunty. True, after his opening three measures, Erickson almost immediately slows the pace to a more sentimental mood for the next three; but this is to set forth at the beginning the kind of range we may expect his four conversants to explore in the course of their opening remarks.

So one listener may approach this music from the perspective of Berg, mindful of the training Erickson received from Krenek, while another may look at the score and note affinities with Gershwin (*An American in Paris* in the second measure, to be exact) and, at the top of the next page, Charles Ives (in the insistent enthusiasms of the three upper strings, climbing in agreement over a busy cello tremolo beneath them). Erickson's Second Quartet continues in this way, in a continuous (though not seamless) twenty-one minutes, with inventiveness, wit, and a sense of urgency. Such urgency, Yates points out,

> has little to do with any attachment to whatever narrative, melodic, referential, technical, or explicatory thread of subject matter is run through the design. The urgency is the continuous discovery of the composer's content within the ... pattern of cross-references of which ... he has reshaped his style. Urgency in art occurs when content, having found the means to concentrate into style, thereby makes imperative every unexpected happening it enforces within the style. [*Twentieth Century Music*, p. 42.]

And there are any number of such unexpected happenings. There's the question of how many movements there may be, for example: four, said the program notes at early performances of the piece; two, says John MacKay in his extended discussion of the work. Whatever the case, there are no extended pauses. The piece runs about twenty-one minutes, with a pronounced break—about ten seconds of measured silence—at the halfway point. The first half of the piece itself falls into three fairly clear sections: the opening two-minute "conversation," whose beginning has been described; a more lively, dancelike response, say a minute and a half long; and a much longer, more eventful, more rambling section based in general on the opening pages, and running to another seven minutes or so.

One does not always follow the thread of this conversation, not even after repeated hearings with the score. But one is always aware of a fascinating series of events, of comments, replies, expansions, and summaries—always in the unique tones of the string quartet. The music is inconceivable for winds, for piano, or for orchestra. Erickson doesn't hesitate to call for virtuoso technique, but within a collaborative context, not as a matter of solo display. Similarly, he balances quick, deft gestures with sections of repose; explores the height and depth of the quartet's range evenly; moves with assurance between the extremes of loud and soft. There is one curious detail at the halfway point: the first violin sustains a very high trill, the viola rocks back and forth on adjacent notes in the middle of its range, and the second violin and cello, across four beats, sweep back and forth across their strings in a loud passage marked both *fortissimo* and, at the foot of the page, in parentheses and in German, "(*Klimax*)." To the eye the allusion is to the climax of the slow movement of Mahler's Fourth Symphony, and this is indeed one of the few passages in Erickson's quartet that would be beautiful and effective played by a full orchestra. It offers some insight into what Erickson may have had in mind as the appropriate performance style of this eloquent and discursive score.

The closing ten minutes of the Second Quartet proceed similarly to its opening. The discussion apparently ranges over different subject matter, but the conversants speak in the same tones, with the same skillful balance of individual statements and collective agreements. Erickson seems in this score to have perfected the two-movement form he was reaching for in the Trio. He avoids the historic requirement of a contrasting slow central movement by including more ample sections within the two halves of the piece. Indeed, we will rarely again meet an Erickson score in contrasting single-tempo movements: in the Second Quartet he evolves the supple, discreet variation of musical pacing that does much to identify his mature work, and to set it apart from the predictably gaited music of most of his colleagues. He has gratefully embraced the *medium* of the string quartet, but has chosen to reject its traditional *forms*, elaborated over the centuries (and generally identical with those of the orchestral symphony): the opening sonata-allegro, the slow arch- or variation-form movement, the energetic scherzo, the clearly structured finale.

By the mid-twentieth century it was clear that to continue with such conventions was to subordinate content—"saying what [one] has to say," in Yates's term—to form, the structural layout of the piece. Musical content, through the previous century and a half, had evolved beyond the stage it had achieved when the original classicists had perfected these traditional forms. To them musical content was either primarily decorative or primarily rhetorical: it served to entertain its audience and performers (no mean assignment) or to participate equally with formal considerations in the structural elaboration of the music. (One could illustrate these two categories, admittedly with absurd overstatement, in two Mozart finales: those to the Concerto for Flute and Harp and the "Jupiter" Symphony.)

The relatively quick but often perplexing development of modernist music, roughly from 1900 to 1950, was concerned with, among other matters, the vexing search for new forms to contain new musical content. The new forms would have to accommodate new idioms—composers' personal musical expressions, and styles—prevailing collective idioms, the result of an accumulating body of work from a given period (and, perhaps, region). The composer and critic Virgil Thomson, considering this phenomenon as it had evolved up to Mahler's time, once described three kinds of traditional concert music (in a lecture given to concert audiences): "strophic," whose structural patterns are outgrowths of song, and whose familiar example might be a Schubert song; "choric," an outgrowth of dance forms, like the movements of a Bach suite or the finale of Beethoven's Seventh Symphony; and "spastic"—one might have preferred "spasmic"—whose patterns are metaphors of body processes. The first two types were in full flower by the end of the eighteenth century; the third was the invention of nineteenth-century romanticism. Erickson, in his Second Quartet, perfects an example of a fourth type of musical organization: for the moment, let us merely call it "thoughtfully conversational." Erickson was the composer, after all, who explained that he "thought sound," rather than thought in sound.

VARIATIONS FOR ORCHESTRA (1957)

Nevertheless, the question Erickson would continue to address remained—the eternal question every composer must learn to address: What is the next note? How does one keep the musical conversation going, the thought evolving? And how does one recognize that the final moment is at hand? *Variations for Orchestra* addresses this question with new directness and in terms completely different from those raised by the Second String Quartet. The quartet, after all, is a relatively intimate affair, performed by an ensemble of soloists, to be heard by an audience of connoisseurs, if not adepts. An orchestral piece, on the other hand, is a public affair: its musical content must be readily rehearsable, apparent throughout a three-thousand-seat hall, interesting to the occasional listener as well as the confirmed enthusiast.

"When I was asked by the Minneapolis Civic Orchestra in 1956 to compose a work for them, I knew only that I wanted to write a piece which would have a budding and branching-out quality," Erickson wrote in a program note to *Variations*.

> That's why I called the composition Variations. The Variations aren't on a theme. A scholar might not want to call them variations at all because what really happens is that a couple of germinal ideas which are

hardly identifiable grow in the separate sections that comprise the composition. These emotionally charged little ideas provided me with a point of view and focus. The work consists of six separate "branches." They make a pattern of contrasts.

The multimovement symphony was the primary challenge, among orchestral forms, to innovative composers in the eighteenth and nineteenth centuries. Its four contrasting movements (occasionally reduced to three) provided ample scope for Thomson's "strophic" and "choric" categories of musical expression, and even provided a hospitable environment for the evolution of "spasmic" expression, above all in the symphonies of Gustav Mahler. But the early modernist composers, aware that the search for continued relevance for the symphonic form would distract them from the more urgent consideration of the evolution of new idioms, turned away from the form. Indeed it is almost definitive of modernist composers that they avoided it: Schoenberg (whose two chamber symphonies stand as evasions of the form), Berg, Varèse, and Bartók, among the first generation of modernists; and Cage, Elliott Carter, Karlheinz Stockhausen, Pierre Boulez, and Luigi Nono, among the following one, ignored the form altogether.[*] Instead, modernist composers turned to the set of variations as the orchestral form *par excellence* as a container for the musical content representing their most public investigations of musical discourse.

There was a historical precedent even for this, in a sense, for the musical nineteenth century was initiated with the symphonic breakthrough of Beethoven's "Eroica," whose last movement, a big set of variations evolved from a smaller set originally composed for piano, revealed new orchestral

---

[*]Krenek was the fascinating exception to this generalization. He composed several symphonies and stated that he had wanted to be the successor of Mahler as a symphonist—but was disappointed by the form after writing his Fifth Symphony. "My only comfort is that nobody else has succeeded any better in continuing the great symphonic tradition." (Krenek, *Horizons Circled*, Berkeley: Univ. of California Press, p. 22). Anton Webern's one *Symphony* is, characteristically, a special case. In two movements, for small orchestra, its title uses the word etymologically rather than in its more normal sense, as does, for example, Stravinsky's *Symphonies of Winds*.

possibilities as Beethoven clothed it, with thitherto unimagined virtuosity, with instrumental colorations. Similarly, sixty years before, J. S. Bach had turned to the variation form for his monumental exploration of keyboard writing in the "Goldberg" Variations. But the style preoccupying both was essentially melodic (because often contrapuntal), and the melodic variations retained the outward forms (often "choric," dancelike) of the subjects of these two gigantic pieces. By the time of Brahms's *Variations on a Theme by Haydn*, in 1873, the relevant style was "spasmic": Brahms used Haydn's theme as a structure, recurring throughout his composition, into which to pour musical content corresponding to various moods of musical discourse, not simply different embroideries of a single musical line.

(A similar contrasting use of the variation form has characterized jazz. Early groups and soloists played "changes" on either a popular tune or an unchanging series of chords, analogous to the cantus-firmus technique of medieval and Renaissance composers. Later groups, particularly bop and post-bop musicians, used such "choruses" much more freely, as opportunities to explore musical ideas that, while they may have arisen from a previous solo, depart considerably from the musical mood and context of that solo. To return to the metaphor of the conversation, we are considering the difference between a trial, when an event witnessed by a group is described successively by a number of different onlookers, each with a somewhat different view, and a brainstorming session, when a number of participants, inspired by one another's ideas, continuously come up with new thoughts, occasionally completely unforeseen, even unimaginable.)

Schoenberg and Webern used their orchestral variations to explore the twelve-tone and serial idioms they were evolving, as Bach used the "Goldberg" Variations to explore contrapuntal techniques, and in his Third Symphony Beethoven orchestrated his "Eroica" Variations, originally for piano, to explore orchestration. Erickson, in his *Variations for Orchestra*, considered his evolving idiom of the "budding, branching" technique of finding the next note, the next melodic gesture or sonorous cluster—and finding it in a way that would be both expressible by a large orchestra and clear to a large audience. The result is utterly convincing: a colorful, memorable, constantly stimulating piece of music, about fourteen minutes long, making full use of the large contemporary orchestra (though neglecting the English horn).

The work begins with a slow, dropping three-note gesture, flute to muted trombones, then reverses through bass clarinet to clarinet, ending in a gradually slowing rocking alternation of two notes. Muted trumpets, in a throat-clearing gesture, quietly introduce a more extended melody in the flute, clearly grown out of the opening gestures, answered by a plucked-string version of the trumpet comment in the violas and cellos. After a hesitation, the flutes extend their melody, ending with a slow rocking figure in the piccolo and a final comment in muted trombones and plucked contrabasses. After another hesitation, a mysterious event in the percussion section, rushing, then subsiding, closes this first "variation," two minutes long.

Erickson marks the opening "Slow and Tender," and alters the tempo rarely. He speeds it up very slightly in the minute-long second section, scored chamber-style for solo violin and cello, clarinet and bass clarinet, and quietly supporting string sections. It takes up the undulating, rocking figure as well as a quick upward four-note gesture, introduced in the first section as an apparently insignificant detail in the violas.

There follows a completely contrasting section, "Fast and Rhythmic," nearly three minutes long, in which the nervous groups of short notes from the original flute melody become flutterings in woodwinds and strings, contrasting with the quietly undulating idea, usually in low-middle voices (violas, horns). The mood is edgier: the oboes make their first prominent appearance, lending pungency to the sonority; and short, detached notes in the strings articulate the buildup to the first real climax of the piece, with full brass, trills in the woodwinds, and a high B by all three flutes. This is quickly dissolved, the mood returning to the meditative rocking-note figure, but a short afterthought rises to another outburst of flurries in the high woodwinds to subside once again, this time in a tender violin solo of a few notes.

The fourth variation is the most enigmatic: quiet tappings of tom-toms and wood-blocks, a pause, a five-note flurry on the glockenspiel, and a sustained sonority—one can't really call it a chord—on high piano and harp. Lasting hardly twenty seconds, this is more a punctuation of the total piece, marking approximately the halfway point, than a fully stated "variation." To take up the composer's "budding, branching" metaphor, it is a nodal point on the stalk, not yet leafed out—but, on examination, a node containing the germs of many of the characteristics identifying the more fully developed sections of the organic structure of these variations. The examination is most readily made by studying the score, of course; but at Erickson's slow tempo, and at the quiet level of sound he stipulates, even the casual listener, prepared by having heard the events of the previous six minutes, will probably feel the connection between these delicate sounds and the apparently more eventful processes that preceded them.

The fifth variation returns to the world of chamber music, opening in solo flute, violin, and cello, answered by clarinets and oboes, then the full string sections, ebbing away in a viola solo to end in a high chord played by the violins—a memory of the closing sound of the preceding section. A little over two minutes long, this section—"Slow, with warmth"—concentrates on the long melodic line originally stated by the flute, a line that combines held notes, quicker gestures of short notes, and subtle references to the steady rocking idea. Erickson's melodies have begun to take on a consistent general pattern, not easily characterized because of their indecisive way of moving from one part of the range to another. Metaphorically, they proceed, both on the page and in the ear, like the flight of certain birds that dart, then glide, then soar, moving upward or downward according to some decision we cannot know, producing an unpredictable but instantly recognizable pattern setting them apart from the steadier flight of less imaginative birds.

In the final section, "Light and delicate," the warmly rocking cellos and violas develop an extended tune under the quiet, high, quivering violins and the dry tappings of the harp. Flutes and clarinets, then bassoons, take up this tune, extending it; and the brass sections punctuate it with contrasting short and sustained notes, providing the section's loud central section. The high woodwinds have another short conversation about the melodic line; the flute drops down its three notes again—to the trumpets this time, not trombones (this may be Erickson's error); muted trumpets and French horn clear their throats once again, summoning the solo flute; the plucked lower strings restate their muttered undercurrent; and *Variations for Orchestra* ends in flutes and piccolo, quietly undulating, set off at the end by quietly dropping gestures in muted trombones, then contrabasses.

DUO (1957) FOR VIOLIN AND PIANO

The Duo, for violin and piano, goes toward the extreme of "private" music after the excursion into "public" music of *Variations for Orchestra*. The Duo is closely written, tightly constructed, hard to grasp intellectually, though clearly written in a manner that makes considerable intellectual sense. If the *Variations* are often warm or tender—and Erickson uses the very words, as we have seen—the Duo is flinty. It is also much harder to pin down. For the first time Erickson makes almost constant use of changing speeds, not only by varying the lengths of the notes, but by varying the speed with which the underlying pulse is maintained. And he very often casts the music over a pulse that is not steady at all, but gradually slowing or speeding. In general the darting, soaring, dipping motions of his melodic lines are made more nervous, quicker: the birds inhabiting this piece are smaller and busier.

The result, especially to the unaided ear, is a piece in which the two instruments are constantly overlapping, often—even usually—apparently unsynchronized with each other. This is a duo, the simultaneous presence of two performers, in contrast to a duet, the collaborative venture of two-performers-as-one. There are moments of solo activity for the piano, but they are rarely extended. And yet the piano rests during only three of the 110 measures in the first movement, one of them the last; and rests are nearly as scarce in the finale. The result is a dense, eventful piece, challenging to listeners as well as performers.

There are two movements—a reversion to the form of the Trio written four years earlier. Violin and piano begin together, with similar remarks, stated simultaneously: brisk, loud, and accented sounds, relaxing only at the end of the phrase, as if unwillingly. For a moment the violin quietly repeats a single pitch, speeding its pulse, while the piano splashes up and down its lower-middle register; then the opening attitudes are restated and enlarged upon. This music is not conversational: it recalls certain couples, so familiar with one another they don't always notice their mutual interruptions and simultaneous speech when addressing a third party. The device is not continuous. The violin pauses on a single repeated or sustained note from time to time, and even drops out altogether after the first two and a half minutes, leaving the piano almost a minute to itself. When it reenters, the violin seems to change the mood, now more reflective; and a dialogue of sorts is achieved for half a minute or so—but the piano, irrepressible, reverts to its earlier way of constantly demanding to be heard. This is another of Erickson's double-entry structures, the second half paraphrasing the first, as we have seen in the Second Quartet.

In Domenico Scarlatti's day the traditional sonata-allegro form began similarly, the first half leading away from the keynote, the second half returning to it. Subsequently the form evolved into the familiar three-part structure of exposition, development, and recapitulation. Erickson typically makes ongoing development the very subject of his exposition, and paraphrases rather than recapitulating the exposition, as if offering views of his musical territory from first one perspective, then another.

The Duo is "abstract," with no hint of a story (my imaginary talkative couple is only a metaphor), no verbal descriptions of tempo (metronome markings determine the changing speed throughout), and only one qualitative adjective to guide a phrase: the word "brilliant" over seven quick notes for the violin, just before the close of the piece. Technical analysis of the Duo is both possible and rewarding, in its own terms if not to the layman (or even, often, to the performers); and it does no disservice to Erickson to point out that he himself has commented on the cerebral organization of the Duo, with three different "fields" of tempi, related in the proportion $2:3:4$, forming much of its underlying structure.

The fifteen years after 1950 were the height of academic modernism, when Stockhausen, Boulez, and Carter advanced their most intellectual and complicated principles of composition, and Erickson was too attentive a teacher (and student) to ignore this. Fascinated with methods of relating different musical pulses, for example, he devised an adaptation of the circular slide-rule to facilitate the move from one tempo to another. If a casual listener were to complain of any of Erickson's music's being too complex to understand, the Duo would most justify the objection. Given the state of chamber-music performance and production, which neglects contemporary music, it's not likely to trouble many listeners—unfortunately. For the Duo is a fascinating, eventful piece of music to those who are content to witness fascinating events even though unable to comprehend intellectually their every nuance.

In the Second Quartet, *Variations for Orchestra*, and the Duo, Erickson had finally achieved full control of his music. He had mastered techniques of melody and counterpoint, from both traditional and modernist examples. He had found coherent forms, even for extended compositions. He had learned the techniques of instrumental performance. He had addressed the very different requirements of "private" chamber music and "public" orchestral music. He knew how to keep virtuosity in line and how to combine undemanding orchestral parts to colorful and constantly interesting effects. Most of all, he had evolved an idiom of his own; each piece was turning in on itself, achieving its own form, at the same time that it reached out, touching its hearers. *Variations for Orchestra* and the Duo were composed in 1957, the year he turned forty. The early period of his career was completed. Music and the mind were one.

II. THE MIDDLE WORK: MUSIC FOR PERFORMERS; EXPERIMENTS IN SOUND, 1960–1977

Further Challenges to the Performers, 1960–1963

Chamber Concerto (1960) for seventeen players; Toccata for Piano, "Ramus" (1962); *Concerto for Piano and Seven Instruments* (1963); *The End of the Mime of Mick, Nick and the Maggies* (1963) for SATB chorus

In hindsight, Erickson took the next logical step in composing his next work, the *Chamber Concerto* for large chamber ensemble. Standing midway between chamber and orchestral music, it is scored for what is essentially a chamber orchestra: a single player on each of the major instruments of the conventional orchestra: flute, oboe, clarinet, bassoon; trumpet, French horn, trombone; violin, viola, cello, contrabass. To these Erickson adds a bass clarinet, harp, piano, harpsichord-celesta (one player), and two percussionists. Such a group can be expected to play both more delicately and more deftly than a full orchestra, and in general such a group can also be expected to invest more time in preparation—both characteristic of chamber-music performances.

On the other hand, so large a group can provide a great deal of color, quite full volume and weight, and requires the presence of a conductor, especially in complex passages. The presence of so many performers on stage also influences the audience's engagement with the music. The result is a different scaling of the musical process itself: where an orchestra is generally heard as an objective unit, chamber music is heard more intimately, the listener participating vicariously with the performers; music for large ensembles frequently develops a sort of dialogue between the two processes. The ensemble can be broken into small units; the music can alternate between solo, chamber-music, or quasi-orchestral textures. Twentieth-century modernists have often turned to this medium, attracted partly by its inherent stylistic possibilities, partly by the greater skill and rehearsal time it is likely to afford. They have often been mindful of the great baroque concerti grossi, which influenced twentieth-century composers as diverse as Stravinsky and Berg. And there may have been a latent affinity between the medium and the big-band phenomenon in American popular music of the 1930s.

For Erickson, the large chamber ensemble provided the logical medium in which to explore further the developments of *Variations for Orchestra* and the Duo: both the "budding, branching" technique, by which small cells are strung together, spun out, and reconfigured into longer melodic phrases whose contrasting parts—flurries of short notes, sustained long ones, dips of pitch and the like—facilitate overlapping and simultaneous sounding; and also the supple handling of tempo, whether in constant flux or in juxtapositions of two or more simply proportionate basic pulses. Metaphorically, the *Chamber Concerto* also provided him with the scope and instrumental variety needed to present a musical drama analogous to the social drama, only too familiar to him by then, of the politics of small groups. One would not want to read too much into this: the *Chamber Concerto* is not program music. But the dynamics of its musical processes are approachable in such metaphorical terms, just as the dynamics of the (admittedly much more evidently programmatic) *Chamber Concerto* for piano and violin with thirteen winds, which Alban Berg dedicated to his mentor Schoenberg for the latter's fiftieth birthday, can be approached symbolically.

Erickson's *Chamber Concerto* opens in an easygoing, attractive mood, its musical content easily taken in by the listener. The first of the four movements is only two minutes long in the CRI recording, laid out in five long phrases. A quiet but intense chord in the woodwinds opens the first of these, from which a low note is sustained by the bass clarinet (a favorite instrument of the composer's, and one whose distinctive voice is easily noted), then a higher one by the flute. A low cello sounds the next sustained note, and then a detached note on the harp introduces a flurry of notes in the brass ending with the first loud note of the piece.

This opening paragraph is stated again, in somewhat different terms, to finish the first half of the movement. The remaining fifty seconds are similar but continuous, fading away at the very end in high quivering notes on the violin. The texture throughout the movement is spare and delicate: Erickson is content to introduce the few basic ideas he will ponder later, in a circumscribed sonic area whose limits reassure any listener concerned about possible disorientation. The mood is quite similar to that of the opening section of *Variations for Orchestra*. It is as if one were standing—seated, even—in the center of an open garden, one's attention being quietly directed to two similar flowerbeds, then to a third, slightly varied and perhaps a bit longer.

The second movement is nearly five minutes long, but we are carefully made aware of the expanded boundaries. Again the music proceeds coherently, in direct lines. The opening paragraph, about forty-five seconds long, restates the opening of the previous movement: chords; sustained notes; punctuation in the harp and, later, bassoon; a chord in the woodwinds; silence. The following paragraph adds to such material crescendi and diminuendi, the swelling and subsiding in volume of the sustained pitches, which begin to be held longer; and, at about two minutes into the movement, a short solo for the trombone. In the third section, occupying the next two minutes or so, the measured silences—abut five seconds at a time—become more frequent, not interrupting the music so much as punctuating it, directing it toward a closing half-minute in which the brass instruments provide the first dynamic climax of the piece, held over scattered notes in the piano, then giving way to a note held strident by the flute, the piano notes growing quieter.

So far, familiar forms: a paragraph; the paragraph somewhat restated. The second movement is a longer analogy of the first, as if we were to notice that this entire section of the garden is laid out just as each bed within it is—an architectural "branching-out" of the first-noticed organizing principle. The third movement, a little over four minutes long, develops the material a bit more—or develops our discernment, making us notice more potential in it; for Erickson's musical idiom, in successfully making music about itself, is beginning to make co-composers of the listener as well. Again there seem to be four paragraphs, made up of the familiar held notes, flurries, mysterious dry tappings, and occasional swells. The solo melodies, often growing out of what begins as a mere flurry of response to a sustained sound, become both longer and more coherent; the bassoon giving one prominent version about halfway through, the violin another, three-quarters into the movement. Again, the formal divisions seem nearly equal, each a quarter of the whole.

The four movements are not equal, however: the last is nearly nine minutes long. It begins much like the others, but after its first three or four paragraphs we notice changes. There are more sliding *glissandi* in the solo melodies, and a greater range of contrast between dry points of sound and the longer, darker chords. After about six minutes, when the scale of the preceding movements might lead one to expect the work to close, a series of solos in trombone, trumpet, bassoon, and violin grows more rambunctious. At this point Erickson invites the musicians to improvise their own solo material—"within the style of the piece," he is careful to stipulate, and beginning and quitting on specified notes. Unusual tone-production is heard: the flutist makes whistling sounds through the instrument; the oboe reed is detached and sounded alone. A slap-pizzicato solo on the contrabass suggests jazz connotations. But lyrical order is restored, and the work ends in a more subdued, meditative mood.

It is relevant to consider what else was being written at this time, 1960. Serialism—the complex ordering of pitches, loudnesses, durations, and instrumental assignments of the notes of a piece of music, according to numerical charts worked out in advance of the actual notation of the music—was giving way, in the musical avant-garde, to new movements. The Polish school, led by Krzysztof Penderecki but inspired by several other composers, had introduced a texture-based style of composition. The German composer Karlheinz Stockhausen, once close to Pierre Boulez in the vanguard of serialism, had moved beyond "pointillism," music based on isolated single notes, to "moment-form" pieces, whose structure was similar to what Erickson had evolved, though Stockhausen's was more convoluted (and more tirelessly promoted).

In the United States the composition of progressive music was settling into two distinct camps. (Neoclassicists and even neo-romanticists continued loyal to the tonal system.) One the one hand—the right, one might say—such academic intellectuals as Milton Babbitt and Elliott Carter evolved further refinements of serialism. Meanwhile, on the left, a "New York School" was growing in visibility around John Cage, grouping the quite different personal idioms of Earle Brown, Morton Feldman, and Christian Wolff under a common banner of revulsion against the conservative tonalists and reaction against the conservative (serial) modernists.

Erickson's position was unique: sympathetic with the desires and values of all three camps, uninterested in the politics of any; bored with the technical and analytical obsession of the serialists; mistrustful of the New York School's apparent renunciation of compositional control. The ear, reassured by an intuitively felt *musical* logic, with its restrained scope and patiently (but not tediously) repeated melodic procedures—the ear does not notice that Erickson's music is *intellectually* coherent, like that of the serialists. Nor does Erickson's allowance of improvisation invite stylistic chaos or an erosion of musical content: the improvised solos branch out from the buds Erickson has carefully nurtured.

Perhaps this is why the position of Erickson's *music,* in the context of that of his colleagues, was also unique—still is. Today one can move with equal ease from a recording of the *Chamber Concerto* to either a Feldman or a Carter piece of the same period—or even to George Crumb's *Night Music I,* which shares the CRI recording with Erickson's *Chamber Concerto.* Their music has in most cases outlived the theories they illustrated. Erickson's music, on the other hand, never promoted any theories—save the internal evolutionary logic Yates demands of the mature artist. The *Chamber Concerto* makes clear the proposal that Erickson's acts of choice—what note to set out next—are based on a rare balance of taste, skill, and self-confidence. He, not a numerical chart or a random chance, would determine the next sound as the need arose, and it would follow from the preceding, within only one context: the immediate one of the composition at hand. This sounds reasonable enough, but it was an independent act in the 1960s.

TOCCATA FOR PIANO, "RAMUS" (1962)

This is not to say that Erickson's music of the period lacks intellectual method or relies simply on an unerring taste—that the composer sits at the piano and picks out exactly the right note to come next, intuitively, without a guiding principle or two. The extent of his planning is evident in the Toccata for Piano, "Ramus," which he composed next. Erickson provided the work with an extensive program note:

> The subtitle of my toccata comes from the Latin word for branch, and expresses the budding, branching and exfoliating structure I had in mind when I composed it. In fact, after I had finished the composition

and heard the first performance I decided to add another branch, the opening section of the piece; and since the work is not a closed form like a box, but an open one like a plant or a tree, there is no reason why other branches couldn't be added.

RAMUS has six linked sections. The first, which has a provision for a short interpolated cadenza, leads smoothly into the second. The second and third sections are linked by a transitional phrase, and the third section cadences on C#. Section four, the center of the composition, hovers around C# and D#. This section provides for two cadenzas: one in the middle, where the player improvises a continuation of a written cadenza, and another growing out of a C#–D# trill, leading to the fifth section. Section five ends with a strong cadence on A, and the final section is on F.

The improvised cadenza passages are conceived as "branching out" from the written parts. The performer is invited but not required to play the cadenzas. However, to my ear the composition sounds incomplete without them.

The rhythms, absolute lengths, tempo changes, accelerandi and ritardandi are all elements of a time field which includes relationships ranging from simple and complex ratios to unmeasured durations.

RAMUS was commissioned by the American pianist, Maro Ajemian, and was composed in 1961.

"Toccata" comes from the Italian word *toccare*, meaning "to touch," and as a musical title usually implies a keyboard piece of considerable virtuosity, meant to display the performer's finger dexterity. "Ramus" does in fact make severe demands of the pianist, in terms of both covering the keyboard and learning the time-relationships. Playing a difficult toccata in a steady tempo is like running an obstacle course against the clock: one must be fleet, but one must also be capable of changing one's gait, taking leaps, dodging hazards, and the like. To these challenges Erickson adds another: in the first and third sections the underlying pulse changes very often, and in the fourth section is in almost constant flux. The situation is so extreme that in the first and fourth sections the composer adopts a new method of warning the player of these changes: instead of simply posting the speed, in the conventional terms of notes per minute, he draws a continuous line under the music, flat if the speed is unchanging, rising or falling when it speeds or slows. The performer must learn and internalize these rules as well as the notes: it is as if our obstacle

runner were being continually told to slow down or speed up, often ir-
respective of the nature of the course.

Of course matters had become this complex and more so in serial music.
By 1961, in fact, the pulses underlying musical performance, organized by the
serialists as cerebrally as all the other "parameters" (pitch, duration, loudness,
instrumental voice, etc.), had grown both so arbitrary and so complex that
their effect eluded the ear—particularly since the *rhythms*, the relationships
among the durations of the notes, were often similarly complex, and quite
likely in an opposite direction. (Make the notes successively longer, while at
the same time speeding up the pulse to which they must be played and by
which they are therefore measured, and the two processes cancel one another
out.)

It may therefore be asked to what end "Ramus" is so detailed and complex
in its rhythm and its tempo. The answer is simple enough: the composer has
heard (or imagined, or determined) a specific choreography of these notes, and
can think of no other way to specify that exact choreography to his performer.
And the fact is that in the 1950s and 1960s a number of performers came
along not only capable of learning such difficult scores, but actually desirous
of being so challenged. In many cases these performers developed, perhaps
from the same psychological motivations, intense loyalties to favored
composers: one thinks of such pianist-composer teams as Aloys Kontarsky and
Stockhausen, David Tudor and Cage. Shortly after Ajemian's premiere of
"Ramus" the piece was taken up brilliantly by Dwight Peltzer, who was
rewarded with Erickson's next score, the *Concerto for Piano and Seven Instruments*.

The layman may be forgiven for entering another objection: Who, apart
from the composer and the performer, can possibly know if a performance is
accurate in so demanding a score? The skepticism latent in this question is not
as easily met, since the listener who can't be sure must take another's authority
on faith. This is something Americans are not trained to do, particularly since
the 1960s, when "Question Authority" became a message commonly met on
bumper stickers. Such skepticism is too frequently justified when applied to
music critics among the press, who, when preparing to discuss a new score,
rarely can or will prepare with anything like the dedication and discipline of

the performer (to say nothing of the composer). One would think that the spectacle of a performer taking on such a difficult assignment would move the audience to faith, not cynicism, but oddly enough it is more often the dismissive critic who is trusted than the demanding composer or the devoted performer. This is understandable: the newspaper critic, in a manner of speaking the representative of the lay audience-member, resembles him more than do the composer and performer, partners in arcana. Therefore the critic is more likely to be trusted.

Erickson was lucky with reviews, partly because San Francisco, in the 1950s and 1960s, was blessed with a critic unusually enthusiastic about novelties: Alfred Frankenstein, who wrote for the *San Francisco Chronicle*; and partly because some of Erickson's own associates went on to become reviewers and maintained their loyalty to him (better put, their shared values and enthusiasms). Alan Rich, for example, who had worked with Erickson at KPFA, had gone on to the New York *Herald Tribune*, where he wrote of the *Chamber Concerto* that the music was "substantial and rewarding" and "proved, as few other proponents of the Webern style have, that this kind of music can be writ large and succeed."[*]

CONCERTO FOR PIANO AND SEVEN INSTRUMENTS (1963)

Erickson may well have wondered, after "Ramus," and particularly if considering it as successor to *Variations for Orchestra* and the *Chamber Concerto*, whether there might not be a danger of his music's growing too remote from its intended audience. Certainly he made no secret of his dislike for the "academic" music of colleagues who showed more concern for musical analysis than for listenability. In any case, the next opportunity for a premiere was particularly conducive to a consideration of this problem, for it involved the pianist Dwight Peltzer, who, having mastered "Ramus," was eager to learn

---

[*]These quotations appear in Carter Harman's liner notes to the CRI recording (CRI 218 USD). It should be pointed out that Erickson, while of course impressed by both Webern's methods and the music that resulted, was hardly a "proponent of the Webern style."

another Erickson score. And so Erickson turned next to the *Concerto for Piano and Seven Instruments*, knowing intimately the skills and sounds of the musicians for whom he was composing, and with the *Chamber Concerto* very much in his ears—he was then in the process of editing the master tape for the CRI release, which required a good many splices to get past rough spots in the recording.

The concerto was commissioned by the School of Music at the University of Illinois and scheduled for performances there and soon thereafter in Berkeley. The latter performance was particularly promising, for it involved a new Bay Area group, Performers' Choice, composed of highly skilled musicians intent on performing the music of their choice, not that of artistic directors with an eye cocked toward the box office. Many, indeed most, of these musicians were associated with the conductor Gerhard Samuel, as members of either the Oakland Symphony Orchestra or the San Francisco Ballet Orchestra, both of which he led. Loren Rush played contrabass; Stuart Dempster played trombone. And Peltzer was the pianist.

The piano concerto is the pinnacle among the range of compositions Erickson had constructed since his student days. It is in one closely stated movement, clearly enough subdivided to keep the listener oriented, loosely enough constructed to allow for an amazing range of techniques, sound-events, and individual statements on the part of its performers. Scored for flute, clarinet, bassoon, trumpet, trombone, contrabass, and percussion, it should really be called a "concerto for piano and eight musicians," because the conductor has a great deal to do with achieving this expressive, continuously fascinating piece. Not that the composer leaves many choices to the conductor: instead, he relies on him, quite properly, to act as navigator and traffic director, keeping track of the present location at all times, bringing in and cutting off the instruments as the composer requires, balancing the general sound-levels to allow Erickson's imaginatively ordained machinery to operate at its most effective level—and, above all, maintaining the proper tempos.

The piece is, to begin with, a bravura opportunity for the soloist, who is nearly always present, in the foreground of the proceedings. Having gained confidence from the gratifying performances he had heard of the *Chamber Concerto* and "Ramus," Erickson went even further with improvisation in the piano concerto. And not only by giving his soloist opportunities to improvise cadenzas: everyone but the conductor is given many solo "breaks," often extending to group improvisation. Erickson was fortunate to be working with musicians who had considerable experience in such collective improvisation: not only did they have jazz in their ears, from the earliest New Orleans recordings to the most recent progressive jazz and bop of their own time; but they had heard, studied, and performed recent avant-garde music involving free improvisation (playing material of their own imagining, preferably made up on the spot, not rehearsed ahead of time), the performance of graphic notation (melodic lines whose general direction, loudness, and speed was indicated by sketches rather than by detailed notes on music paper), and the navigation of open-form pieces (whose structures were like mobiles, allowing the performers to decide at the last moment just what musical material might come next).

Depending on the length of a couple of solo cadenzas, the *Concerto* is about twenty-one minutes long—with the second quartet and the *Chamber Concerto*, as long a piece as Erickson had yet composed. But its apparent length is less: the piece is continuously eventful, even its slower middle section sustaining the intensity established at the outset. It opens with a now-familiar Erickson gesture: a trill, a flurry of five sounds, a note held for two or three beats, another flurry, this time of six quick sounds followed after a very short pause by three more; and a very long-held note—"at least ten seconds," the score stipulates, often closer to half a minute in performance. That's the first page of forty-nine; it calls for only the soloist, an almost unnoticed dry bark from the percussionist (vibraphone, cowbell), and a quiet flute on the last long note. Then, after another quick seven notes from the piano, everyone jumps in.

Because of the unusually free nature of its content—more music is improvised, in one way or another, than not—various performances of the concerto take on quite different characters. Erickson provides for a wide range of moods in any case: quiet introspection, collective statements, interchanges between single instruments as dialogues or confrontations, sudden unprepared outbursts. Sometimes an instrumental entrance will seem to be completely ignored by the rest of the group; at other times it will influence a decided change of direction. In traditional romantic fashion, the soloist is sometimes an onlooker, more often the leader of things, establishing mood and texture.

While the piano begins an improvisation as early as the second page of the score, Erickson's requirements of the accompanying instruments are fully detailed at the beginning of the piece. Instruments are allowed to place a very few specified notes anywhere they want within a specified beat, but the pitch, volume, and other characteristics are assigned, and the characteristic dips, flurries, and sustained notes are indicated as precisely as they were in previous pieces. After the first long solo cadenza, between eight and eleven minutes into the score—that is, about halfway through the piece, and at the beginning of what might be its third major section—Erickson allows the flute and then the contrabass to improvise for a few seconds on a given note. Two or three minutes later, after an extended piano solo, contrabass and then flute are requested to improvise duets with the soloist and one another; and then, after another half-minute of slowly building intensity, a few measures of graphic notation are given to the winds: the general shape of musical gestures is indicated, but the precise pitches are left up to the players. Then, immediately, free improvisation is begun, only the instrumental entrances, exits, and general dynamic level being indicated.

The climax of the piece follows, fifteen to eighteen minutes in: a free collective cadenza, each instrument given merely a few words of instruction. Directions for the clarinet, for example, are:

> Cadenza. Tempo free. Fast notes, sharp accents. When [trombone] enters finish phrase segment and drop out. [*Later:*] Interrupt [flute]. When [trombone] enters, finish segment & drop out. [*Later:*] 4 interruptions: 1. Tight 2. Looser 3. Tighter 4. Tightest

Six accompanying instruments are given similar instructions, the piano soloist and percussion being silent for the moment. The conductor shapes the four sections, each of which is marked by successive interruptions, from high instrument to low, woodwinds first. Then the conductor guides the final moments toward an improvised duet cadenza in piano and percussion. There follows a gradual subsidence of three minutes or so, in which the instruments alternate between improvised material and carefully set-out sustained notes, with occasional melodic flurries, with the piano either silent or quietly in the background. Twice this gradual decline is interrupted by noisy outbursts, but both times the mood relaxes again; the piano recalls the loud flurry that opened the piece, over twenty minutes earlier (but with an "error," playing the third chord a bit lower than before); clarinet, trumpet, and trombone sound a last chord, and the flute closes the piece with a thirty-second meditation over a very quiet background in the piano.

It is an extraordinary piece, combining the expressionistic outbursts of Berg and Schoenberg, the delicacy of Webern, the long-held near-inaudibility of Feldman, the unpredictable healthy violence of Cage, and the ironic wit, born of detached observation, that was Erickson's own specialty. The shapes of these events are clearly foretold in *Variations for Orchestra*, the Duo, and the *Chamber Concerto*; and the secure and rational but completely hidden organization was perfected in "Ramus." But in the *Concerto for Piano and Seven Instruments* Erickson made something of a kind that hadn't existed before. Tightly constructed for dramatic effect, encyclopedic in its instrumental techniques, uniquely balanced between the composer's and the performers' creativity, it is a collective effort under benevolent leadership. There is something very American in this piece, which so readily permits so many voices to work together. Perhaps the last composer to achieve such a result was Debussy, who learned from Balinese gamelan, at the 1889 Paris Exposition, about the collective transcendent beauty of simultaneous individual melodic statements. Debussy, however (and Berg after him in the *Altenberg Lieder*), had to feign the effect, writing it out fully for his enormous orchestra in *La Mer* and *Jeux*. Erickson trusts his nine musicians to improvise, and obtains a new version of the real thing. He completed the work in January 1963; it was an early contribution to the gathering expansion of energy and liberation of styles the 1960s would ultimately represent.

THE END OF THE MIME OF MICK, NICK AND THE MAGGIES (1963)

Before beginning work on the piano concerto, Erickson had finally taken up a long-postponed commission: the request, now over ten years old, for an unaccompanied choral piece for Robert Holliday. It was just as well Erickson had taken so long to get to this, for his stylistic approach to this commission would suggest the approach to the purely sonic drama of the *Concerto*. For the text inspiring this new development, Erickson turned to one of the greatest of the sacred modernist icons, James Joyce's last novel, *Finnegans Wake*. Erickson described his attraction to this book in the liner notes to the recording of *The End of the Mime*:

> What drew me to *Finnegans Wake* was especially its polyphony. That quality of multiple levels was what I have tried to bring out in my setting of this passage....

There is no plot in *Finnegans Wake*—almost all of its themes appear on every page—but in this particular passage there is an event sequence that may be helpful to those who are new to Joyce: the children come home from play; they study their lessons; they become noisy; their father chases them off and slams the door; they flee to the bedroom; a prayer ends the chapter.

> Joyce's meanings fan out from this domestic scene to the life and history of mankind; all fleeing, all thunderous door slams, all sexual relationships are woven in. The multiplicity of meaning can become very confusing, although there are no nonsense words. Everything has a meaning—more likely, several.

Erickson chose the closing pages of the chapter (Book 2, chapter 1) in which Joyce introduces the saga of the twin sons of Tim Finnegan, the eponymous hero of his novel. In the course of the book Shem and Shaun stand for a number of familiar antagonists, from Cain and Abel to Jonathan Swift and Laurence Sterne, and to the Ant and the Grasshopper. This chapter records their enactment of a little play, *The Mime of Mick, Nick and the Maggies*—St. Michael, Old Nick the Devil, and a chorus of nagging temptresses. Joyce had published the chapter separately in 1934, in a sumptuous edition printed in Holland for the Gotham Book Mart in New York. When *Finnegans Wake* finally appeared five years later the chapter had grown considerably, for Joyce composed it in layers, adding and elaborating to successive drafts, even after the book was set in type.

Erickson set the closing passage, beginning on page 256 of the (first) Viking edition:

Home all go. Halome. Blare no more ramsblares, oddmund barkes! And cease your fumings, kindalled bushies! And sherrigoldies yeassymgnays; your wildeshaweshowe moves swiftly sterneward! For here the holy language. Soons to come. To pausse.[1]

[*A partial paraphrase*: Go home, everyone. Hallow me, follow me. No more ram's horn blowing, old man odd-mouth barks! Stop fuming, kids; stop smoking, burning bushes! ... Your Wilde Shaw show moves swiftly back, Jonathan Swift-style, toward (Laurence) Sterne! ...]

The text continues like this for three pages, warning of coming lessons in French, history, and science; describing little Isolde (the twins' sister) dallying on her way to bed; recalling the old story of Father Barley dallying with a couple of platinum blondes; meditating on the crack of doom (as Finnegan slams the door to one of Joyce's famous "hundredletter" words); lapsing into paraphrases of Old Testament battles; and finally saying their nightly prayers, yawning, and falling murmuringly silent:

Loud, heap miseries upon us yet entwine our arts with laughters low!
Ha he hi ho hu.
Mummum.

Erickson turned this text into a choral *tour de force*, setting it for twelve solo voices, sometimes grouping into the normal four-part chorus, more often breaking up into various overlapping combinations of solo voices. The text suggests a polyglot setting, not only because of its multilingual puns, but also because of the wide range of references. Erickson responds, inventing mock-liturgical chants, sea chanteys, counterfeit Irish folksong, graphically notated approximations of speech.

The score, dated June 1962, is laid out with exceptional clarity on thirty-nine pages: it had to be easily read by singers confronted with a difficult text, a variety of vocal styles, and a frequently changing tempo, indicated once again by a "tempo line" ranging from twenty-four to ninety-six beats to the minute. (All the different speeds are related in simple ratios.) And the music, especially if heard with score in hand, is relatively clear as well, in spite of the overlapping and sometimes simultaneous sentences. Erickson even improves on Joyce's complexities, for in the book words must necessarily follow in sequence, however jumbled their syntax may be; in the choral setting, phrases may overlap, collide, pile up on top of each other, or proceed simultaneously but at different speeds. Erickson distinguishes such phrases by assigning them to separated vocal ranges (basses, sopranos); or by tucking isolated words from one phrase into the interstices of another; or by asking his chorus to sing one, speak or chant another.

The result is utterly convincing to one who knows *Finnegans Wake*: the listener can only regret the fact that Erickson was never encouraged to attempt a more ambitious setting. True, its twelve minutes are both challenging and sufficient for unaccompanied chamber chorus; and at that rate a setting of the entire book would run to forty hours of music, not counting purely instrumental episodes—a full work-week, to perform or to hear. Joyce once said he'd written *Finnegans Wake* for an "ideal reader" who would dedicate his life to its perusal—after all, Joyce had given the book eighteen years of his own life. Erickson was not about to become such a reader, let alone devote all his composing to one subject. *The End of the Mime of Mick, Nick and the Maggies* was more than a successful setting of Joyce: it showed Erickson how to develop his own complex but entertaining drama in purely musical terms, without recourse to someone else's text, without the specific verbal baggage of a narrative, even one as rich as Joyce's. As we have seen, that drama was the *Concerto for Piano and Seven Instruments*.

SIRENS AND OTHER FLYERS III FOR ORCHESTRA (1963–1965)

The improvisations allowed in *The End of the Mime* and the piano concerto led naturally to Erickson's next works, but these were informed by other liberating influences as well: extended virtuosity on certain instruments that rapidly became favorites in the composer's inventory; unusual sounds from homemade instruments and from altered tape recordings; and, especially, the enthusiastic experimentation of the younger composers who came to him for instruction and who went away having brought new energy to him. This in spite of the transitional nature of these seven years, which saw him complete his work at the San Francisco Conservatory, travel for a year, and then make the eventful move to San Diego, where he helped start a new department, settled twice into new homes, continued his experimentation and research, and rapidly began the series of works that led to his final quarter-century of composition.

This fecundity was not easily found. After finishing *The End of the Mime* in 1962, Erickson spent over two years working on a long music-theater composition. Many sections of the score demanded a large and unusual orchestra, whose musicians were required to play from specified positions, often moving from one to another. Instead of conventional melodies and harmonies, Erickson planned the music in terms of texture and tone color and above all the motion of sound within the concert hall. Only one section of the score survives: calling for a relatively conventional orchestra, it struck the composer as immediately practical, and so he scored it fully before apparently abandoning the larger work. The result is *Sirens and Other Flyers III*, a big orchestra piece with a curious personality. In it, for the last time, Erickson hesitates between following his own ear and acknowledging the forces of the musical styles emerging at a feverish pace in every corner of the world.

It is a poignant moment in the development of Erickson's musical style. He is aware of the great strides in postwar modernist music being made by composers in Poland, Italy, Germany, France, and Japan, as well as his own country. At the same time he is somewhat isolated: geographically in San Francisco, which continued to receive more information from the outside world than it managed to impart; and psychologically in the tension between the composer and the teacher, the creative artist and the scholar of artistic creation other than his own.

Sirens and Other Flyers III was to be Erickson's last orchestral score for ten years, and it embraces two ideas that would preoccupy him increasingly in the work to come: an increasingly dramatic, even argumentative interplay among the instrumental voices, and a surprising turn toward an almost inhuman kind of sound.

The twelve-minute piece begins with a burst of activity in the strings, set off by a single note struck on the kettledrum. For a minute and a half there is a cluttered sonic landscape of eventful contrasts: rapidly repeated notes in the strings, sliding tones, low brass sonorities, edgy attacks in the higher brass. Then for half a minute or so the activity pauses. High woodwinds emerge, as if regarding this landscape from aloft, to be answered by quiet muttering in the trumpet, then an unusual solo in the highest notes of the bass clarinet.

A quiet section follows, lyrical but very sparse, with high plucked notes in the violins establishing a nocturnal kind of atmosphere within which a solo violin emerges to be answered by a solo contrabass, then by a muted trumpet. Again the activity increases over a minute or so, and again it is spurred by rapidly repeated notes and tremolos, only to dissolve, about five minutes into the piece, into clouds of plucked notes and a curious passage of high scraping sounds in the violins, evocative of birds—not only of their song and calls, but also of the beating of their wings.

At the halfway point in the score there is a sudden low chord. A solo cello emerges from this new context, introducing a very sustained, quiet, soloistic section, a sort of restatement of the second section of the piece. The woodwinds take up this mood, cross-fading to the strings. A solo-clarinet comment prompts replies from the strings, whose glissandi prompt a response in turn from the trombone; and a series of calls and responses continues among the brass. The dramatic curve of the section intensifies, not in a loud climax but by ascent, with the solo violin again prominent, repeating high sliding notes in a setting that dissolves into solo burbles ending in brittle sparkles. The last quarter of the piece is a kind of coda, with quiet birdcalls in the flute, various whistlings in the high woodwind and strings, contrasting chirpings and sustained notes in harp, flute, and trumpet, and then, in the last minute, a completely unprepared surprise (except in retrospective analysis): literal birdcall imitations, first from toy birdcalls, then in the high winds, ending in a fade to a violin tremolo, then a quietly sustained trumpet.

As we have seen, *Sirens and Other Flyers III* looks outward to many "gestural" orchestral scores by other modernist composers. Erickson was responding in part to the recent compositions of the Polish school then led by Henryk Górecki, Bogusław Schäffer, and Włodzimierz Kotoński, whose percussive, "pointillist" music, characterized by flurries of rapid short notes, sudden outbursts of percussion, and clusters of sustained steady or sliding notes, was familiar to him from KPFA's broadcasts of the annual Warsaw Autumn Festival of contemporary music. (This festival represented an island of innovative activity in the otherwise bleakly rigid climate that prevailed in the musical life of the Soviet-bloc countries until the late 1980s.) The Polish school itself was a response to the challenge of the great early-twentieth-century innovator Edgard Varèse, whose announced creative intention had been the "liberation of sound" from the straitjacket of traditional musical forms and techniques—not only the traditional foundation of tonal harmony and counterpoint, but the traditional concepts of melody, too, and even the traditional inventory of accepted musical instruments. (The Poles must also have been aware of the advances that had been made by John Cage, whose music was more influential in Europe than in his own country in the 1950s and 1960s.)

Sirens and Other Flyers III responds also to the dramatic gestures of the Italian composer Luciano Berio, whose most innovative music had climaxed in the 1960 *Epifanie* for soprano and orchestra and in the 1962 *Circles* for soprano, harp, and percussion, becoming less radical later in the stylistic pastiche of the Mahlerish *Sinfonia* for orchestra: Berio taught at Mills College in Oakland during the 1960s, contributing to the vigor of new-music activity in the Bay Area during those years. And *Sirens* is aware, too, of the rich, saturated style of the music then coming from the Hungarian composer György Ligeti, whose *Poème Symphonique* for one hundred metronomes represented both a materialistic piling-up of otherwise unremarkable sounds, minimal in themselves, and a poignant expression of negative entropy, the natural tendency of active systems to move from order to chaos, from activity to stillness.

Sirens and Other Flyers III is impressively competent in its embrace of these various elements of international modernism, and in its extension of their ideas to the symphony orchestra. It is more impressive, though, in its statement of purely personal musical values, and in its extension of the earlier characteristic Erickson gesture, familiar from the Duo, *Variations for Orchestra*, and most recently the piano concerto, to the new fascination with high pitches and uncanny sonic events. These events seem to be grounded in, or prompted by, an internal logic of their own, coherent but ultimately mysterious, evading logical analysis. The musical drama seems no longer a matter of conversation or dialogue, but rather of something analogous to geology or meteorology.

It's tempting to consider this new development as a response to John Cage's recent championing of indeterminacy, his own approach to the "liberation of sound." Cage, from about 1951, had famously taken up chance techniques, abandoning the composition of "music that is about something" in favor of composing methods of "letting the sounds be themselves." In *Sirens and Other Flyers III* Erickson seems to have hit on his own approach to solving the problem of the intrusion of too much personal expression on the musical statement. This intrusion had by the middle 1960s become both too introspective and too limiting to deal fully with the unprecedentedly huge number of possibilities facing the modern composer, freed from the restrictions of traditional musical discourse and resources, but at the same time challenged to find some degree of order in a personal response to an entirely new world of sounds.

1. James Joyce: *Finnegans Wake* (New York: The Viking Press, 1939, p. 256).

Finding Sound on Tape, 1965–1967

Piece for Bells and Toy Pianos (1965); *Roddy* (1966); *Birdland* (1967)

The relative excess of the orchestral *Sirens and Other Flyers III* may have prompted Erickson to work on its successor, the *Piece for Bells and Toy Pianos*, written rather quickly in 1965. The piece grew naturally out of Erickson's experimentation with relatively unusual sounds, which had led him to investigate the quiet but penetrating timbres available in small high-pitched bells, wind chimes, and in certain toy pianos—not the familiar, inexpensive variety, in which metal plates are struck by the hammers, but a more carefully manufactured sort that uses metal rods for their purer and more resonant effect. (Such instruments may be sold as toys, but they can put full musical resources at the disposal of serious players, including up to three fully chromatic twelve-note octaves.)

The Erickson home became a sound-studio:

> *The first sound-producing thing I made was an indoor version of a wind chime—a construction of metal rods, small bells, and assorted junk. Strings of bells, clappers, glass strips and chunks of metal expanded throughout our kitchen and dining space until they were a hazard to foot traffic. A push or two would start a marvelous sequence of tinkling, rattling, thumping, and clicking that could continue for five or six minutes.*

To convert this experience into a work for the concert hall, Erickson captured these sounds on magnetic tape. With the moral support of his students Ramon Sender and Pauline Oliveros, who had by then established the San Francisco Tape Music Center, and with the technical assistance of Bill Maginnis, he re-recorded and edited the natural bell sounds, often altering them by speeding or slowing the tape to change pitch, and by electronically filtering the complex bell timbre to emphasize certain bands of sound.

The final result of this process was a fourteen-minute tape whose technically primitive quality seems to enhance its dreamy, free-form effect, a poetic adaptation of the "marvelous sequence of tinkling, rattling, thumping, and clicking that could continue for five or six minutes"—a deceptive structure, apparently artless, yet utterly controlled by physical laws of cause and effect: once set in motion, the sounds continue, gradually slowing and fading, in a process unmistakably suggesting organic processes. Erickson planned the tape as one component of the final piece: the other consisted of a single performer seated (rather uncomfortably) at a pair of toy pianos, one atop the other, playing a response, much of it improvised, to the sounds on tape.

Through Bill Triest, who had been an announcer at KPFA and had gone from there to the fledgling public television station KQED, and who had been a friend of Erickson's for a number of years, the idea came about of using the *Piece for Bells and Toy Pianos* as film—not as musical accompaniment, but as the substance of a film whose relatively crude yet immediately expressive visual technique was suggested by the low-budget, free-fantasy technique of the music. (An unlikely convergence of two influences seems at work here: the grainy black-and-white hand-held cinematography of the Italian cinema vérité and the Dada- and surrealist-influenced theater-piece musical form that was just then developing at the San Francisco Tape Music Center and elsewhere.)

Erickson asked a student, Warner Jepson, to perform the *Piece for Bells and Toy Pianos*. Jepson was interested in film and theater: he had performed in the classic James Broughton film *The Pleasure Garden*, and had written the score for the popular *San Francisco's Burning*, which enjoyed a six-month run in the San Francisco Playhouse in 1960. The final film of *Piece for Bells and Toy Pianos* was shown several times on KQED, and the sound-track makes persuasive listening to this day, but the music is even more interesting for its esthetic workings-out of several considerations that would preoccupy Erickson for the next few years—a transitional period, following such early masterpieces as the Second String Quartet and the piano *Concerto*, and preceding the second wave of masterpieces that would begin in 1978 with *Night Music*.

As it would turn out, the most significant aspect of the *Piece for Bells and Toy Pianos* is the communion it develops of listener and sound. This is expressed by the relationship of the performer and the tape, of course, which resonates with the relationship of audience and performance. In addition, the tape itself records Erickson's communion with the tangle of bells and wind-chimes in his home. *Piece for Bells and Toy Pianos* is a contemplation of sound, and a musical metaphor of the state in which man contemplates nature. It turns inward the kind of awareness that is required by the group dynamics of the *Concerto for Piano and Seven Instruments*: instead of awareness and response to other musicians, the performer—and hence the listener—contemplates the sounds themselves, and the state of hearing them.

This aspect, however, was not to be fully investigated until five years later, in the "environmental" pieces *Pacific Sirens* and *Nine and a Half*....Until then, Erickson explored further two other aspects of *Piece for Bells and Toy Pianos*: the technical medium of recorded sound, and the theatrical nature of the performer's response to a sonic context.

For all his interest in unusual sounds and musical techniques, Erickson produced only two compositions for tape alone, *Roddy* and *Birdland*. *Roddy* was a direct consequence of *Piece for Bells and Toy Pianos*. As we have seen, Erickson built for it what he laconically described as "another non-instrument," clamping lengths of welding rods to the sounding board of a grand piano. After sketching out rough scenarios of what he wanted on his tapes, he gathered musicians to join him in improvising on the instrument, striking the rods to produce deep bell-like sounds, bowing them, rubbing the piano strings, and striking rods, strings, and the piano itself (as well as its bench) with wooden dowels. The gifted recording engineer George Craig captured the results, and then Erickson returned to the Tape Music Center, by now installed at Mills College, to alter, superimpose, and edit the tapes to produce the final seven-minute composition.

Roddy is, then, a work of *musique concrète*—a musical work existing only on a recording medium, taking as its sources sounds produced not electronically but with actually existing objects. The medium had been pioneered in France in the years after World War II; according to John Vinton's *Dictionary of Contemporary Music* the "term was coined in 1948 by Pierre Schaeffer, a broadcaster for the French radio." Erickson was well acquainted with the history of the medium, in part through his own broadcast experience at KPFA. The French *musique concrète* was soon answered by a rival medium, electronically synthesized music, whose development centered first in Germany, where Herbert Eimert and Karlheinz Stockhausen built a studio in

Cologne, sponsored by the Northwest German Radio, and in New York, where Vladimir Ussachevsky and Otto Luening established a similar studio at Columbia University. The polarity of *musique concrète* and electronically synthesized music was often, though not always, similar to that of figurative and abstract painting, for *musique concrète*, as Schaeffer and his colleague Pierre Henry had shaped the medium, always had narrative, poetic implications, while Eimert and Stockhausen insisted on a "pure" music, devoid of programmatic dimension.

In part this devotion to abstraction was understandable: the first electronic sound-synthesizers were crude and cumbersome affairs, generating pure waveforms that were subsequently modified through various manipulations. Such equipment did not satisfy the tastes for urgency and expression of performing composers, who were used to real-time production of sounds on conventional instruments, and in 1966, after three years' work, Berkeley engineer Don Buchla installed the first modern music synthesizer for the San Francisco Tape Music Center. (There is a controversy as to whether this was the first modern synthesizer anywhere; Robert Moog produced one, at about the same time, on the East Coast.)

In his next (and final) piece for tape alone, *Birdland*, Erickson turned to the Buchla synthesizer at UC San Diego to mediate the polarities of *musique concrète* and electronic music. He worked with pure electronic synthesis, but, as his title suggests, retained his characteristic contemplation of natural sounds. But where *Piece for Bells and Toy Pianos* conveys the physical cause-and-effect of wind chimes, once set in motion, gradually coming to rest, and *Roddy* records the familiar human activity of a group of musicians, however unconventional their technique and instruments, *Birdland* is a composer's study of a third kind of organization of sounds: birdcalls. An immediate influence may have been Pauline Oliveros's *Trio for Accordion and Bandoneon with Possible Mynah Bird Obbligato*, performed by Oliveros, David Tudor, and the composer's pet mynah (who turned out to be mute) at the Tape Music Center in 1965. But Erickson had long been interested in birdsong, and had already explored its musical use, as we have seen, in *Sirens and Other Flyers III*.

Birdsong had interested other composers. Haydn's "Lark" Quartet may have been suggested by the bird Vaughan Williams celebrates in his *Lark Ascending*; some motives in Anton Bruckner's symphonies sound similarly inspired. Beethoven's allusions to the nightingale, quail, and cuckoo, in his "Pastoral" Symphony, are well known. Ottorino Respighi uses a recording of a nightingale for atmospheric purpose in *The Pines of Rome*, and Olivier Messiaen transcribed birdsongs for their melodic substance in many of his works, even titling one *The Catalogue of Birds*. Erickson's interest in birdsong was not sentimental, pictorial, or even melodic, however, but "compositional"—grounded in a curiosity as to how the sounds of birdsong were generated, how they combined, and how such sounds could be adapted to musical purpose. We have suggested that in such works as *Variations for Orchestra* he had developed musical phrases whose structure was "like the flight of certain birds": the phrases of birdsong, built up of trills, steadily repeated figures, flurries of sounds, and occasional sustained sounds, is also an analogy of the swooping, darting, soaring patterns of their flight. And in addition to this metaphorical suggestion of birdsong, certain technical implications caught Erickson's fancy—"heterodyning," for example: the phenomenon of very high sounds producing a kind of metallic warbling when they collide with one another, or when they alter their pitch as they move quickly through the air. (A familiar example is the sometimes painful effect produced by shortwave radios being tuned between stations.)

Birdland is also significant as an early example of what soon becomes Erickson's fascination with steady rhythmic patterns, both for themselves and for the effect produced when they overlap. Until the middle 1960s his rhythmic organization had tended to be quite in the other direction: he avoided steady pulses, preferring rapidly changing tempos and, in such pieces as *The End of the Mime*, constantly fluctuating speeds. In 1964, though, with the appearance of Terry Riley's epochal *In C*, a new kind of rhythmic organization seized the imagination. It too had been inspired by work at the Tape Music Center, where Steve Reich, especially, had developed a kind of sonic equivalent of the moiré effects of op art, then in vogue, by simultaneously playing a number of endless loops of magnetic tape. Each bore the recording of a simple phrase, but there were differences in their length—

differences too slight to be noticed in one repetition, but which grew more noticeable over a number of repeats. Riley took this phase-pattern music in a new direction, writing out short phrases for a number of live musicians to play in a collective performance, individual musicians repeating each of these cells as they chose before moving on to the next. The result was an utterly new kind of rhythmic organization growing out of contrasts: the shifting patterns of moves from one cell to the next; the contrast of lengths of cells, some only a note or two long, some much more extended; and the contrast of the lyrical phrases with the steadily repeated C obsessively providing the quick pulse of the music.

Two aspects of *In C* immediately caught Erickson's attention, and *Birdland* records his immediate use of them: the obsessively repeated "looping" rhythms and, growing out of them, the phenomenon of "hocket"—the aural illusion of continuous activity resulting from quick alternations of sound and silence, overlapping and interlocking in multiple voices. Hocket (the word derives from the French *hoquet*, "hiccough") is an ancient device, much practiced by medieval composers. Erickson was familiar also with its recent appearance in the music of Webern. *In C* extends the concept, by analogy, to alternating and (especially) overlapping phrases, not merely individual notes. And that put a new emphasis on an aspect of musical performance always present but conventionally taken for granted: communality of activity. All three aspects—loops, hockets, and the joy of communal ensemble playing—combined with Erickson's characteristically forward-tumbling phrase and bright textures, already familiar in the *Concerto for Piano and Seven Instruments*, to express a new kind of free-wheeling playfulness in the pieces that closed out the decade of the 1960s.

Fun, Games, and Virtuosity, 1966–1969

Ricercare à 5 (1966) for trombone and prepared tapes; *Scapes* (1966) for two groups of instruments (a "contest"); *Ricercar à 3* (1967) for solo contrabass; *Down at Piraeus* (1967–68) for soloists, chorus, and tape; *General Speech* (1968) for solo trombone; *Cardenitas 68* (1967–68) for soprano, tape, and ensemble; *Do It* (1968) for solo speaker, chorus, and instruments; *High Flyer* (1969) for solo flute

The lively mood of the late 1960s combined with the collegial atmosphere at the San Francisco Conservatory (and later at UC San Diego) to inspire Erickson to compose a series of uniquely high-spirited works. Exuberant, often extremely funny, and insouciant, they are nevertheless serious pieces that continue to extend the composer's emerging style. At the same time they take full advantage of the late-sixties interest in "extended techniques" calling on vocalists and instrumentalists to push virtuosity to previously unknown limits.

Again, the development had begun in Europe, where a few singers and instrumentalists, perhaps bored with the standard repertoire, perhaps seeking to distinguish themselves among the growing number of soloists, had encouraged the composition of new music to show off their virtuosity. The flutist Severino Gazzelloni, the oboist (later composer and conductor) Bruno Maderna, the pianist Aloys Kontarsky, and the cellist Siegfried Palm worked with such composers as Pierre Boulez, Luciano Berio, and Karlheinz Stockhausen, among others. In this country, David Tudor evolved a piano technique that inspired John Cage's epochal early indeterminate scores. Luciano Berio set poems of e. e. cummings, in *Circles*, for his wife, the celebrated mezzo-soprano Cathy Berberian. Erickson himself was to assist the development of two other masters, the trombonist Stuart Dempster and the contrabassist Bertram Turetzky.

He did this in two pieces deceptively titled *Ricercar*. The word, Italian for "to search for," has a long application to music—so long that its connotation now is primarily academic. Originally the word seems to have been applied to prelude-like pieces "for lute or keyboard instrument (as in the expression *ricercare le corde*, 'to try out the strings')";[1] by the sixteenth century it implied a severely contrapuntal composition. Perhaps the best-known ricercar today is the monumental one *à 6*—in six voices—by J. S. Bach (in his *Musical Offering*), which Erickson discussed in his book *The Structure of Music* in a section titled, significantly, "Virtuosity, Craft and Play." "Riddles, delight in craft, virtuosity, technical display, all appear in abundance in Bach's *Musical Offering*," Erickson points out. Ten years later, with his piano concerto behind him as a first step on the road, Erickson took up Bach's example.

He began with *Ricercare à 5*, composed, as we have seen, for Dempster's 1966 solo recital at the San Francisco Tape Music Center. Music for instruments and prerecorded tape was already in the air. Berio's 1959 *Différences* for flute, clarinet, viola, cello, and harp included a prerecorded tape to be prepared by the quintet in advance of its performance: it had been heard at Mills College, where the clarinetist and composer Morton Subotnick, one of the early associates of the Tape Music Center, led the Mills Chamber Players in many new-music performances. Rarely, however, could prerecorded tape have been so closely allied to live performance as it was to be in *Ricercare à 5*.

The very process of its composition confounds the traditional image of a composer lost in inspiration at his writing-desk. Erickson and Dempster worked together for long days, exploring every kind of sound to be got from the trombone. The conventional method of producing tones was not overlooked, ranging from the lyricism of a Tommy Dorsey to the authoritative snap of a Sousa march, from the deepest notes of the contrabass trombone, whose range drops below that of the grand piano, to the highest notes of the alto trombone, which lie above the treble staff. Other effects were explored: percussive tapping on various parts of the instruments; slapping the palm of the hand against the cup-shaped mouthpiece; muting the instrument with appliances ranging from the conventional fiberboard cones to rubber plumbers' plungers; making rude noises through the trombone after the manner of Spike Jones; and whistling, humming, and singing through the instrument while simultaneously playing it, conventionally or not.

The composer reduced all this to rather a dry description in the liner notes to the Acoustic Research recording:

> In the spirit of the baroque model the *Ricercar a 5 for Trombones* [sic] is through-composed and characterized by imitation between the voices. The technical demands made on the trombonist are manifold and include simultaneous singing and playing; whistling, whining and bellowing into the instrument; and the imitation of percussion sounds.

In his memoirs Erickson reveals two sources of the sound he was looking for—one musical, one unexpectedly extramusical:

> On a trip to Southern California I had recorded a herd of hungry cattle bellowing for food and water, and some of the larger bulls produced remarkably trombone-like upward glides with a characteristic breaking-up at the end of the bellow. Stu quickly learned to make similar sounds by listening to my tape. We were both influenced, in the sounds being developed for the *Ricercar*, by a composition by Jan Bark and Folke Rabe, *Bolos*, for four trombones. These young Swedish composers and trombonists were on grants to work at the San Francisco Tape Music Center and they brought as much to the Bay Area music scene as they carried away.
>
> I never intended to mimic the real sound of real cattle in my *Ricercar à 5*, any more than the quarreling section of the piece was meant to represent real quarreling or the ocean or traffic sounds in other compositions were meant to mimic real sources. My intent has always been quite different—to make musical transformations in which the recognition aspect and semantic elements are so leached out that the sound can exist in its own right as musical material, uncluttered by its everyday associations. Fake bellowing, properly composed, is musical for me; real cattle bellowing in a pasture may not be musical but the sound might tickle out a musical idea, and that is what happened in this instance.

"Properly composed." This is the part that's harder to investigate: the actual process by which a composer considers, edits, and organizes the sounds he has heard, in the concert hall, the studio, or the environment; gradually evolves them into a single time-span; and then finds a way to write enough down that the purely mental construct may be achieved in sound. "Ricercar" is an appropriate title for a piece both as complex and as allusive as this: much of the composer's work involves both research and investigation.

Erickson has not written about the scoring of *Ricercare à 5*. Written music is often thought of as visual symbols for sounds, and indeed conventional European music notation is best at symbolizing the pitches of tones and the ratios of their durations, which determine their rhythmic patterns. But there is another kind of written music, perhaps more accurately considered as instructions to the performers by which they are to produce the sounds desired by the composer. Guitarists are familiar with chord symbols that show, pictorially, where to place the fingers of the left hand on the strings in order to produce the desired chord.

The decade after World War II saw the evolution of an extensive vocabulary of pictorial notation, some of it purely symbolic of sound, some of it expressive of the affect of the sound, some of it descriptive of the process by which to make the sound. This "graphic notation" was especially suited to various kinds of indeterminate music, since it admitted of a greater range of interpretive freedom than does conventional notation. Usually less precise than conventional notation, it can often take less space on the page, an advantage for solo performers who are thereby freed from constant page turning. But it is also a feature lending itself to sudden "intuitive" decisions involving different paths through "mobile-form" compositions whose sections can be arranged in different sequences for different performances.

Erickson had used some graphic notation, as we have seen, in the piano concerto, but he turned to it much more freely in the *Ricercare à 5*. Each of the five lines is fully written out, and the exact pitch of the many sustained notes, slides, and trills is stipulated, because pitch—the exact placement of a musical tone within the range of hearing—is always a central concern in Erickson's music, even when he takes unpitched natural sounds for his source material.

The exact notation is required by another concern: the careful interplay among the five trombone voices. *Ricercare à 5* is "about," among other things, the role played by individual expression in an ensemble. The pun on "hearing among a herd" is metaphorical: in its twelve minutes, *Ricercare à 5* manages to present an aural drama on its first level, an extended commentary on the nature of solo participation within a group on a second level.

It begins, not in the feedlot or pasture, but on the freeway—perhaps driving past an airport: for the low growls, rapidly accelerating to an extended higher-pitched warbling in four voices behind a gruff solo statement, suggest both speed and space. The pristine natural landscape of *Sirens and Other Flyers III* has been followed by an excursion through a man-dominated landscape: this pairing will be met again in the sequence of *Pacific Sirens* and *Nine and a Half*. . . .

The opening growls subside into a quietly glittering tapping on the instruments, which soon serves as background to animal-like sounds: the trombonists are barking through their instruments. These give way to vocal growls, the "jungle" growls found in classic Duke Ellington recordings, and a dialogue develops, subsiding into lyrical sustained musical tones in a duet over percussive accompaniment.

A quieter interlude follows, with chords providing a contrasting texture, first produced on single trombones (the musicians humming one pitch while playing another to produce complex chordlike sounds), and the atmosphere is tranquil though still moody. Soloistic behavior again emerges, however: individual trombones provide variations on a single held note, some smooth, others edgy or strident, others pulling the entire ensemble into a texture of trills that become stronger, more eventful, finally descending into the low growls that opened the piece.

The "herd" episode follows. By now the listener's ear is fully prepared: what may have seemed humorous at first is now taken on its own sonic terms, an interesting, evocative voice within a carefully invoked texture. One can hear the "bellowing" as expressive commentary by sentient life; and, hearing it so, one can appreciate the communicative (because communal) nature of calls and responses. A pensive solo transforms the texture once again, reintroducing the chordal quality of an earlier episode; solo voices separate out from the chords, playing with alternating neighboring notes, finally settling on a single quiet note to end the piece.

Much of this description suggests a deliberate program on Erickson's part, but he has never expressed one. Programs inevitably lessen even descriptive pieces of music, because they focus the listener's reception of the music on a single set of "meanings," excluding others—including interpretations that might be utterly unpredictable by the composer or performer. In any case musical "meaning" is elusive. We have suggested earlier (in discussing John

Cage) that it emerges from "the possible concepts [the] sounds and procedures [of any composition] could relate to," that the point of a piece of music—beyond the mere attraction of its beauty—consists in the intellectual and emotional (but, unfortunately for a writer, not verbal) concepts it suggests to its listener. In this case, and certainly in the case of the articulate and evocative *Ricercare à 5*, "The multiplicity of meaning can become very confusing," as we have seen Erickson write of *Finnegans Wake*, "although there are no nonsense words. Everything has a meaning—more likely, several."

SCAPES FOR TWO GROUPS OF INSTRUMENTS, FIVE OR MORE IN EACH (A "CONTEST" WITH THE FORMAT OF TIC-TAC-TOE) (1966)

The composer's natural response to the composition of *Ricercare à 5* was the contrasting *Scapes*. In it Erickson continues his exploration of graphic notation, but chooses a form very different from the fully determined dialogues of the *Ricercare*. *Scapes* is an elaboration of the "mobile form" that had evolved by 1960, reaching perhaps its highest form of development in *Credentials*, the setting (for narrator and eight musicians) of a passage from Samuel Beckett's *Waiting for Godot* made that year by the Polish-Israeli composer Roman Haubenstock-Ramati. A San Francisco performance of *Credentials* by Cathy Berberian in the early 1960s had a profound influence on the Bay Area avant-garde, among young composers as different from one another as Robert Moran and Loren Rush.

In *Scapes*, as in the mobile-form pages of *Credentials*, the written music is set out divided not into the conventional measures of so many beats but into rectangular frames representing boxes. Performers are free to choose their own route from one box to the next, resulting in an "open" form, whose structure is variable, as contrasted with the conventionally "closed" form, whose structure is determined once for all by the composer. The analogy is the sculptural "mobile" invented thirty years earlier by Alexander Calder.

It is worth noting, though, that the implications are very different for sculpture and for music. The various planes and volumes of even a conventional sculpture assume different relationships as the viewer regards it from varying positions; this is the challenge faced by the sculptor. Calder's mobiles simply allow the sculpture to present these relationships in even more subtle variations, to an unmoving viewer. In music, on the other hand, "open form" scores inevitably result in "closed form" performances. As performed, even a mobile-form composition results in a musical structure whose relationships are fixed for that one experience. It is only when different performances of the same mobile-form piece are heard, preferably in succession, that the changes in relationships allowed by the form can be perceived.

(Of course the attentive listener stores in mind constantly changeable responses to the musical events heard. This is why certain compositions, whether open or closed in form, continue to yield rich meaning even after repeated hearings, and why they can change their "meaning" even when merely being considered without actually being heard.)

Like *Ricercare à 5*, *Scapes* is a dialogue—not among five musicians, but between two groups. Its three movements, each set out on a single square page, are arranged as a game to be played three times. And so it is, of course, rich in implications, suggesting political and athletic metaphors of the musical process. It is not farfetched to think of other examples: Degas's painting *The Spartan Games*, Stravinsky's ballet *Agon*. *Scapes* is, among other things, a musical embodiment of the dialectical process so familiar to Erickson through administrative politics, and it resonates with his emerging interest in ancient Greece.

Characteristically, though, it is grounded in familiar American vernacular: the game of tic-tac-toe. The boxes of musical notation are arranged nine to a page, like the squares of that game's grid. The leaders choose the route through the square, marking them with Xs or Os (the audience and performers watch by means of an overhead projector). Erickson takes care to provide contrast: some squares are nearly empty, resulting in a very quiet passage; while others are cluttered with markings: conventional notes; letters representing vocal sounds [HU(gh), HI(c), Shshsh]; sand- or woodgrain-like areas representing busy improvisation on percussion; and cartoonlike constellations of exclamation points, spirals, pointing fingers and so on, representing "a vehement quarrel" produced by combining instrumental sounds with vocal ones. ("Instruments that are unable to produce quarreling should remain tacit during these passages," the composer stipulates.)

The three pages of actual score are supplemented by three pages of instructions. (An oddity of "free-form" music has been the extensive instructions so many composers need for its elucidation.) In them, Erickson is careful to balance the sport and the musical implications of *Scapes*:

> Progression from square to square need not, should not, be at a regular rate. If interesting interactions are taking place between the two groups, or if one of the groups is producing music of interest, stay there longer. If a square is not producing worthwhile musical results, move quickly to a new square.

Two versions of *Scapes* were prepared: the second, commissioned by the University of Illinois ensemble for a European tour, requested three navigations of the score, with improvised passages separating the movements.

Erickson asks that the performing groups be "of about the same strength, but not necessarily identical in instrumentation. Five or more instruments on each side. No high strings." And yet while they vary considerably as to instrumentation, length, and dramatic curves, different performances of *Scapes* have sounded not only remarkably similar, but recognizably Ericksonian. The musical drama recalls that of the *Chamber Concerto*, the piano concerto, and *Ricercare à 5*. There is humor, and lyricism, and substance.

RICERCAR À 3 FOR SOLO CONTRABASS (1967)

In the *Ricercar à 3*, Erickson returned to exclusively conventional musical notation for the first time since *Sirens and Other Flyers III*. But the result is hardly conventional music—certainly not the conventional image of the contrabass. Writing to commission from Bertram Turetzky, Erickson carefully catalogued the many possibilities of that neglected instrument, whose large size and deep voice is capable of producing many nuances of pitch and tone color.

Erickson treats the instrument essentially as a big guitar, not using the bow until about halfway through the ten-minute piece. The performer first records two solo tracks on tape, then performs the middle voice live standing between two loudspeakers. The music of the three contrapuntal voices is closely similar, consisting of rapidly repeated plucked notes, upward scalewise figures, a recurring "turn" (three rapidly descending adjacent notes followed by a return to the central one, a familiar baroque ornament and a frequent motive in Mahler), and long-sustained lingerings on certain pitches.

The result is an unusually introspective piece, the first of many that Erickson was to compose. The rapidly strummed long-held notes at the beginning, and the filigree around other long-contemplated pitches at the center of the piece, suggest a mantra in the sense of a sound contemplated as an aid to meditation. In his score Erickson suggests dramatic intentions, calling for roaring chords from the plucked open strings, for "brilliant" scale passages, and for a "dramatic" utterance growing out of a "dolce" opening to begin the second half of the piece. But the essentially lyrical nature of the contrabass mutes these intentions, perhaps taking the piece in another direction entirely from that originally intended.

Erickson had composed quietly lyrical, even introspective passages before: the close of the piano concerto and the touching passages over low chords in *Ricercare à 5* are memorable examples. But never until now had he produced an entire piece so deeply meditative. It is the first unaccompanied composition for solo instrument he had produced in nearly twenty years, since the 1948 Piano Sonata. (The trombone *Ricercare* had been written with a trombone quintet in mind as the ideal performing medium.) Before turning to *Ricercar à 3* Erickson had completed his two pieces for magnetic tape, *Roddy* and *Birdland*. It is possible that the sustained close-range study of sound required for those pieces generated this contemplative mood; and certainly *Roddy* and the earlier *Piece for Bells and Toy Pianos* can be heard with this meditative quality in mind.

Then too, for the first time since *Sirens and Other Flyers III*, Erickson was composing at the desk, not in the studio. He collaborated with Turetzky, as he had with Dempster, in finding potential material in the instrument and the performer, and working out notation for the unconventional effects to be produced. But this collaboration was conducted through the mail, for Turetzky was teaching in Hartford, Connecticut. The sounds and procedures of *Ricercar à 3* were unusually abstract after the many years of work with bells, toy pianos, and sound on tape. Erickson was returning to "*thinking* sound" as a viable alternative to hearing it.

Both *Ricercars* became widely heard and studied, partly because of the many appearances made by their first performers, partly because both Dempster and Turetzky were subsequently commissioned to write on their respective instruments for monographs in the series published by the University of California Press, where Erickson was cited among the composers actively extending the horizons of those instruments. The *Ricercar à 3* was published in score, too, by the UC Press, in 1973; and both *Ricercars* were released on recordings fairly soon after their creation.

DO IT FOR SOLO SPEAKER, CHORUS, AND INSTRUMENTS (1968)

Even in the studio it was impossible to avoid the sounds of public life during 1967 and 1968. Demonstrations were virtually omnipresent, especially in the San Francisco Bay Area. A presidential campaign was under way. The Vietnam war, and the protest against it, had reached a climax. Erickson turned the sounds of all this to creative use in *Do It*, for double mixed chorus, a solo speaker, and a group of drone instruments (two contrabasses and a bassoon are preferred, but alternatives are sanctioned). Much of the piece develops the communal repetitive structure of Terry Riley's *In C*, as the two choruses, one on each side of the stage, begin by rhythmically speaking relatively short repeated chants, moving from one to the next on the conductor's cue and staying "about an item apart" through the first third of the piece.

At that point the choruses drop out of their coordinated rhythm, murmuring as individual voices behind the soloist, who speaks the poem by Donald Peterson that provides the central imagery of this protest:

> Move twenty paces from start
> Do not go to jail
> Do not pay two hundred fifty dollars
> If of course you choose to pay the two fifty
> And that to the right person
> You can get out
> Someone will take your place....
> Let him wear your suit and your number
> Let him drop the bombs and the napalm....
> Whatever you do do not forget to sell him

> The name of the game is selling
> Be aggressive....

The soloist speaks the entire poem twice, separating them with a few phrases from General Douglas MacArthur's farewell address ("Duty, honor, country..."). Meanwhile the choruses have resumed their rhythmic chanting, their rhythms growing more complex, more at odds with one another. Against all this, but silent during the speaking of the poem, the drone instruments play notes from a B-flat chord, choosing them ad lib. The stability this gives the piece is emphasized by the conductor's cues to the choruses, given not with gestures but with soft strokes on a gong to change from one item to the next, on a tuned metal bar (B-flat or F) if the chorus too is to begin singing a note from the B-flat chord.

It is difficult to describe in words the tension *Do It* generates. All this sounds relatively innocent at first, the chorus suggesting a high-school cheering section, its words, taken from broadcast advertisements, almost impossible to understand, heard as abstract sounds rather than expressive exhortations. Gradually, however, even before the words of Peterson's poem are understood, *Do It* turns into an experience first mesmerizing, finally almost frightening. The droned chord lulls the listening ear into submission; the insistent rhythm drills the texts into the mind—not the text, in fact, but the subtext. *Do It* succeeds in revealing the threat of politicized communication by imitating it. "I wanted to transform these rhetorics into musical experience," Erickson stated in a program note. "...[M]any aspects of language have been deliberately distorted or re-formed in order to lay bare emotion underlying the overt semantic content."[2] The fun and games of *Scapes* has been set aside; an uglier side of competing issues has taken its place.

DOWN AT PIRAEUS FOR SOLOISTS, CHORUS, AND TAPE (1967–1968)

Down at Piraeus is a fraternal twin to *Do It*. The political aspect of communal activity is again present, but the direction is not to contemporary American issues but to ancient Greek ones. Erickson refers to the piece, in *Hearing Things*, as "a mostly rude commentary on Plato's ideas about music, [with] a determinedly anti-antiquarian bias." The composition began as a project for tape, using a number of sounds provided by Stuart Dempster during visits to Erickson's studio, along with recordings of specially produced sounds on toy zithers, pitchpipes, an electric guitar, and Turetzky's contrabass. A solo soprano sets the ancient atmosphere, inflecting her long-spun phrases with microtonal glides suggesting Greek, Turkish, and Arabic musical accents.

The chorus, generally intoning repeated octaves, sings a catalogue of moral virtues (taken from the story of the Pythagorean Damon and Pythias) interspersed with Plato's condemnation of certain musics as degenerate and wrath-producing.

> The text is a severely cut and adapted section from Plato['s] *Republic* where he is putting down all the harmoniae except Dorian and Phrygian. I'm having the men be Socrates and the women the assembled young, with their "yes, you are right, that is true" etc., and I think it will be pretty funny. [Letter to the author, June 30, 1967.]

Around and behind the singing is a network of repeated pulsing beats from the tape, often featuring nasal or buzzing qualities not calculated to soothe the listener. ("It really sounds like a giant jews harp, all on G# and symphonic," Erickson wrote.) The piece is curiously static in spite of its quick-tempo repetitive pulse, but fascinating to the connoisseur for its use of the exotic tuning systems Erickson studied so closely, both in California and, on his Guggenheim year, in Greece.

CARDENITAS 68 FOR SOPRANO, FIVE MUSICIANS, AND TAPE (1967–1968)

Maintaining the principle of composing by contrasts, Erickson followed *Do It* and *Down at Piraeus* with *Cardenitas 68*, a monodrama for solo soprano accompanied by recorder or wooden flute, bassoon, trombone, contrabass, and percussion—the latter including three instruments Erickson invented himself: a marimbalike instrument comprising slabs of travertine marble, a set of bongolike drums made of tin-can lids and plastic sewer-pipe shells, and a set of brass rods whose eerie whistling was set into play by stroking them with rosin-coated gloves. (The instruments were perfected and fabricated by Ed Hujsak, an engineer and acoustician who worked in the aerospace industry in San Diego.)

Cardenitas was composed for the soprano Beverly Ogdon, married to Erickson's friend and colleague Wilbur Ogdon, as a sort of celebration of their collaboration on the creation of the UC San Diego music department. Erickson wrote his own text, a kind of contemplation of contrasting emotions and psychological states: among them tension, confusion, tenderness, beauty, flight, water, aging, and freedom. The structure of the long piece—at nearly a half hour, much the longest piece Erickson had yet composed—is free-form, proceeding by association with the text, often quiet and lyrical. The instrumental writing is as emotional, as intimate and introspective, as is the vocal line, particularly in the long keening prelude to the soprano's confrontation of coldness and age, beginning the last third of the piece. Here too Erickson comes close to evoking non-Western music in the slow slides of the soprano, responding to similar gestures in the contrabass: the effect recalls Chinese opera, or Japanese music for the Noh theater. (Soon, too, there is a fleeting reminiscence of the last movement of *Das Lied von der Erde*, the first Mahler reference to appear in Erickson's music, not to reappear for a number of years.)

Cardenitas 68 will not be widely heard: it is tied to its specific instrumentation. Those who have heard it have had an unusual glimpse into the most inner significance of sounds to Erickson's own personal values, so closely guarded otherwise. The soprano voice accentuates this innerness, symbolizing innocence and purity, recalling the marvelous coloratura writing Luciano Berio provided his wife, Cathy Berberian, in setting the seabird episode of James Joyce's *A Portrait of the Artist as a Young Man* in his early masterpiece *Epifanie*. The tenderness and near-nostalgia of a *Cardenitas* is surprising at this point in Erickson's development, especially in the context of *Do It* and *General Speech*, but it would turn out to be a major component of his music in the next two decades.

GENERAL SPEECH FOR SOLO TROMBONE (1968)

A more ingratiating development of the premise of *Do It* was found next, when Dempster's success with his *Ricercare* was rewarded in 1969 with *General Speech*, a theater piece that combines political satire, instrumental virtuosity, and the composer's continuing research into the no-man's land thitherto existing between speech and music. The idea was brilliant: the trombonist, dressed and made up to look like General Douglas MacArthur, would deliver the ringing peroration from his farewell address, given at West Point—speaking the text through the trombone, while simultaneously playing a pompous, dirgelike line in the bass register of the instrument. Lenore Alt-Erickson provided the costume and setting; Erickson found wonderfully mocking notes to play against MacArthur's unconscious pathos ("You are the leaven which binds together the entire fabric of our national system of defense"), and Dempster played the role to the hilt.

The score carefully prescribes the presentation. The trombonist wears MacArthur's trademark oversize dark glasses and "full dress (tails) to simulate a full dress military uniform." He stands behind "the most opulent lectern one can muster," provided with a pair of miniature American flags and a glass and pitcher of water. He is to walk brusquely on stage, face the audience sternly, and maintain strict military address throughout the performance—in spite of the frequent irony of Erickson's treatment of the text.

General Speech ends in an appropriate *coup de théâtre*: house and stage lights go instantly to black; a dim red light plays in a ghostly fashion on the general's hat and medals, and then he fades out of view. The technical requirements for this are minimal, and they are carefully worked out and explained in the score. The result, unlike *Cardenitas*, is a piece that travels easily and addresses the audience directly, never failing, in Dempster's performances, to make a big hit.

The score provides the text of the speech in phonetic spelling: at the beginning, DOO-TEE ——YON-OR ——CUNT˄TREEEEEE. Underneath this, the text is provided in its correct spelling for the performer's convenience, in smaller letters; and underneath that, the musical staff with the trombone part. A number of pauses, most of them five seconds or so long, punctuate the text: in them the performer is directed to survey the audience with a hard stare, or to remain immobile, or to lean forward slightly. Twice there are longer pauses during which the performer drinks water.

The text cannot be clearly made out, of course, but its inflections are unmistakable, and enough of the words do come through to make Erickson's extramusical meaning clear. This is not high-minded pacifism but a burlesque of militarism, certainly informed by the composer's own tedious army career as well as by the mood prevailing among most artists and teachers during the Vietnam war. Its theatrical element clearly links *General Speech* to the many theater pieces presented at the San Francisco Tape Music Center, where Anthony Hopkins provided overhead projections and lighting to complement performances by such composers as Ramon Sender, Pauline Oliveros, and Morton Subotnick. The direction of influence between those artists and the then-emerging rock scene would be impossible to establish: suffice it to point out the shared energy, willing to subordinate elegance to effectiveness, that characterized both. Erickson seems to have found in *General Speech* exactly the right vehicle to make use of these developments.

HIGH FLYER FOR SOLO FLUTE (1969)

Erickson's final solo composition of the 1960s was *High Flyer*, for flute. It reflects Erickson's fascinations with birdsong, flight, and the spoken word—and his sense of humor. It recalls the importance of the natural world in Erickson's work, too: it was "worked out," in the composer's words, in collaboration with the flutist Peter Middleton, in the summer of 1969, and largely completed at Lake Tahoe that September. *High Flyer* also continues the series of pieces for which he provided his own texts, but—even more so than in the case of *General Speech*—the intelligibility of the text is a decidedly subsidiary element in its performance. As the composer notes:

> In much of *High Flyer* the player is asked to shape his mouth and vocal cavities to various vowels and consonants. The "text" of these passages is mostly nonsensical—it functions as a very precise notation of the composed timbre of the music. The words are, therefore, not meant to be projected distinctly. There are, nevertheless, moments when a word or a phrase (albeit distorted) will filter through the texture of the music. Air sounds, multiphonics, humming while playing, and other extensions of traditional flute technique are used freely, as are both finger and lip glissandi.

Every musical sound has an "envelope," in the composer's jargon: a complex mathematical description of its pitch, loudness, tone-color, and boundaries— the nature of its attack and its decay. Intone the syllable "ahh," sustaining it, and you can hear the attack as the throat abruptly opens to release air across the vocal chords; without interrupting the sound, change the syllable to "ohh" and you can hear a change of "envelope" even while the pitch and loudness are unaffected.

Erickson's text provides his flutist with descriptions of similar changes in the mouth and throat, changes that affect the tone-color of the flute. The four pages of *High Flyer* look like conventional (though decidedly modernist) solo-flute writing except for that running text, placed underneath the notes. Nonsense syllables would have served but might have been hard for the performer to memorize, so Erickson used a series of random comments he'd overheard once made by a nearby drunk passenger on an airplane: "Hoo—wuh take-off quick. Hoo—ah wish away. Hawaii." A cadenza, placed early in the piece, sets a syllable against each quick note:

> How do you do, cutie. Yoo hoo, hey! How ah ya oh? What if, what if we coo, a kiss kissy coo. Wassa matta catcha talk?! ...

Interestingly, the text links the *Finnegans Wake* of *The End of the Mime of Mick, Nick and the Maggies* and the wistful world of *Cardenitas 68*. Did we not know the true origin, the text might seem to transcribe comments from a pet bird, a mynah or more likely a budgerigar—another ironic layer in the meanings of Erickson's music. The text, and its influence on the flute envelope, central as these are to the piece, only heighten the effect of this piece. It is only a short divertimento, a sort of display-piece perfect as a recital encore, but it easily comprises the whole range of techniques worked out in the 1950s and 1960s for the flute: key-slappings, slides, simultaneous sounding of two or even three pitches, microtonal inflections, loud breaths through the instrument, and the like.

1. *The New Grove Dictionary of Music*, p. 835.
2. *Erickson Celebration*, p. 29.

III.   MUSIC IN ITS PLACE; RHYTHM, MANTRA, AND
       SONORITY, 1968–1975

Music Expressing the Environment, 1969–1970

Pacific Sirens (1969) for instruments and tape; *Nine and a Half for Henry (and Wilbur and Orville)* (1970) for instruments and tape; *Oceans* (1970) for solo trumpet and tape

With *Pacific Sirens* Erickson seems to turn away from the politics, humor, and extroversion of the pieces of 1968. Quiet and contemplative, it combines conventionally produced instrumental sounds with specially altered recordings of surf. These latter sounds, after being carefully recorded on portable tape machines, were processed in the studio through electronic filters, limiting their range somewhat but, more to the point, focusing their pitch and tone-color to the composer's taste. The musicians are instructed to collaborate in performance with the finished tape produced from these sounds, resulting in a kind of duet of ensembles, as in *Scapes*. But *Pacific Sirens* is not a contest of opposed forces; it is a conversation of separate (and different) yet complementary ones. Its sources may have included the traveler's experience of the harbor at Piraeus, the time-filling sound-effects from tapes of surf occasionally broadcast over KPFA, the long hours experimenting with filters and resonance in the electronic studio, and ultimately childhood enchantments of brooks and boats near Lake Superior. Its final effect duplicates such solitary meditation in music of unusually contemplative natural orientation: the technology of the electronic studio is used to enact a musical poetic that Thoreau might have approved. (John Cage, in many ways quite a different sort of artist, produced his *Water Walk* at about this same time, and would later produce music for *Inlet* using water sounds and conch shells, among other instruments, using drawings from Thoreau's *Walden* as elements of his graphic score.)

Erickson was inspired by the old stories of quasi-musical moans and sighs heard by sailors passing a cliff in southern Italy, but the intent of *Pacific Sirens* is not descriptive or pictorial—in this it contrasts interestingly with Virgil

Thomson's true "picture for orchestra," *Sea Piece with Birds*, and Debussy's *La Mer*. Nor is it an expression of the composer's feelings on being at the beach, though in fact it was prompted by the setting of Erickson's first home in southern California. It is, instead, the first of a distinguished series of works in which Erickson was to develop a hypnotic, entrancing effect out of carefully chosen, repeated, and sustained pitches, substituting them for the traditional function of the keynote in conventional European tonal music; "grounding" the listener so as to assure a feeling of coherence, while weaving an increasingly filigreed skein of melodic sound around these constant notes—as thoughts and memories, elaborating themselves, intrude on the constant and focused structure of the mind.

Erickson chose his instrumental ensemble carefully: flute, clarinet, and bass clarinet; trumpet, horn, and trombone; strings; and percussion. Most of these instruments are capable of "bending" pitches to match and respond to the tape Erickson provides; additionally, the low instruments (except the bass clarinet) can slide evenly from pitch to pitch. John MacKay has noted the result of this careful match of artificial and natural sound-production:

> ... [T]he piece offers many spontaneous revelations of the relationship between the focused sounds of our conventional awareness of musical pitch and the phenomenon of pitch in natural sources, but for the most part its intrigue is in the margin of distinguishability of the instrumental sounds and the play on the immense sonic ambiguity of ocean sounds in which much can be imagined that is not heard directly. [*Music of Many Means*]

Given the nature of its organization, *Pacific Sirens* can vary considerably from one performance to the next. The overall effect of different performances is remarkably consistent, though, thanks to the instrumentation and, of course, the given of the length of the tape. It was featured on the disc made for Composers Recordings by the Arch Ensemble of Berkeley in 1984, a recording that did much to introduce Erickson's music—particularly the haunting, introspective music of his final period—to a wide audience.

NINE AND A HALF FOR HENRY (AND WILBUR AND ORVILLE) FOR INSTRUMENTS AND TAPE (1970)

Composers often produce works in pairs: Mozart's *Musical Joke* and *Eine kleine Nachtmusik*; Beethoven's Seventh and Eighth Symphonies; Charles Ives's *Unanswered Question* and *Central Park in the Dark*. *Pacific Sirens* was answered by *Nine and a Half for Henry (and Wilbur and Orville)*, another piece based on environmental sounds, but this time decidedly technological and urban, not nature-oriented. (Erickson consistently gives the title as a numeral, not spelled out.) Instead of surf, the four-channel tape is based on airplane and freeway sounds: Erickson has turned away from the Pacific and is facing the freeway and the airport.

Again the printed score is deceptively simple: a single sheet of paper with two five-lined staves drawn on it, measured off in ten-second intervals. Again the composer recommends, but does not stipulate, the instrumentation: two woodwinds (flute, piccolo, or clarinet), two brass (trumpet or trombone), two percussion (no mallet or timpani this time), one contrabass (no high strings). The musicians are asked to play specific pitches—an F-sharp major chord, in fact—for the first quarter of the piece, holding them quietly; to play louder through the third minute of the piece; then to subside for a minute. Shortly after the halfway point the texture changes; the instruments play more loudly and in a lower range; two passages of nearly a minute each represent climaxes in the work, and then the piece subsides again.

In addition to the instrumentation and the thirty-one notes indicated on their staff, Erickson provides only six instructions, laconically and pragmatically stated:

1. Musicians should relate to the timbre of the tape sounds (abrupt).
2. No half or whole-step pitch changes. No tunes.
3. Bend pitches with descretion [sic].
4. Air sounds are O.K.
5. Relate to auto, airplane, jet, etc. without direct simulation of sounds.
6. Tune carefully to tape pitches and other players. Percussion should tune skin instruments to chief pitches of tape and/or octaves of those pitches. Wild pitches should ornament the structural pitches in significant ways.

The title nods to the sixtieth anniversary of Orville and Wilbur Wright's pioneer triumph with heavier-than-air flight, and of course to Henry Ford's success of nearly the same period. Erickson took particular glee in carrying out the camera-work preparing *Nine and a Half for Henry (and Wilbur and Orville)*, which was commissioned by the San Diego public television station, KPBS, for a national film series, *Artists in America*. Wearing a bright orange industrial jumpsuit and a hard hat, and carrying his portable tape recorder and microphone, he roamed freeways, climbed refinery towers, and soared in a glider, seeking the right noises for his musical response to this aspect of the San Diego environment. The film then demonstrates his studio alterations of the gathered sounds and finally ends in the first public performance of *Nine and a Half for Henry (and Wilbur and Orville)*. It is a persuasive integration of art, technology, documentation, and entertainment; completely opposed to the Thoreauvian *Pacific Sirens* in effect, but similarly focused and intent on its awesomely different object.

OCEANS FOR TRUMPET AND PERCUSSION (1970)

Oceans, composed the year after *Nine and a Half for Henry (and Wilbur and Orville)*, is a final comment on that pair of ensemble contemplations, and another excursion in collaborative work with instrumentalists: it was "composed directly with [the trumpeter] Jack Logan's live sounds and a few verbal directions; it has no written score." It exists (apart from any live performance) only as a recording, like *Piece for Bells and Toy Pianos*, *Roddy*, and *Birdland*.

In one dimension it is minimal music *in extremis*, as a schematic description will suggest:

0:00 small gongs (bowl gongs?), B flat, occasional other pitches in B flat chord.

0:30 a faraway trumpet plays a middle-range B flat, holding it, repeating occasionally.

1:45 gongs continue; the trumpet is very slightly nearer.

3:00 little changed, but sound slightly more present still, and more evident overlapping of trumpet notes.

3:30 trumpet plays a D above its B flat, then returns to the original
B flat. High metallic sharp-attacked bell joins gongs.

5:25 trumpet plays an F, filling out its B-flat chord, then returns to
the original B flat. Percussion continues.

9:00 trumpet adds a top B flat to complete its chord, then returns to
the original B flat. Percussion continues.
Quiet slow percussion continues, with original trumpet B flat,
overlapping as the gong notes subside, beginning to die away
after about thirteen minutes.

14:30 Silence.

Oceans is in many ways a transcription of *Piece for Bells and Toy Pianos* for new instrumentation. Whether because of the title, though, or because of the intervening compositions (especially *Pacific Sirens*), the introverted, meditative quality of *Oceans* seems to have taken on an entirely new meaning. In another dimension than that of the sheer number of events, *Oceans* is quite vast. On the most immediate level it is "about" two things: the way we relate pitches to one another, and the way slow rhythms expand to fill a long stretch of time. In the end, the two things approach one another, recalling Karlheinz Stockhausen's proposition that pitches, tempos, and forms are ultimately simply three different scales of a single phenomenon: a regularly recurring beat. Repeat any pulse fast enough—anywhere from about thirty to four thousand times a second—and it becomes audible as a pitch, from about the lowest C on the piano to the highest. Slow down the pulsing, from sixteen times a second to once every eight seconds or so, and the pulse is heard as a steady rhythm, from the quickest playable to the slowest perceptible. Slow the pulsing down further, and the repetitions are heard as defining structural units. "The ranges of perception are ranges of time," Stockhausen concludes.[1] *Piece for Bells and Toy Pianos* was meditative in an apparently intuitive way; *Oceans* is a meditation on a now-known proposition. It is a contemplation of the essence of music—the simultaneous filling-out and comprehension of the nature of time.

Oceans is therefore another expression of Erickson's mounting interest in the phenomenon of tuning and in the ancient Greek philosopher Pythagoras. A musician tuning his instrument is analogous to a mechanic tuning an engine, an athlete fine-tuning his technique. It is a question of bringing distinct elements into exact relationship. For *Oceans*, Erickson chose (and manufactured) percussion instruments whose pitches were precisely in tune: the octave higher vibrated exactly twice as fast; the fifth higher, three-halves as fast; and so on. Accurate tuning, in this acoustical sense, is pleasing, sounds "right," because it relates pitches according to even proportions. If the pitch A (tuning A) pulses 440 times per second, its octave will pulse at 880; its fifth, E, will pulse at 660. The four notes of a major chord, like that forming the material of *Oceans*, will be laid out in an immediately satisfying manner:

unison	octave	fifth	major third
[B♭:B♭]	[b♭:B♭]	[F:B♭]	[D:B♭]
1:1	2:1	3:2	5:4

Having set our ears at rest with respect to tuning—the relating of pitches to one another—Erickson can now turn our aural contemplation to that other dimension, rhythm. In *Oceans* he is concerned with the rhythms of long periods, what we conventionally think of as phrases. Stockhausen pointed out that just as we hear eight octaves of pitches, each pulsing twice as fast (or slow) as the next, so do we notice about eight "octaves" of structural units, from entire movements of sixteen minutes or so down to short motives, a few seconds long, composed of individual notes. *Oceans*, fourteen and a half minutes long, is at one end of this range; its individual notes are at the other, taking a few seconds to die away. The most noticeable structural events are the new trumpet notes: the original B flat, then D, then F: these are placed at times whose relationships are analogous to those of the pitches. In other words, the musical structure of *Oceans* stands for the musical structure of an octave. Its duration is marked off exactly as are pitch distances within an in-tune octave.

Thus baldly stated, *Oceans* sounds formulaic. No more so, though, than any naturally occurring simple relationship. Thanks to the title, we are reminded that such relationships, complicated it is true by the intrusion of innumerable events too small to be otherwise noticed, determine the reassuringly regular rise and fall of the swells of a calm sea. Time and tide are linked phenomena; the observation of natural rhythms undoubtedly led the ancients to embark on the analytical inquiries leading to our science and philosophy. Music was central to classical education because it led to, proceeded from, enhanced, and facilitated a concern for just proportion. *Oceans* is the beginning of a return, rare among contemporary composers, to that concern. It would be a protracted return: it underlies all the music Erickson was subsequently to compose.

1.   Karlheinz Stockhausen: *Stockhausen on Music: Lectures and Interviews*, compiled by Robin Maconie (London and New York: Marion Boyars Publisher, 1989), pp. 92–95.

The Rhythm of Mantra, 1968–1973

Drum Studies (1968); *Cradle* (1971) and *Cradle II* (1972) for drums and instruments; *Loops for Instruments* (1972–73); *Percussion Loops* (1973)

Oceans was a study in structural rhythm, but Erickson was also preoccupied, in the pivotal period between 1968 and 1973, with a more familiar kind of musical rhythm: motor rhythm, the underlying pulse propelling a musical line onward. In those years Erickson composed five percussion works focusing on motor rhythm as their content; the last, *Percussion Loops*, almost excludes all other musical concerns.

The earliest, *Drum Studies*, is Erickson's only music written specifically for educational purposes. There are twenty studies in all, written not for music students but for nonmajors taking music courses in the department Erickson was then establishing at UC San Diego. The études are in asymmetrical rhythms—that is, rhythms whose strongly accented beats do not arrive at regularly repeated intervals. (These are often heard when dance-band drummers—Gene Krupa, for example—wander far away from the steady beat during solos, always careful to keep the contrasting symmetrical rhythm going with one hand.) A few of the final études use rather long rhythmic cycles, repeated "loops" of fairly extended spans of these asymmetrical rhythms.

Each étude calls for two or three sets of tuned tube drums. At about the time of his move from San Francisco to San Diego in 1967, during his period of experimentation with homemade instruments, Erickson became interested in the possibilities of such fiberboard cylinders as those used for forming concrete columns, or for the storage and shipping of carpeting. Available in various weights and diameters, they could be cut to length to produce various pitches. The resulting tone quality was rather diffuse and "hollow," nicely mediating between the sharply defined pitch of a kettledrum and the throatier sound of an unpitched drum. (In fact, the sound of these fiberboard cylinder drums approaches that of the Indian *tabla* and is not that far from the hauntingly wooden but resonant sound of the plucked contrabass of *Ricercar à 3*.)

To allow the tone to ring out with resonance the tubes were suspended on cradles of rope: hence the title of the next pulse-piece, composed in 1971. Erickson provided a program note:

> *Cradle I* came out of a long standing interest in rhythm, especially asymmetrical rhythms, and in rhythmic cycles. It also reflects my fascination with the rhythmic polyphony of African, Indian and other musics. The tuned tube drums, which I had invented for an earlier composition, provided the instrumental means. Three percussionists play progressively more complex overlapping rhythmic cycles to create a highly detailed polyphony, static and hypnotic, while an instrumental ensemble provides a drone background of slowly changing color. Three of the percussionists play interpolated solo cadenzas.

The subject of cross-cultural influence and borrowing is complex and not to be investigated here; but it should be noted that the issue came to a head in American music, especially on the West Coast, in this period—the close of the 1960s, when even the Beatles found irresistible the sitars and tablas of the Indian subcontinent. After composing *In C*, for example, Terry Riley turned to the serious and profound study of Indian Kirana-style singing. After his early work in the San Francisco Bay Area, Steve Reich took up a similar study of West African drumming at the University of Ghana. An Ethnomusicology Institute had been established at the University of California at Los Angeles as early as the 1950s, soon including a full-scale Indonesian gamelan. In the early 1970s the gamelan found new vigor elsewhere in the United States, with ensembles of instruments bought or built for such campuses as UC Berkeley, Mills College, San Jose State University, and California Institute of the Arts in California alone.

Erickson had no illusions that exotic musical cultures could be fully assimilated by American composers:

> *I have done my best to be influenced by the musics of India and Africa, because I have been particularly attracted to the rhythmic richness and variety that permeates them. But there are puzzling difficulties ... I think that in order to understand, really understand, Indian rhythm*

or African rhythm I would have to think music in the way that they do, that I would have to have learned it in their ways and produced it with their kinds of mental operations. I come to this view reluctantly, and not for want of trying. Certainly some of my thinking about African and Indian rhythm has found its way into my compositions. Nevertheless, some aspects of their rhythmic organizations seem very hard to grasp, maybe even ungraspable.

He had already noted the curiously false accent of jazz played in Warsaw, of Balinese music played by Los Angeles students. He noted, in the unpublished essay "Other Worlds," connections between music and language: "The relationships between Indian rhythm and language are very close, according to Fox Strangways in his classic study . . . in some parts of Africa the relationships between language and music are even closer." He found the languages of Balinese dance and shadow-play, when he attended performances there in 1974, a "closed book" but enjoyed it hugely for its "musical nuances."

Whatever the music, it carries a potential for many levels of understanding and misunderstanding. We always miss some of the meanings, no matter if it comes from our very own cultural back yard. Some musics, whether close to home or half a world away, are more difficult to cope with than others, and that is probably as it should be. Some musics stretch my powers of understanding too far—I may fail to get aboard at any level at all; other music sounds as though it had been invented especially for me. And there is that occasional delicious shock of certainty when one senses human to human communication that somehow has found its way through the thickets of cultural difference. At those moments one is in touch with whatever it is that is universal in music, and brotherhood is not too large a word to use for the feeling one has.

A fascinating idea emerges here—we have met it before in contemplating Erickson's compositions. A piece of music may be, ultimately, "about" *music*—about its relation to language, its function as a sort of language; and about both its ability and its refusal to assume familiar aspects of language and communication. And the development of a personal artistic style, as we see taking place in our survey of Erickson's music as it developed over the years, may be "about" this too. The use of music, and the need we feel for it, may lie in this aspect of music: it is, and represents, the way we note and grasp events and concepts, the way we take them in, relate them to previous experience, and express them. There is no doubt that Erickson was thinking of music in these terms in the early 1970s, not only in his own music, but also in his research papers and in the thinking that was evolving toward his second book, *Sound Structure in Music.*

In *Cradle*, as in *Do It* and *Down at Piraeus*, the expression is above all else communal. The three percussionists play steady, ingratiating rhythms; the drone instruments enter and drop out, individually swelling louder, then softer on their individual pitches. As in *Oceans*, the listening ear is lulled, the analytical conscious mind dampened, the receptivity to nonverbal sonic information heightened. It is fascinating to contrast this music with the more familiar repetitive-pulse music composed in the same years by Steve Reich and Philip Glass: all "minimal" music is by no means alike. Reich's music, because of its generally fast tempo, insistent and unvarying volume, and percussive attacks, sounds more highly machined; Glass's, for its gentler dynamic, often slower and abruptly varying tempo, is often quite lyrical, but his instrumentation often lends a brittleness to the texture. Erickson's, particularly in the two *Cradles*, is gentler and more engaging: the percussion instruments have soft attacks and quick decays, and the quietly changing pitches of the drones, whose own attacks are minimized, veil the sonic atmosphere.

This veiling was central to *Loops for Instruments*, a tantalizingly elusive study composed after *Cradle II*, in 1972–73. Scored for flute, clarinet, trumpet, alto saxophone, bassoon, and marimba, it remains unpublished and unrecorded. Resembling an orchestration of the rhythmic music of *Cradles*, this is hocket music at its most focused. The individual instruments interchange isolated quick notes, as if the entire ensemble were a single instrument—a thumb piano, say, each instrument representing a single finger, playing only in alternation with the other instruments; not always the same pitch, to be sure, but never a significant note of soloistic importance: only notes with significance to the larger context of the entire ensemble. John MacKay writes that "The central issue of the *Loops* pieces is the perception of linear continuity in sequences of essentially isolated sounds" and continues by quoting Erickson's commentary from an unpublished research paper, "Loops: An Informal Timbre Experiment":

> Clearly one is able to listen to this delicious confusion in more than one way: (1) one may follow the tune through its hinges of timbre; (2) one may begin to form perceptual streams on a pitch basis ... (3) one may follow the line of a single instrument ... (4) one may listen—and this is most likely—in a mixed manner, using (1) (2) or (3) depending on the detailed musical situation at any particular moment.[1]

With his hocketing technique, then, Erickson was investigating the phenomenon of selective perception: how the mind interprets incoming sounds as parts of a pattern. We are all familiar with the urge to recognize patterns in apparent clutter: the satisfying linings-up of rows of trees as we drive past orchards, for example; or the occasional and suddenly significant groupings of vehicles speeding in the other direction on the freeway. What became increasingly evident in the years after 1968, when so much changed so quickly within societal structures, was the need to recognize the presence of this patterning interpretation—if only to understand better its pervasiveness in the communications and encounters of daily life.

In the early 1970s this patterning was a central problem addressed by composers (of minimal music, for example), painters (op art), poets (especially "sound poets," who would evolve the genre of "language poetry"), and particularly by researchers into artificial language and speech recognition, extremely significant aspects of the emerging research into computer technology. Through the Defense Department, the federal government subsidized intensive research in the area. Loren Rush, who had succeeded Erickson at the San Francisco Conservatory of Music, joined John Chowning in establishing a Center for Computer Research into Music and Acoustics (CCRMA) at Stanford University. (This institution was one of the principal models for the Institut de Recherche et Coordination Acoustique/Musique established subsequently by Pierre Boulez, in Paris.) Great amounts of time and energy that might have gone into the composing of music were invested instead in the very early stages of computer research: it was important, as Rush noted at the time, that composers make the underlying decisions that would affect future generations of computers, if computers were to evolve capable of dealing with music. A similar institution, the Center for Music Experiment (CME), was established at UC San Diego.

Erickson observed these developments sympathetically but somewhat skeptically. In another context he had recalled Darius Milhaud's comment on the rise of conductorless orchestras in the Soviet Union in the Lenin days: the results were successful, but a conductor would have obtained the same results, no doubt a little faster. Large organizations and abstruse technologies impose a certain inefficiency and stiffness. The inquiring scholar-artist, using the traditional tools of travel, observation, reading, and listening, might come to conclusions quite as fundamental and visionary, without spending as much government money (or as much of his own time). There was another danger:

> The trouble with computers is that fiddling with them is a kind of trap and seduction. The seduction of the input end. Music is heard music, not tinkering with some engine that will have perfect power or perfect specifications. As long as one is dealing constantly with live musicians that fact is constantly in front of one, and the results are ultimately BETTER than any brainy "perfection," because live human beings occasionally do better than they are able to do. [Letter to the author, Jan. 26, 1980.]

So in the first half of the decade of the 1970s Erickson pursued these investigations—tuning, rhythm, tone-color, speech, hocketing techniques, virtuosity, and communal performance—gradually seeing them all converge on the central but diffuse and extensive issue of music as an activity that imprints the mind, rendering it open to outside influence while shaping it to process that influence. Erickson was fascinated with these investigations, but under no illusion that they would necessarily turn into music:

> Neither science nor music theory is of any great value to the practicing musician when performing or composing. Theory is a separate and distinct world that exists to satisfy our curiosity. Making music is a unitary process. Imagination, invention and memories of sounds are mixed with thinking, and the thinking is not like theoretical thinking or the thinking that goes on in science. ["Psychology and New Music," pp. 534–535, quoted by MacKay in *Music of Many Means*.]

Erickson's investigations into hocket, and his writing for percussion, reach their climax, oddly, in a work for solo performer. *Percussion Loops*, composed for Ronald George, began, as Erickson noted,

> as nothing more than some experiments with fast change of timbre played by a single percussionist. As the instrument list grew longer, Ron George devised new racks until a rather large console of thirty-five easily accessible elements was evolved. This flexible instrument sounded so impressive that I wrote a composition for it. There are seven categories of percussive sounds and five pitch levels within each category. The pitches are not integrated to any tuning plan; the emphasis here is on timbre ... and in the contrapuntal effects which come about through perceptual channeling.[2]

The seven kinds of sounds are: skin (drums), wood, dry metal, ringing metal, gongs, cymbals, and rattles. Each is indicated by a symbol, which required that the score be rather more than usually laboriously drawn out by hand, and there are twenty-seven pages of score. (George plays the work from memory.) These seven kinds of sounds do the hocketing: one of the challenges of the piece is its (unstated) requirement that the performer not attempt to smooth over the differences among the thirty-five sounds (actually there are more, for Erickson occasionally asks for sounds produced from the bodies of the drums) or their seven families.

Percussion Loops begins in a sparse, tentative texture of sounds, flexibly arranged without a regular rhythmic pulse: it is the quiet exploratory prelude to a toccata. After a minute or two this leads to the main movement—in both senses of the word: the long central section is in a steady quick rhythm, four notes to the beat, a steady ticking on the various instruments in recurring longer patterns—"loops"—that slowly evolve. Again, the historical source is the loops of tape dangling from racks of recorders at the San Francisco Tape Music Center.

The listener distinguishes the individual loops primarily by their instrumentation: bright crisp metal, ringing gongs, hollow wood-blocks, resonant low drums. Passages primarily for one or another of these groups alternate with others in which a more complex interplay of instruments is featured. The steady beat is maintained, like Krupa's driving snare drum; with cross-accents provided by shifts of instrument, like Krupa's rim-shots. Erickson also lets certain gong or cymbal notes hang over from rhythmic passages, to inject a sense of memory, to project anticipation of change, or (particularly after the ten-minute central section) to slow the tempo.

At eighteen and a half minutes, *Percussion Loops* is a major work in its genre. Emphasis on percussion instruments has been a hallmark of twentieth-century music, especially since Varèse's pioneering *Ionisation* for thirteen players (1931). Other modernists have written memorably for solo percussionist: among them, Cage in *27' 10.554" for a Percussionist* (1956) and Stockhausen in *Zyklus* (1959). *Percussion Loops* is an important contribution to this catalogue, almost unique for the delicacy of nuance and expression it demands of its performer. This characteristic reveals its deep kinship with *Ricercar à 3*: in a good performance, it can be meditative and soothing. Its overall shape, slow four-minute introduction and epilogue framing a ten-minute trance, recalls the extended gamelan pieces of Indonesian music; but it is not tempted by local color or the exotic. It stands unique but organically within Erickson's evolving catalogue.

1. MacKay: *Music of Many Means*. The Erickson quote is from a paper written for the Center for Musical Experiment at UC San Diego.

2. *The Ninth Annual Contemporary Music Festival* (program booklet), California Institute of the Arts, 1985, p. 33.

Sonority and the Sound Structure of Music, 1974–1975

Rainbow Rising (1974) for orchestra; *Sound Structure in Music* (1975); *White Lady* (1975) for wind ensemble

Erickson's first book, *The Structure of Music*, was intended as a layman's guide. His second is addressed to composers. It is concerned with a subject so elusive as to lack even a proper English name: like many writers on music, he settled on the French word *timbre*. It is most easily described by describing the difference it makes: what differentiates a trombone and a flute, both playing an identical pitch at an identical loudness, is the difference in the timbre of the instruments. A frequent approximation in English is "tone color."

The book was preceded, as was customary for Erickson, by a long period during which he mulled the subject over, discussed it with students, explored it in his music, read about it in scholarly books and journals, and considered it in recordings. Fairly simple approaches to the subject have been noted in the *Loops for Instruments*, in which Erickson noted his interest in the gradual changes from the sound of one instrument to the sound of another. He was not the only composer to study the subject: the gradual transformation of sound between two dissimilar instruments was a popular assignment in the early days of music synthesis. Today we call this "morphing," and it is familiar in visual terms: the head of a tiger is gradually transformed, through computer technology, into the face of a young woman. In the middle 1970s the sound of a lion was similarly transformed smoothly into that of an intoned word.[1]

There were historical precedents as well. Preëminent among them was the third movement of Arnold Schoenberg's *Five Pieces for Orchestra*, op. 16. This movement, titled "Summer Morning by a Lake (Colors)," presents a nearly static melody resting on a subtly changing chord intoned, in turns, by two sets of instruments: low viola, bassoon, clarinet, and two flutes, handing the pitches off to contrabass, muted French horn and trumpet, bassoon, and

English horn. The five pitches are identical, and the tone colors, which are very close, vary them in the slightest amount. It is significant that Schoenberg, still generally (and mistakenly) thought of as a composer of "abstract" music, produced this pioneering example of pictorial music. In fact the analogy seems apt, as anyone can attest who—like the young Erickson—had contemplated the subtly shifting visual inflections of light on the surface of a lake on a still morning.

Erickson's first orchestral essay into this contemplation was inspired by a similarly visual experience, as described in the program note quoted above (page 70). *Rainbow Rising*, a two-part work commissioned by Thomas Nee's La Jolla Civic Orchestra, was composed for orchestra with a large percussion section including Erickson's beloved rods—now made of aluminum—carefully tuned to exact frequencies and bowed. It is a two-part work with an epilogue. About sixteen minutes long, it opens with floating pitches, then introduces a cloud-scatter of notes with a final return. It is somehow "overtonal": certainly not "tonal" in the traditional sense, not using conventional tonality as did George Crumb, George Rochberg, and other "quotationists" of the period, but clearly a piece whose sense is that it is tonal, using our perception of the relationships of pitches to make its effect.

And the effect is novel. The "tonic," the benchmark pitch we take as basic to the music, gradually shifts from one frequency to another, as would happen in any conventional piece of tonal music. But conventionally the result is a "modulation" of the key. Instead of a scale of eight notes all relating to a basic C, say, the composer takes us to another scale resting on G four note-steps higher—but the mutual relationships of the eight notes in the new scale are identical to those of the first. It is as if one were to put three-inch blocks under the legs of one's dining table: the plates, silver, glassware, and so on would be three inches higher, but their mutual relationships would be unchanged. Ignore the floor itself, and one perceives no alteration.

In *Rainbow Rising* it is not the keynote but the tuning system itself that "modulates," changing the way the ear takes in the relationships among the many overtones of a basic pitch. It is as if one were to examine closely the triangulation of plate, wineglass, and napkin, choosing the napkin as the focal point; then, shifting the reference point to the wineglass, reconsider the grouping for a moment before taking note of the saltcellar and the vase of flowers, which without one's realizing it distract one from the napkin and plate.

It is a very simple piece whose method is hidden in the first hearing, for Erickson never publicly revealed his approach to the musical material of *Rainbow Rising*:

> In the case of *Rainbow Rising*, I did a lot of pretesting. The sequencing of the harmonies was tried out with 16 insts at CME in various improvised situations which I recorded and studied. The stacc. notes, the dots, was another written out experiment played by the same group. I then recorded and rerecorded dots to get the feel of how they would come out in a full orchestral texture, played them and studied them. Some things ... were invented as they turned up or were needed, but the pretesting allowed me to feel very sure footed. [Letter to the author, Sept. 18, 1980.]

> *Probably I should have been more explicit about how I had mixed, separated, and manipulated single tone colors, and ensembles of tone colors, but aside from my aversion to technical discussion in program notes, my understanding of what I was doing was not really clear enough to be put into language. I knew what I was doing compositionally, but neither the compositional ideas, nor the impetus and clarification they got from seeing the rainbow were formed into words, phrases, sentences. It was several years after composing Rainbow Rising before I was able to say anything sensible about how the piece works. When I composed it I had a nucleus of clear and muddy feelings, all wrapped up in seeing that rainbow, and that is why, I suppose, I thought it important to share with my listeners.*

The result, to the composer's chagrin, was frequent misunderstanding on the part of the public. "Dozens told me how wonderfully I had described rain, thunder, storm and clearing in music. Some of their stories were very detailed, and took a long time to tell." We meet here an intriguing and perhaps inescapable dilemma: the utter intransferability of the private "meaning" of a piece of music from one listener to the next—and particularly from the composer to the listener. For starting with *Rainbow Rising*, Erickson's music takes a decidedly "narrative" turn. "Narrative" in quotes, for his music is narrative in manner and perhaps, metaphorically speaking, even in method; but it is not narrative in the explicit procedure that depends, reflexively, on the existence of the story it narrates.

This is not the place to study closely the differences among verbal, visual, and musical narrative, as exemplified in, say, *Hansel and Gretel*, *The Adoration of the Magi*, and Beethoven's Fifth Symphony. Any culturally literate person will instantly recall the matter narrated in any of those examples, and will probably agree that instrumental music could not "narrate" the story of the two children, or the birth of Christ, any more than painting could express the Fifth Symphony. Yet *Hansel and Gretel* could be presented in a painting (thanks, it is true, to prior knowledge of the story), and the *Adoration* was first told through words, not visual images.

No doubt one of the great sources of the emotional power of music is this very resistance to verbal and visual translation: it rises, perhaps, in a more basic, more "primitive" area of the mind.* While the narrative of music resists translation, still it is made up of relationships that are analogous to those of verbal and visual narrative, even of logical and mathematical thought. It was this realization that urged Erickson to write his second book. He remained unaware until the book had gone through press that its very title, *Sound Structure in Music*, revealed his concern for finding, in the relationships of our perceptions of sound itself, well-formulated fundamental approaches to his art.

SOUND STRUCTURE IN MUSIC (1975)

As we have seen, *The Structure of Music* was written for the layman. The new book, *Sound Structure in Music*, is differently addressed. The preface, couched in technical language, makes this clear:

> This book was written for musicians, especially for composers, with more than a glance in the direction of performers of contemporary music. It aims at gaining some understanding of the role of timbre in

---

*See the persuasive argument for this view in Julian Jaynes: *The Origin of Consciousness in the Breakdown of the Bicameral Mind* (Boston: Houghton Mifflin Company, 1976), pp. 367–370.

> music and at locating principles upon which a theory of timbre organization might be constructed. [*Sound Structure in Music*, p. ix.]

Though written for professionals, it is more speculative than doctrinaire:

> I wanted to look closely at how we have used timbre in music, at our assumptions about its functions, and at our traditional ideas about what we are doing. I hope I have offered no recipes for constructing timbral music. That needs ears and imagination above all. This is more a what-might-be than a how-to-do-it book, for all its emphasis upon practice.

Erickson's speculations proceed from the general to the specific. His first chapter, on "The Sounds Around Us," opens with a striking observation: "We cannot close our ears; we have no ear lids." He considers the various modes by which we organize our hearing experiences: sounds as signals (telephone bell, automobile horn); "music mode," in which we pay attention to the sound itself rather than interpret it as a cue for action; "speech mode," in which we process sounds as patterns within a linguistic context.

Erickson notes the extreme difficulty of separating these modes, of tracing single strands of mental activity during the process of hearing a sound. There has been considerable study into these matters, of course, and attempts at localization of such mental activity, within the brain, are now familiar even to the layman. But the complexity and redundancy of any human mental activity is daunting, and Erickson is careful neither to oversimplify nor needlessly complicate his approach as he closes in on his subject: timbre. It is a fascinating subject, because it is primarily through perceptions of timbre that we can follow a single line in a complex piece of music, even learn to keep track of several simultaneous lines. We do this without knowing how: any music-lover can tell a clarinet from an oboe (though there are ways to trick the ear), but only the professional neurobiologist can begin to tell *how* we do this. The explanation is fascinating to the composer, for if one *could* learn how we do this, one might exploit this knowledge when organizing sounds into musical compositions.

Erickson closes his first chapter by citing the opening of Anton Webern's orchestration of the six-voice ricercar from J. S. Bach's *The Musical Offering*, which does precisely this. Webern breaks Bach's nineteen-note theme into two halves, then four uneven quarters, and assigns each of these fragments to similar but distinct tone-colors or timbres. Once having used timbre as a tool for analyzing a single cohesive theme into its fragments, in the ricercar, Webern goes on in an original composition, the *Five Pieces for Chamber Orchestra*, to use timbre as a tool for integrating a group of tiny thematic fragments—"motives"—into a coherent unit.

Webern's approach to building a cohesive musical structure through timbre, systematic though perhaps equally intuitive, was a historical necessity, for concert music had by then evolved past the point of organization through tonality, the reference of melodic shapes to a keynote. Webern's situation was analogous to that of Braque and Picasso a quarter-century earlier, when the forfeiture of traditional perspective and illusionistic "realism" in painting was answered by the development of similarly cohesive methods of organizing space and markings in cubist painting and drawing. It's interesting to note that cubism itself went through two phases, characterized as "analytical" and "synthetic" cubism.

Erickson turns next to a close consideration of "Some Territory Between Timbre and Pitch," as he calls his second chapter. The pitches of notes—their position in a scale of notes—is the basis of traditional musical theory, as codified by Rameau and d'Alembert in the eighteenth century. (Their work is one of the triumphs of the Age of Reason and the Encyclopedists: Jean-Jacques Rousseau, however, thought otherwise, arguing that the preconscious source of all music lay in speech—an argument that resonates with some of Erickson's investigations.) Twentieth-century studies into psychoacoustics, however, have revealed greater complexities than were available (or significant) to these eighteenth-century theoreticians, and Erickson notes that the boundaries between pitch, chords (several pitches simultaneously sounded), and noises (sounds without definite pitch) are vague and easily crossed.

A whispered vowel, for example, which would normally be thought of as a "noise" in a musical context, can seem to have pitch when put in a special context. Whisper the vowel sounds only (not the consonants) in the words "her he hay hot / her hay he her / he hay her hot / hot hay he her " and you produce the tune of the Westminster chimes. (Erickson had used this phenomenon in *High Flyer*.)

Again, noise—like the whoosh heard when a radio is tuned between stations—can be narrowed down to "pitchiness" (a word Erickson favors) by filtering out its highest and lowest components, leaving a frequency range of only a hundred cycles or so—about the range between tuning A and the C above it. One can then juxtapose different such bandwidths, using them as if they were notes, either alone or combined with conventional instruments, as Erickson did most notably in *Pacific Sirens* by filtering the sounds of surf.

Certain twentieth-century composers have used aggregations of sounds—sonorities—that can't usefully be thought of as either chords or noises: Erickson cites Debussy's pioneering work in *Jeux*, sonorities in Stravinsky's *Rite of Spring* and *Agon*, and, supremely, passages in music by Edgard Varèse:

> With the composition of *Déserts* Varèse achieved many of his lifelong desires: to compose sound-masses projected in space, free from the straitjacket of tempered tuning, where no one parameter should enjoy privileged status, and where the entire work is an intermixed unity which "flows as a river flows." His vision about composing the sound itself, rather than certain abstractions more or less related to sound, opened up the sound world we have been colonizing ever since. [*Sound Structure in Music*, p. 57.]

Erickson turns next to a consideration of time in music—what happens to sounds during their time of sounding. "Every sound is in motion," he points out, and even the untrained ear recognizes the authenticity of a single piano note, as contrasted to a synthesized one, by the tiny changes in its sound as it fades into silence. Similarly noticeable though tiny components are built into the different possible attacks of a note, as Erickson explored in *General Speech*, where the consonant attack sounds of the syllables "duty, honor, country" were made, for example, to influence the playing of the trombone notes assigned to them. Expressive (some might say "excessive") vibrato, familiar from sentimental violin-playing and fading opera singers; beats, as are produced by vibraphones or by two instruments not quite in tune; and rustle noise, like that made by rattles and cymbals, all contribute to the changes in sounds over time. All these microscopic variations, too small to be noted individually, add up to what Erickson calls "grain"; and our brains, complex sound- and pattern-analyzers that they are, attend to these variations whether we know it or not (which may be why hearing some music leaves some of us so fatigued).

There is reason to believe there is biological resonance in this procedure. Erickson quotes Wladimir Weidlé:

> The tissue of a work of art seems alive because it closely imitates—as closely as possible—the cellular tissues of organisms. And this is how it does so: it is entirely composed of units of brief duration or of reduced size which, in turn, imitate the internal structure of living cells."[2]

Erickson notes that different species respond differently to sounds, repeating an observation of Donald R. Griffin: "Where bats catch fruit-flies at rates of several per minute, blind men cannot... fly airplanes to catch birds."[3] There are microscopic patterns in the crow of a rooster that only the rooster, apparently, responds to, and birds in general seem to note much quicker events than we do. Conversely, as Erickson notes, "whale song presents a different musical problem, more like learning to understand and appreciate an extended musical composition, one with few clearly defined motives but long and diffuse phrases."[4] This does not mean that birds are superior to humans and humans to whales, of course, but that all animals are capable of responding to intricate patterns at a scale appropriate to their biology, even though these patterns are heard on a preconscious level. (This relates to the discussion noted earlier in Julian Jaynes's contemplation of the association of music with the right hemisphere of the brain.)

Composers have taken advantage of the mind's ability to perceive similarities between juxtaposed sonorities in carefully planned sequences. The quiet chords alternating just before the noisy conclusion of Beethoven's Eighth Symphony; the quiet plucked strings, bowed strings, woodwinds, horns, and percussion in the "March to the Scaffold" in Berlioz's *Symphonie fantastique*, and passages in the "Nachtmusik" of Mahler's Seventh Symphony preceded Schoenberg's epochal "Summer Morning by a Lake (Colors)." (Erickson does not cite the Beethoven.)

There follows a short but intense chapter on drones, which will prove central to the work of Erickson's final period. Rare in Western concert music until the twentieth century—the prelude to Wagner's *Das Rheingold* cited as "the only well-known drone piece in the concert repertory"*—drones have become commonplace in the music of the last few decades. Erickson speculates that this is partly because they leave the listener free to attend to other components—timbre, texture, rhythm, and so on—when pitch is constant and unchanging. He cites music by Loren Rush (*Hard Music*) and Folke Rabe (*Was??*) and his own *Down at Piraeus* as examples, efficiently noting the specific sound details exploited in these pieces.

He then turns to more "primitive" examples of drone: the jaw harp (mouth harp, Jew's harp), central to ritual music in New Guinea, China, and Southeast Asia (and no doubt familiar as a folk instrument in Erickson's childhood); the didjeridu, a buzzed-lip wooden tube used with great sophistication by the aboriginal people of North Australia (and taken up with considerable enthusiasm and success by Stuart Dempster in the late 1960s).

Most fascinatingly, Erickson considers the vocal drones of India and Tibet: "When used in secret and sacred ceremonial songs the sounds of speech are inseparable from the musical sound as a whole," he points out;[5] and it is impossible, in this music, to separate music, speech, ceremony, secrecy, and pattern. First-century Egyptian priests, twentieth-century Chinese lovers, Australian shamans, Tibetan lamas—all use drone as a means of expression, of expression of nuance and concept that may elude the precision of conventional left-hemisphere verbalization.

> What are we to make of all this? More than pitch must be involved....
>
> Indian musicians speak of the sound of the [drone] tambura as the ambient in which the music moves....
>
> No overview of drone music can neglect this conception of the sound as ambient....
>
> The conception of drone music as an ambient or an environment is at the root of much contemporary music ... and is, I think, only at the beginning of a long and fruitful development. If we are interested in the "whole sound" we shall have to use that whole sound, even if we need

---

*Erickson overlooks Alexander Borodin's *In the Steppes of Central Asia*, whose horizon-line drone makes the work an unusually appropriate choice for programming next to a late Erickson score.

to give up some of the frenetic darting about from pitch to pitch, so typical of our music, in order to hear and appreciate other musical dimensions. [*Sound Structure in Music*, p. 104.]

Then Erickson indulges in a rare revelation of his contemplation of the spiritual content of music: "Varèse's dream of a living, unbounded music ... and Schoenberg's conception of a melody of timbres ... are reverberations of attitudes that are deeply imbedded in Eastern music and musical thought.... A concern with numinous aspects of sound is at the center of Tibetan religious thought...."[6]

And he ends the chapter quoting Schoenberg, who believed that a music capable of transcending conventional classifications of timbre and pitch

> would bring us closer to the realm which is mirrored for us in dreams; that, in fact, it would expand our relationships to those things which seem not yet alive to us by giving from our life to the life which appears dead to us only because we have so little connection with it. [Arnold Schoenberg: *Harmonielehre* (Leipzig and Vienna: Universal Edition no. 3370). Erickson's citation, *Sound Structure in Music*, p. 105: translation uncredited.]

Having discussed pitch, timbre, time, and drones, Erickson turns to the problem of organizing a music of sounds beyond pitch. The conventional Western European musical organization of pitch, as we have seen, was largely crystallized in the Age of Reason, then radically reformulated (especially through the "twelve-tone method") early in the twentieth century. "[E]ven today [1975], after sixty years of experience with such sequences [of timbres, rather than pitches], composers and theorists have written little or nothing about the logic of that rather large variety of linear formations usually tagged with the convenient term 'klangfarbenmelodie.'"[7] (Perhaps this is because composers and even theorists have come to be suspicious about the validity of all-embracing "systems," since new information is continually surfacing, forcing revision.)

In conventional Western music, timbre has been left largely to the performer, but other musics—Erickson cites Chinese *ch'in* music—carefully notate timbral details. (In *ch'in* notation, timbre is specified at the expense of detailed rhythmic notation.) Of course changing timbre relationships are possible and effective in instrumental music of the Western style, as Webern's orchestration of the Bach ricercar shows. These changing relationships can even be organized into patterns, as pitches are into scales and melodic patterns, and Webern was the early master of this kind of organization—though Erickson believes that a listener follows either the tone colors of the patterns, or the pitches as they relate to one another, taking in both patterns simultaneously only after becoming familiar with such pieces as Webern's *Five Pieces for Chamber Orchestra*, op. 10.

Webern's middle pieces, Erickson notes, make a more systematic use of timbral organization, often with particular clarity resulting from repeated pitches played by contrasting (though usually related) timbres. These "channels" of particularly clear pattern-threads, once we are aware of them, can be woven together into a unified larger pattern, as one can attend to either the windows in the facade of a large modern office building, or the blank walls between them, or the interplay of both elements. Rhythmic motives arising in this kind of interplay—"hocket"—are a significant component of much sophisticated African music, where they have a clearly societal significance; and from West Africa they found their way into the equally societal "minimal" music Steve Reich composed for his performing group in the 1970s.

Erickson investigates even more radical Western music: the kind that results from the suppression of any kind of motive, whether melodic or rhythmic. Even here—in John Cage's *Atlas Eclipticalis*, for example—timbral contrast offers a kind of implicit organization, whether or not intended by the composer.

Erickson turns to South Indian drumming, however, for examples of the most highly evolved organization of sound patterns:

> In the West we have learned how to make musics from selected pitches. We have hardly begun to think of timbres in fixed relationships, and perhaps such limited sets of fixed timbres are not a fruitful direction for us, but those musicians who see that direction as a possibility may find that Indian music can give them more than an inkling of what such a music might be like. [*Sound Structure in Music*, p. 138.]

Sound Structure in Music ends with a contemplation of the most complex, seemingly abstract aspect of the new music: texture. Perhaps the most succinct description of the difference between twentieth-century concert music and the music that preceded it—though the description may be simplistic—would concern its dimensionality. Traditional concert music of the baroque, classical, and romantic periods tended to lie in two dimensions: forward-moving melody, led through a more or less steady rhythmic pulse; and "vertical" chordal harmony, whose more pronounced changes often mark off the structural divisions. By deflecting attention away from melody and harmony, the new twentieth-century music gave the listener a more evident third dimension.

Since "every sound is in motion," as Erickson stated boldly in his third chapter, it follows that every sound occupies a sort of space. The final chapter of *Sound Structure in Music* is concerned with this aspect. Erickson investigates the performing space of the orchestra, as Berlioz, Charles Ives, and Henry Brant, among others, have composed for it. He investigates the psychological phenomena of the apparent location of high pitches above lower ones. He discusses computer-assisted dispositions of sounds in space, taking note of such pioneers of computerized spatial distribution as John Chowning, of Stanford University, and of the technologies of electronically enhanced concert halls—a rapidly growing industry twenty years after his book was published. (Two Erickson students, Loren Rush and Pauline Oliveros, are involved in Good Sound Foundation, one of these hall-enhancement companies.)

Such extended musical "space" provides greater room for the "grain" of music, which can be composed in such a way as to provide for a number of layers of different musical sounds, analogous (though Erickson quotes Ives's caution against spatial analogies) to the foreground, middle distance, and background available to a painter.

In contrast to these layered textures, "fused textures" are also available: in them, many layers of sound can collapse into one, or expand to surround their own space. Erickson cites examples by Pierre Boulez, Alban Berg, and Ernst Krenek to demonstrate these rich, ambiguous sonorities, and his own *Pacific Sirens* as well—simply, but not retiringly: "An attractive aspect of the sound of the reconstituted waves in *Pacific Sirens* was its sense of multiplicity and its bigness. I could sometimes hear (or could imagine I could hear) the distant singing of a chorus of voices."[8]

Erickson calls for further investigations of the resources of musical space, even for codifications of their results:

We have composed as though orchestras were as unchangeable as architecture. Certainly some of the works of the past twenty years might have profited from a disposition of instruments not so cruelly bound to older orchestral specifications. Composing should include composing the orchestra; then the orchestra can be for the composition rather than the other way round. Unless orchestral music is to go the way of the dinosaur it must have the potential for extended transformation, and no doubt this means a new form of organization. If the economics of modern life and the nature of orchestra organization is such that orchestras cannot adapt to changing musical ideas, then they will freeze into what they all too often are now—a very expensive device for accurately projecting the music of a rapidly receding past. [*Sound Structure in Music*, p. 177.]

Erickson does not shrink from an enthusiastic comment on John Cage's *HPSCHD* (composed in collaboration with Lejaren Hiller, 1967–69):

Listening to the recorded version is an amazing experience, full of surprises and perceptual kinks. Tunes and other coherent borrowed musical materials slip in and out of perception, their beginning and ending points masked by the multitude of less-patterned sounds. It is like a walk through a forest. One sees the pine among the maples or the maple among the pines, and sometimes, if there are many varieties, one sees only the forest....

HPSCHD could not work without the history of music and our memories of that music.... These recognizable bits are constantly emerging and submerging in a rather mysterious way, and the listener may feel that he is in motion, because these experiences of changing perspective of the details in a mass are so much a part of modern life, where we see things (and hear things) from moving automobiles and airplanes." [*Sound Structure in Music*, pp. 190–192.]

Erickson ends the book, appropriately, with a description of Charles Ives's *Universe Symphony*, unfinished and perhaps unrealizable (though the attempt has been made), with its several orchestras and huge choruses placed in valleys, on hillsides, and on mountains, sounding the musics of heaven and earth.*

---

*As this book goes to press a commercial recording of Larry Austin's performing version of the *Universe Symphony* has just been released, with Gerhard Samuel conducting the Cincinnati Philharmonia and the Percussion Ensemble of the College-Conservatory of Music at the University of Cincinnati (Centaur CRC 2205).

Sound Structure in Music is sound scholarship, tightly presented, extremely wide-ranging in its 193 pages. But it is neither dense nor humorless. It is full of homemade verbal descriptions, charmingly apt: the "shingling" of sounds spilling out of layered chords, the "pitchiness" of loosely tuned drums. There are dozens of practical comments: "If [a certain chord] were part of a composition of mine I would explain to the conductor what I had in mind, put an accent on the lowest note and hope for the best," Erickson observes at one point; at another he notes that the prelude to *Das Rheingold* is usually played too loud. There is the occasional ironic comment: "The advent of electronic music played through loudspeakers makes for less visual distraction—indeed, many theater pieces have come into being from a desire to give an audience some sort of visual distraction *from* the music...."[9]

In short, the book, while directed to the professional, and though ostensibly arguing the need for an evolved theory of music progressing beyond mere pitch-organization, is limpid, sensible, almost conversational. It is as if the author of *The Structure of Music: A Listener's Guide* had followed his ideal reader, a quarter-century later, into an ideal society in which music, especially orchestral music, were an avidly sought diversion that addressed the realities and values of its own time.

Alas, such is not the case. The many fascinating scores Erickson cites are neglected by the musical establishment. Ligeti, Berio, Cage, Stockhausen, Webern, Erickson himself most of all—all are shamefully ignored at the close of the century whose events and experiences they translate into art. The history of music, as performed by the symphony orchestras and opera houses of our time and place, remains so overwhelmingly devoted to the two dimensions of melody and harmony that we have been trained to ignore all other aspects of music—and even to object to them on the rare occasions when they are forced on our attention. It is as if painting had been exclusively preoccupied with line, and had altogether ignored color, perspective, and the contrast of foreground and background.

Yet with the writing of *Sound Structure in Music* behind him Erickson turned to the practical demonstration of his ideas in an impressive series of fully mature compositions, orchestral pieces among them. They are works that explore color, sonority, drones, microscopic texture, and extensive vision. He began, rather disarmingly, with a short piece based on a single chord.

WHITE LADY FOR LARGE WIND ENSEMBLE (1975)

Sound Structure in Music had required extensive research into orchestral scores, and this had rekindled Erickson's enthusiasm for the orchestral medium:

> My big difficulty is that now that I have gotten back to the orch. I am its suitor, lover, gigolo and slave! I do have the hots for that hundred man sound. Nevertheless I am trying to be sane and reasonable; a friend has been after me to do a piece for wind band and I am going to see if my libido can be transferred to that extent. Wish me luck. [Letter to the author, May 20, 1975.]

The result was *White Lady*, perhaps the most easily "heard" of Erickson's investigations into these "sound structures." It is scored for the wind section of a large orchestra: four flutes and alto flute, two oboes and English horn, two clarinets, piccolo clarinet, bass and contrabass clarinets; two bassoons and contrabassoon; three saxophones; three French horns, three trombones, euphonium, and tuba—nearly thirty instruments in all. Alone or combined, these instruments produce rich, dark sonorities, irresistibly suggesting those of such jazz bands as Duke Ellington's and Stan Kenton's, dissimilar as they are from one another.

White Lady is "about" at least two things: the changing colors of the instrumental timbres, and the drift through the various chords that make up the single sonority of Erickson's pitches. One hears *White Lady* in somewhat the manner one would contemplate a twelve-storey building on a dark night, noting rooms now on one floor, now on another, as lights are lit or extinguished over the course of a warm evening. At the center of the piece our attention is on a single level, its rooms coming to life one after another. Then the lights begin to go on and off at an increasingly rapid pace, only to subside. At the close, blocks of windows on adjacent levels are illuminated, one after another, the building's grid taking on more coherent, orderly, "organic" rhythms than were at first apparent.

White Lady is a three-part piece, beginning with quietly changing chords handed around various sections of the orchestra, occasionally hesitating for a note or two from a solo instrument; pausing at the center for a minute and a half in which the only pitch, middle C, is given from one instrumental voice to another; then returning to changing chords, now sideslipping more distinctly through a series of minor triads to end quietly in flutes, oboes, and clarinets.

All but one of the twelve notes of the scale are heard in the first chord, quietly but rather sharply attacked, then growing louder. (Erickson's score is ambiguous, for the missing twelfth note, G, is indicated in the "short score" reduction at the foot of the page, though not assigned to any specific instrument.) With a few strategic exceptions these remain the pitches of the entire piece. As the composer notes, "there is no 'progression' of chords in the composition, because the two, three, four, five and six element chords that succeed each other are simply extracted from the registrally fixed chord."

In *White Lady* Erickson again responds to the powerful stimulus of Schoenberg's "Summer Morning by a Lake (Colors)," this time carefully avoiding the programmatic distractions of *Rainbow Rising*—except in his title, meaningful to the composer, potentially misleading to a later generation assaulted on all sides by "political correctness." Erickson was thinking about the cool elegance of a satin-clad Jean Harlow or Carole Lombard, and there is something of Art Deco about the slow, rich sonorities of this music.

---

1. James A. Moorer: "Lions Are Growing," a computer-synthesized setting of a spoken delivery of the poem by Richard Brautigan (Elektra compact disc 9 60303-2).

2. Weidlé: "Biology of Art: Initial Formulation and Primary Orientation," in *Diogenes*, 17, Spring 1957: 1–15 (cited in *Sound Structure in Music*, p. 81).

3. Griffin: "Echolocation and Its Relevance to Communications Behavior," in *Animal Communication*, ed. Thomas A. Sebeok (Bloomington: Indiana University Press, 1968), cited in *Sound Structure in Music*, p. 78.

4. *Sound Structure in Music*, p. 84.

5. *Sound Structure in Music*, p. 98.

6. *Sound Structure in Music*, pp. 104–105.

7. *Sound Structure in Music*, p. 106.

8. *Sound Structure in Music*, p. 175.

9. *Sound Structure in Music*, p. 144.

IV. CLOSURE: MUSIC AND THE INTERIOR MIND

Introspection: Solo Music

Summer Music for violin and tape (1974); *Kryl* for solo trumpet (1977); *Quoq* for solo flute (1978)

While working on the essentially orchestral concepts discussed in *Sound Structure in Music*, and before completing the larger pieces *Rainbow Rising* and *White Lady*, Erickson composed a final piece for solo instrument with tape accompaniment. In the ten years since *Piece for Bells and Toy Pianos* his mood had sobered, his vision had extended. In those ten years he had also neglected the instrument he first played as a small boy, the violin. In fact, he hadn't written a note for that instrument since the 1960 *Chamber Concerto*, except for the two orchestral scores, *Sirens and Other Flyers III* and *Rainbow Rising*. (This most likely reflects a lack of sympathetic and enthusiastic players of the instrument among his associates.)

When he did finally return to the violin it was in rather a nostalgic mood, and the result ushers in his final period—sixteen years of contemplative, generally quiet, uniquely expressive music. Of all the music of that period, *Summer Music* remains among of the most haunting, partly because of its intimate scoring. The music is slow and rhapsodic, somewhat recalling slow South Indian violin improvisation, but as if played by a Michigan farmhand sitting on his front porch on a quiet evening.

The score is as simple as it sounds. The violin's line is written on one staff; the accompanying sound on tape is indicated on another, below it. The tape, in the first and last sections, produces only a sort of burbling sound: this was made by passing the recorded sound of a babbling brook through electronic filters to accentuate certain pitches, as the sound of surf had been treated in *Pacific Sirens*. At the beginning there seems to be no rhythmic measure: instead, a vertical line marks each passing second. *Summer Music* opens with a characteristic Ericksonian slow introduction, the tape alone for fifteen seconds, the violin then entering on its lowest note, rising through three note-steps to middle C only after fifty seconds have elapsed—and then falling silent for another ten seconds.

After two and a half minutes the first quick notes are heard, ornamental filigree passages punctuating the quiet mood. The violinist is directed to "call to the tape," and a dialogue of sorts is established—each "word" lasting several seconds, and answered, at first, only by silence. Erickson's resources are minimal. Until the fourth minute the only pitches used are those of the C major triad, with F and A added. The tape carries only two kinds of sounds: the filtered brook, which John MacKay describes as sounding like "a mildly percussive cross between cello and tube drum colored with the rushing water ambience," and barely audible high whistling sounds, possibly produced on aluminum rods. The violin is always bowed, never played muted, and its few double-stops are always octaves. But if the resources are few the music is effective: though slow and quiet, it is continuously absorbing. In the fifth minute the violin begins to play quickly reiterated notes, an echo of the "pulse" of Terry Riley's *In C*, but much filtered, by now, through the drones and hockets that have preoccupied Erickson since the late 1960s. These quick notes gradually subside into a more lyrical, melodic kind of violin writing, taking it into the octave above the staff, and the "bubbles" on the tape give way to "high stuff," as Erickson plain-facedly describes the extremely high, barely audible whistlings that begin to appear behind the violin.

For over three minutes, at the center of the piece, the violin plays only the pitch C in various octaves. For a minute and a half only *middle* C is played, alternating with silences of ten or fifteen seconds' duration. In this section the tape is all but inaudible. At one point there is a silence of twenty-five seconds—an unbearably long silence in almost any musical context, but in *Summer Music* Erickson somehow keeps the ongoing melodic impetus from flagging. The burbling tape is reestablished and the violin filigree returns, slowed down; the violin climbs once more through its middle register, even playing in octaves, finally instructed to "sing!"; and then, in a closing minute and a half, the piece subsides, the tape dying out altogether as the violin lingers over three octaves of the pitch G.

Summer Music, as Erickson comments in an unpublished program note, has much to do with rhythm: the dancing rhythms of myriad sound particles; the way they coalesce into larger musical units; the rhythmic implications of "small sounds"; the superimposed phrase organizations of the violin. Textures undergo transformations too, and the music depends upon several textural dimensions for the composed ambience of the "small sounds." It is Summer Music because it hardly sounds like a winter piece—maybe a spring piece, not likely an autumn piece. It may not sound the way summer sounds, but to me it sounds the way summer feels.

It is likely that the easily sung melodic line of the violin is another afterthought to *In C*, which was the first gentle volley fired in the battle against the established dissonance imposed on twentieth-century music by the European modernists. But in Erickson's hand consonance is never bland or sentimental. *Summer Music* recalls instead the fresh strong sweetness of the Charles Ives violin sonatas. For all its awareness of Asia—and many commentators have noted suggestions, in *Summer Music*, of Chinese, Indian, and Indonesian inflections—the piece has a Yankee twang, perhaps because of the clearly homemade nature of the accompanying tape. In the liner note accompanying the Musical Heritage Society recording of the work, Joel Sachs has referred to the music as a "unification of an intense love of nature and an expressive simplicity that arises only from complete inner piece," but this is not an exotic, Taoist inner peace; it is that of every camper who has ever sat contentedly in a national park—which is, in fact, as Sachs notes, where Erickson recorded the brook heard throughout *Summer Music*.

Commissioned by the San Francisco violinist-composer Daniel Kobialka, *Summer Music* has since been taken up by a number of violinists. It is fascinating to compare their different interpretations: the tempo of the piece is relatively set by the tape, but the violin part leaves a great deal of expressive nuance to the performer. Technically easy, it nevertheless rewards the sustained focus and lyricism of a seasoned musician.

KRYL FOR SOLO TRUMPET (1977)
QUOQ FOR SOLO FLUTE (1978)

After *Rainbow Rising, Sound Structure in Music,* and *White Lady,* two years were to elapse before Erickson's next work, *Kryl,* for unaccompanied trumpet.

This is a *divertissement* for virtuoso player. In its way *Kryl* is another contemplation—again related to *Ricercar à 3*, but meditative of nothing particularly lofty or spiritual. After a sort of warm-up consisting of quick filigree leading to held notes, the trumpeter begins the main body of the work: constant running sixteenth notes, either of neighboring pitches or of wide skips.

The technical demands are considerable. Erickson requires quarter tones (the notes "in the cracks" of the piano keyboard), notes very low in the bass register, and frequent changes of the trumpet's slides to lengthen, shorten, or entirely disable portions of its intricate plumbing. In addition the player must sing (and occasionally scream) through the instrument, either in quick alternation with played notes, or simultaneously with them in two-part counterpoint.

Performances of *Kryl* are almost inescapably humorous, for the sight and sound of a professional musician squealing through his trumpet, while removing and reinstalling its attachments, is unconventional in the extreme. The source of Erickson's mood in the piece may lie in his explanation of its title:

> When I was about twelve years old the famous cornettist, Bohumir Kryl, brought his touring band to Marquette.... Kryl was a dazzling player, with a smooth, liquid technique and a remarkably sweet tone. He made everything sound easy, even the low tones (in the trombone range) that he introduced into the cadenza of *The Carnival of Venice*.

Erickson had worked with Jack Logan, who premiered *Oceans*, in exploring these low trumpet notes; and in 1977 he entered into a similar collaboration with Edwin Harkins, for whom *Kryl* was written. Harkins had studied composition and had performed in a number of new-music ensembles before joining the UC San Diego faculty. He prepared the carefully annotated edition of *Kryl* ultimately published in 1984 by Smith Publications.

Quoq, another solo *divertissement*, followed, using similar techniques to those in *Kryl* but to less frankly humorous, more lighthearted purpose—appropriate to its instrument, the flute. Erickson opens with a quick burst defining the flute's upper and middle range, bringing in the vocal sound underneath in the second measure, then rushing through flurries of notes recalling those of his music of the 1960s—but with the quarter-tone filigree that distinguished *Kryl*. Hockets, in *Quoq*, take the form of isolated silent key-slaps in quick running passages, allowing the flutist to catch a breath without allowing a sudden silence to intrude.

Comparatively little vocal production is required. The flutist occasionally hums a note, an octave (or two, or even three) under that played on the instrument, and once or twice quietly sings an independent melody against the flute, but these are punctuating moments in *Quoq*'s eight and a half minutes, not continuous activity, and the vocal sound seems intended rather to reinforce the typically weak bass end of the flute's timbre than to assert a contrasting voice in the texture.

Quoq was composed for another UC San Diego colleague, Bernhard Batschelet. The title word, from the inexhaustible *Finnegans Wake* ("Quoq! And buncskleydoodle! Kidoosh!"),[1] had leapt out of context near the center of *The End of the Mime of Mick, Nick and the Maggies* when Erickson set that text fifteen years earlier.

Again, Erickson was joining distinguished company in writing for unaccompanied flute. The Italian virtuoso Severino Gazzelloni was one of the pioneers in the extension of instrumental techniques after World War II: Olivier Messiaen, Pierre Boulez, and Luciano Berio had all composed music for him. Again, however, Erickson brought an individual personality to his contribution to the literature. Witty, lyrical, and deft, *Quoq* offers flutists a short display piece content with entertaining its audience.

1. *Finnegans Wake*, p. 258.

Introspection: Small Ensembles

Garden (1976–77) for violin and orchestra; *Night Music* (1978) for solo trumpet and ten instruments; *The Idea of Order at Key West* (1979) for soprano and five instruments; *East of the Beach* (1980) for orchestra

In 1976 Erickson returned to orchestral composition for the first time since *Rainbow Rising*. Surprisingly, he set aside the complex fused textures he had described in *Sound Structure in Music* in favor of further investigation of the simple melodic contours of *Summer Music*.

The result, completed the next spring with a grant from the National Endowment for the Arts, was *Garden*, for solo violin and small orchestra—modest string sections and single winds. This is a tranquil, sunny piece, about seventeen minutes long, with open textures and a relaxed, lyrical mood that manages to suggest both Mahler at his most cheerful and Chinese music at its most accessible. It is in an entirely new mood:

> I have such weird feelings about this piece; I like it, even after it has sat for 9 months, but I feel all my colleagues will think it giving in to a conservative impulse. I'll have to hear it with an audience a few times before I can even begin to guess what its tendencies are. It is lyrical, so lyrical and long phrased that I can't help liking it (my god, look at that, I must really be worried). It is so unintellectual that I can hardly believe it, though there are some satisfying tonal secret things that I don't comprehend yet. [Letter to the author, July 25, 1978.]

There are two basic motives: a held note, often approached through either a "turn" (a quick passage through the notes immediately above and below the main note) or a slide; and free-ranging, rather slow, songlike melodies wandering through a series of consonant notes, often in a five-note scale. The held note very often turns into a drone, sometimes taken up by entire sections of the orchestra, sometimes hanging out of the solo line—"shingling"—in isolated relief.

These two ideas are presented in a minute-long introduction in the strings before the solo violin enters, to confirm their centrality to the piece. After two minutes the first winds are heard: trumpet, then horn, still maintaining the pitch that opened the piece underneath a rising melody in the solo violin. By the beginning of the fourth minute the strings have moved to a very high range, the orchestral violins playing harmonics above the solo violin, itself well above the staff. The musical space is very open and unrestricted; the quality recalls Sibelius's slow movements, spacious and untroubled. *Garden* is a long way from Sibelius, of course, but it is even further from *Pacific Sirens* and *Nine and a Half for Henry (and Wilbur and Orville)*.

After subsiding into a narrower range for a minute or so the woodwinds make their first entrance, their single tones sounding rich and important by virtue of their long delay. (We are more than five minutes into the score!) The brass respond, and the first real discords are heard when the string sections play clusters of notes, repeating them always lower, taking the orchestra to its lowest depths, to a droning cluster carrying solid notes from the cellos, contrabasses, and bass trombone.

This signals the beginning of a central section, with more assertive melodic lines (especially, at first, in the cellos), clusters of notes (horns), and high shimmering tremolos in the strings. The solo violin is silent for nearly two minutes, then returns, still untroubled. The music by now sounds rhapsodic, improvisational: Erickson has internalized the principles of melodic contour, of phrase-lengths and rhythmic looping, to such an extent that compositional process is the furthest thing from the listener's attention.

It is misleading to mention such composers as Sibelius, let alone Frederick Delius: the substance of Erickson's expression is far from theirs. But there is an affinity of unhurried contemplation among these composers, so far from the heroics of nineteenth-century romanticism or the evident structural craftsmanship of twentieth-century modernism. At the middle of this center section there is even a suspiciously Mahlerish tune, low in the orchestral violins, fleeting: it introduces the lowest point of the score in terms of activity and density. Gradually the texture gains in complexity, with orchestral notes again placed in isolated relief against the solo violin. A short folklike solo tune emerges in the clarinet, followed by more strident clutter in the trumpet and high strings, whose whistling sounds recall the stroked rods heard in *Summer Music*.

A final section begins, about twelve minutes into the score, with suddenly increased textures: a brass cluster, tremolo in the violas, the sudden appearance of bell sounds. The atmosphere of the opening section returns, and after another absence of a minute or two the solo violin reappears against drone horns and clarinet. Long phrases range through five-note scales giving a "Chinese" effect; a mood of utter tranquility is established, and the music fades to its end.

It is hard to resist the conclusion that *Garden* is *about* something. The title suggests a quiet stroll through an outside space, natural but man-made. Gardens originated as enclosed, protected, artful havens set apart from the threat of the wild and the confines of the interior. It is their nature for gardens to be metaphorical: they stand for relationships of people to their spatial contexts, and for the relationship of order to delight. In *Garden* Erickson works out, in purely musical terms, an effective combination of his own creative style, as it has evolved over the last twenty years, with the conclusions he has drawn from his absorbed study of Debussy and Mahler, Chinese and ancient Greek music, Indian rhythms, and the psychoacoustical principles of our perception of sounds and sound-patterns. It is amazing that after all this *Garden* is so tranquil, so effortless.

NIGHT MUSIC FOR TEN INSTRUMENTS (1978)

In its tranquil, sunny mood, *Garden* is music for a summer day. *Night Music*, its companion piece, Erickson's next score, is another matter. Its restless pulse, dark timbres, and haunting melodic cantillations suggest a mood more anticipatory than participatory. Hushed and expectant, it is music for an intimate setting. In Erickson's words, "it invokes the kind of night that belongs to dreaming, an oceanic night."[1]

Night Music was written for the SONOR ensemble, in residence at UC San Diego, and exploits the technical mastery of its players judiciously but thoroughly. Erickson stipulates the disposition of his ten instruments carefully: clarinets and flute to the conductor's left, trombone and cello to the right, two contrabasses at center, two percussionists behind them, and trumpet centered at the back.

Lasting about eighteen minutes, the piece is in three sections but sounds in two: a long, quiet drone opening followed by a quicker, dancelike movement. There is an unexpected precedent for Erickson's form: the "Night in the Tropics" Symphony by the nineteenth-century American composer Louis Moreau Gottschalk. It would be delightful to hear the two on a single program: both open with a haunting, expectant, slow-moving nocturne, then conclude with a supple, languorous dance.

Night Music combines many previous Erickson ideas in pursuing its completely new program. The restless timpani, whose pacing recalls the opening of Charles Ives's "In The Dark" (from the *Set for Theater Orchestra*), have been prefigured in the tube drums of *Cradle I*. They pulse on a reiterated C, over an F drone in the dark, low instruments, recalling the opening of *Garden*. After a minute or two the trumpet enters, unnoticed at first in its deepest bass register, then quietly joining the drone—now on C—decorating it with a turn, and with microtonal filigree. This develops into the sinuous cantillations we heard in *Kryl*, and these are taken up by the other instruments, building to a climax, subsiding through a bass clarinet cadenza into a broader statement in the cello, then building again to a striking moment in which the contrabasses call out five times with downward-sweeping slides (marked "seagull gliss." in the score) under trills in the wind instruments.

This is followed by a two-minute pause on a drone C, relieved, a few times, nearing the end of the moment, by quietly struck gongs. Without a break the pace is picked up, still at the same tempo but seemingly faster because of the steady sixteenth-note toccata in the solo trumpet, which by now is assuming the leading role in the ensemble. The melodic line now takes up the hocketed vocal sounds and tappings of *Kryl*, combining them with the undulating filigree heard earlier, but the effect in *Night Music* is not humorous: instead it sounds exotic, lending a Near Eastern quality to the musical atmosphere. The vibrant plucked contrabasses have added their own insistent insinuations, and the mood is frankly erotic.

The droned C is reasserted under a lengthy melody plucked by the first contrabass, recalling the poignancy of *Ricercar à 3*. This is taken up by trombone, trumpet, clarinet, and finally flute, high above the staff. The tension drops down into the pulsing timpani; the trumpet calls out one last quiet song; and the piece fades into its drone, finally on F.

Garden seemed to be "about" something: *Night Music* does not. It is all hushed expectancy. Graceful as a dancer, it nonetheless waits, like the dancer's audience, content with its unique mood, half trance, half awareness. The trance rests on a carefully worked-out cycle of rhythmic loops (though in fact they may have been intuitive to Erickson by the time he came to the piece), but the listener needn't know that: it is enough that the piece seems, because it is, *right*, each of its details taking a perfectly ordered place in the whole.

THE IDEA OF ORDER AT KEY WEST FOR SOPRANO AND FIVE INSTRUMENTS (1979)

The Idea of Order at Key West, Erickson's next score, is a setting for soprano and instrumental ensemble of the poem by Wallace Stevens. It is not a song, but a chamber cantata, faithfully setting all seven stanzas. The words are easily understood throughout, for Erickson sets them almost as chant, on now-characteristic drones, the rhythm determined by that of the poem.

> I am trying to set it without destroying the poem. That creates a number of interesting problems: the tempo must be close to that of speech; melismas few; the rhythm of the line must be felt, along with the individualised rhythms of words, punctuation, speech articulation etc. . . . I am having a very good time with it, drawing rhythmical sustenance from Stevens' own reading of the poem, which is a revelation when compared with printed versions. [Undated letter to the author, spring 1979.]

Like other pieces for soloists, *The Idea of Order at Key West* involved collaboration with a willing performer. Erickson provided Carol Plantamura with early sketches, asking advice on dynamic indications and about "naturalness and comprehensibility," and offering her a choice among three different pitch levels in the case of one florid phrase. Presumably he listened to performances of these sketches before making his final decisions.

Jonathan Saville noted a model for *The Idea of Order at Key West*:

> Monteverdi's *Il Combattimento di Tancredi e Clorinda*. And as in that work, the declamation in Erickson's *Idea of Order* blooms, at specific

dramatic moments, into a lyrical cantilena all the more thrilling in that it arises out of such a restrained background.[2]

These moments are the introduction, nearly two minutes long, sung wordlessly to slow melodies similar to those of *Night Music*, two intermezzos surrounding the center section, the longer about a third into the piece, the shorter introducing the conclusion Stevens reaches in his last two stanzas; and a half-minute wordless coda rounding off the score. Certain key descriptive words interrupt the chant with sudden darting gestures: "fluttering," "artificer." And key phrases and sentences are set to expansive melodic contours, rising to greater eloquence, or subsiding into thoughtfulness.

In what might be a tribute, the opening section is sung against overlapping notes whose rhythm recalls the changing chord of Schoenberg's "Summer Morning by a Lake (Colors)": but Erickson reduces Schoenberg's poignant chord to a single noncommittal D. There are very occasional gestures toward pictorial phrases in the instruments: the cello quickly crossing its four strings at the words "dark voice of the sea / That rose"; suddenly louder notes in the winds at "bronze shadows heaped / On high."

Erickson's muse had visited the sea before, of course, notably in *Pacific Sirens* and *Oceans*. But those pieces were about the environment and our relationship to it. Stevens's poem is bigger even than that, and more abstract: it is about the mind that embraces such concepts—tellingly, for a composer, the mind that embraces such concepts through sound.

It is probably foolish to attempt this sort of summary of the subject of *The Idea of Order at Key West*, certainly to speculate on precisely what it may have meant to the composer. Erickson warns, in a program note, "This great poem (it makes me tingle!)... says so much more than anything that can be said about it...."

That noted, the subject of the poem is what Erickson's musical thought had been tending toward for many years, in his composition, his research, his teaching, and his writing. It is "the idea of order," which lifts the singer "beyond the genius of the sea,... More even than her voice, and ours," an idea, apparently built into our human patternmaking mind, that enables us (or at least leads us to attempt) to impose structure on the experiences of time and space in the world around us, "And of ourselves and of our origins."

The Idea of Order at Key West is stark, though the outbursts of cantilena serving as introduction, intermezzi, and close are florid. Much of the time the singer is paralleled by a single instrument, and the accompanying quintet, lacking deep bass and percussion, never intrudes on either the soprano or the poem. Again, the melodic contours favor supple cantillation, including micro-tonal inflections; again, the texture is built of hocketed drones. The free rhythms are determined by the prosody of the poem itself—those of the phrases, of the lines within stanzas, and of the long Latinate lines across the stanzas.

The lines follow upon themselves unceasingly, like the waves of the sea. The listener's perception of their relationships changes as they pile up new nuances. *The Idea of Order at Key West* is about the intelligence that is within natural accretions: of notes, of waves, of phrases—whether their organic context is that of the sea, the song, the singer, or ourselves. This "Idea" was intuitively present in *Pacific Sirens*, metaphorically the subject of *Garden*, and enigmatically anticipated in the hushed *Night Music*. By accepting the challenge of setting the poem itself in this scenic cantata, curiously breathless yet stable and poised, Erickson finally revealed—or perhaps first consciously understood—the content that had been emerging within his evolving compositional style.

EAST OF THE BEACH FOR ORCHESTRA (1980)

Erickson next moved away from the sea, inland, in a piece for Tom Nee's New Hampshire Festival orchestra. *East of the Beach* is pictorial music, once you know the setting. We have seen that he was surprised by a New Englander's response to the title: in New Hampshire, only the sea lies east of the beach. Where Erickson's house stood, east of the Encinitas beach, one's view took in ocean to the west, rolling foothills to the east; beyond the ridge, one was always aware of the high desert.

East of the Beach is a lighthearted pastorale, combining the energy and occasional humor of *Kryl*, the drones and melodic invention of *Garden*, and the two-part drone-and-dance of *Night Music* with the geographical contem-plation (but not the philosophical meditation) of *The Idea of Order at Key West*. A hearing of *East of the Beach* can almost be thought of as an aerial trip across a slice of southern California, beginning with the warm droning of the ocean, passing over the grainier, more active beach communities, crossing the complex freeway-dominated multiple relationships of the inland strip-cities, ultimately rising to clear the ridge and contemplate the broad expanse beyond.

The opening drone is on E this time, and remains virtually the only feature of the music for the first four minutes—though so richly varied in color and texture that one's attention never wanders. (It is fascinating to note that the pitch E has been associated in the minds of many composers with depth, even specifically with the sea. Rimsky-Korsakov, for example, chose it as the key for *Sheherazade*, associating the sound of E with the deep blue of the Mediterranean.) The textural elements come from attack sounds, especially in the flute, oboe, and trumpet, and from occasional use of drumrolls, on timpani or unpitched midrange drums. At the third minute a gong rings quietly underneath the drone, now in the brass, briefly adding what seems to be a dissonant pitch. But it is only at the end of the third minute that the steady E gives way to other pitches, first generating a cluster of them, then developing into lyrical minor-key phrases in the dark middle range of the cellos. (These tunes are similar to those occasionally interrupting the meditative chant of *The Idea of Order at Key West*.)

The melodic line climbs higher in the cellos, and first the trumpet, then the flute "shingle" notes out of the line, first holding them, then projecting them into melodies of their own in a duet. This is interrupted by a sharp attack in brass and strings, introducing a more complex texture from which is extruded a new, more insistent drone. Clusters of jagged tunes arise in the strings, ultimately ending in a particularly acrid dissonant cluster in strings and brass. The trumpet drone that evolves from this breaks into octaves, and then, not quite eight minutes after the opening, the second section begins.

This is in Erickson's dancing, "perpetual-motion" hocketing style, a steady jog-trot of sixteenth notes alternating in different (but usually related) instruments, pitches often repeated, but occasionally jumping suddenly off the track. The texture is light and bouncy, and stabilized by long-held notes in the strings, underpinning the dance. These droning notes occasionally jump up or down by octaves, and this turns into a new kind of melody, slower than the dance, but giving it the rhythmic background it needs to flavor its offbeat responses.

Quiet drumbeats are heard at the nine-minute mark, and again forty-five seconds later, as if we were passing over landmarks of some kind. Then the high violins sound a few sliding *glissandi*, just as the contrabasses had in *Night Music*, and low timpani interrupt the hocketing dance, aided by growling low trombone, piano, and bassoon. The perpetual motion quickly returns, now in a lower middle range of the orchestra, and the clarinet picks up the slower string melody, only to hand it on to the brass. By now, twelve minutes into the score, the hocketing has settled on the high bassoon and clarinet, and sounds suddenly Stravinsky-like; a minute later, the slow string melody, expansive in its octaves, recalls Copland. But the references are not quotes or even allusions: they are the listener's sudden awareness of Erickson's completely new, completely individual use of properties hitherto associated primarily with other composers.

In the meantime the texture has thinned, the activity is sparser, and the mood is even lighter. This began with the more delicate sounds of plucked high violins, very short but unaccented notes on the flute, and quiet ticks on wood-blocks, answered by high muted timpani and unpitched wood-drums. The open spaces of the violin's melody settle, almost suddenly, into overlapping unison statements of a single pitch, growing louder, and the piece ends, decisively, almost abruptly, on the E with which it had begun.

East of the Beach sounds seamless, but this effect cost Erickson more pains than usual:

> I had ideas in mind—cloudy ones—for a first section, or movement, a second section or movement, but I was a little worried about how the last section or movement would work out, so I decided to write it first. Then, when I came to complete the second section and join it to section three, I had trouble! I had forgotten how I had planned to make that delicate and intimate relationship, and now I wondered (sweated too) if I could manage it. I did, and to my full satisfaction, but I decided to never work that way again if I could help it. [Letter to the author, Sept. 18, 1980.]

Only fourteen minutes long, *East of the Beach*, while complete in itself, provokes thought about orchestral programming. It is an orchestral scherzo, recalling Mendelssohn and Berlioz, and its geographical program brings Borodin's *In the Steppes of Central Asia* once more to mind. It would be fascinating to hear *East of the Beach* in such company: perhaps the older pieces would be stripped of their overfamiliarity, at the same time lending some of their accessibility to the newer music.

Another, more problematic consideration arises: could pieces like *East of the Beach, Garden,* and *Night Music* be combined on a single program? Do they amount to individual movements in a larger Symphony, perhaps contemplated but for whatever reason never actually undertaken by the composer? Remembering Erickson's study of Mahler makes it fascinating to contemplate these "character pieces" as analogous to the twin "Nightmusics" in the Austrian's Seventh Symphony. Had the American orchestral climate been more promising for contemporary composers in the 1970s, Erickson might well have considered such a large-scale context for his musings on texture, sound-color, the growth of melody from background drone, and the combination of melodies into complex tissues. He had developed a masterly ability to hold attention over spans of fifteen, even eighteen minutes. It is a great pity—and a loss for the orchestral repertoire—that the opportunity to extend this architecture into its next logical development never arose. Erickson, ever a practical man, was not about to repeat the lesson learned in *Sirens and Other Flyers III*: he wrote for the forces at hand. "Writing for orchestra these days is writing for one of those black holes in the universe—play once, then oblivion." We are lucky Thomas Nee continued to request scores for his festival and community orchestras.

1. *Erickson Celebration,* p. 26.

2. *Reader,* San Diego, June 4, 1981; quoted at the head of the published score (Baltimore: Sonic Art Editions, 1984).

Introspection: Voice and Violin

Postcards (1980) for mezzo-soprano and lute; *The Pleiades* (1981) for solo violin; *Three Songs for the Five Centuries Ensemble* (1981–82)

In 1980, spurred by a request from the soprano Carol Plantamura, who specialized in early music as well as that of the twentieth century, Erickson turned to songwriting for the first time since 1945. He had written for voice, of course, notably in *The Idea of Order at Key West*, which Plantamura had performed splendidly for him. But, as he confessed in the note heading the score of *Postcards*, he had never been comfortable with song texts, feeling that his music got in the way of the music in the poems. For *Postcards* he wrote his own texts. "They may not be very nourishing as poetry," he noted, "but they fit the music."

Plantamura had requested songs with lute accompaniment, and Erickson's texts are an appropriate (if characteristically unexpected) choice for the medium. The lute is a quiet instrument and best accompanies songs of a lyrical, intimate, contemplative, perhaps amorous nature. Erickson's texts represent the musings of a woman on vacation in Europe, writing down her disconnected thoughts in a series of six postcards from London, Stockholm, Paris, Venice, and Capri. It's important to note that the texts do not represent the postcard messages themselves: Erickson writes an interior monologue expressing the woman's state of mind and her intended messages. A distant impetus was probably his reading of James Joyce's *Ulysses*, many years previously. (That book's second chapter, describing Stephen Dedalus's meditation on the strand on Dublin Bay, may have influenced such works as *Pacific Sirens*.)

The anachronism of writing twentieth-century music for the Renaissance lute may have unconsciously influenced the disconnected logic, vocabulary, and prose style of these texts, which combine the simultaneity of cubist expression and Joycean stream-of-consciousness with the vernacular slang and prosaic imagery of Erickson's own surroundings—San Diego in the seventies and eighties. Characteristic lute-technique is preserved: the arpeggiated chords sounded quickly across open strings, the fleet toccatalike running-note passages on adjacent pitches. These touches are found in the vocal line as well, which alternates between repeated-pitch declamation and florid scalewise passages. And pictorialism, so dear to medieval and Renaissance song composers, crops up in birdcalls, bell sounds, and echo-passages.

The melodies themselves, apart from scales and chants, are in the minor-key voice first noted in *Garden* and *Night Music*. This again brings the music of the Near East to mind, and we recall the lute's origins in the *oud*—even the word is ultimately the same—introduced to Spain by the Moors and further popularized by returning Crusaders. Medieval troubadour song is close to its Arabic source, and *Postcards* reminds us that Western European art music, even in the twentieth century, is merely another branch of world music.

Each song is about two minutes long, the first a little longer, the slow fourth song nearly three minutes. The fourth, portraying a travel-weary woman feeling the aftereffects of bad shellfish, is an unaccompanied lament taking the singer down nearly an octave below middle C. The two last songs are surprisingly tonal, comfortably fitting the conventionally tuned lute, and appropriately nostalgic for Venice and Capri, visited by the Ericksons fourteen years earlier.

THE PLEIADES FOR UNACCOMPANIED VIOLIN (1981)

Though three years had elapsed since *Kryl* and *Quoq*, and in that time Erickson had written the introspective masterpieces *Night Music*, *The Idea of Order at Key West*, and *East of the Beach*, he next returned to solo instrumental writing with a piece for unaccompanied violin. Like *Kryl*, *Quoq*, and *Postcards*, *The Pleiades* was composed for a colleague at UC San Diego: the violinist János Négyesy.

The contemplation of nature is apparently again at work in this music, though the composer's comment on the title, printed at the head of the published score, is remarkably unenlightening:

> The title refers to the well known constellation of stars—a formation carrying in its orbit a multitude of stories, associations and myths.

Erickson is more forthcoming concerning the musical source of the remark-
able violin technique he demands:

> Ever since I was ten years old and first heard the remarkable passages
> in Bazzini's Dance of the Goblins, I have been fascinated by mixed left
> and right hand pizzicato, and certain passages in *The Pleiades* are rich
> in such sounds, often in close proximity to bowed sounds, of which a
> wide variety is also used.

The music falls into three sections. A slow-pulsed, graceful opening, six minutes or so long, introduces the rocking minor third A–C—the notes of "I'm
coming" in the old song "Old Black Joe"—in various octaves, set off from time
to time by microtonal scales. The mood is generally quiet, even during the
frequent quick reiterations of single pitches. Toward the end a very high tune,
sliding among the five notes of its pentatonic scale, adds an exotic, quasi-
Oriental color.

The two- or three-minute center section requires a specially tuned violin
that has been prepared in advance: the lowest string tuned up a step to A, and
the highest tuned down a full five steps to the same pitch as the adjacent
second string. This center section is louder. It begins with the left-hand
pizzicato Erickson recalled from the goblin dance, moves through fast fiddle-
style passagework, and closes on an extended pizzicato phrase.

The final movement returns to the original instrument. It offers considerable rhythmic contrast with the earlier sections: sections of fast, irregularly
accented lyrical lines alternate with trills and quickly reiterated notes (especially on "open," unfingered strings, facilitating left-hand pizzicato on the
remaining strings).

Erickson allows the piece to be performed in a relatively normal concert
presentation, but suggests a theatrical production recalling that of *General
Speech*, with a "pretty girl" assistant to the violinist,

> dressed as a magician's helper, in a rather skimpy sequinned
> costume.... She stands motionless in her own (whole body) spotlight,
> eventually moving very very slowly to make the violin exchanges.
>   The soloist should be behind a lectern that hides the lower part of
> the performer's body. A spotlight should light up the head, shoulders
> and arms—not much else.

In a "variation," the composer suggests the assistant face the back of the stage during the second movement, and that her motions be "slow, languorous, like a sleepwalker." Unlike *General Speech*, *The Pleiades* has neither verbal content nor program. One can only wonder if the assistant—who is actually directed to play a few notes, as if tuning the instruments—may somehow stand for the composer himself as a child, attending the great visiting virtuoso (or the trick-fiddler railroad conductor) capable of playing the "Dance of the Goblins." The "pretty girl" was a stock assistant figure in vaudeville magic acts; *The Pleiades* might better be staged, for our time, with a child in the role.

THREE SONGS FOR THE FIVE CENTURIES ENSEMBLE FOR SOPRANO, COUNTERTENOR, VIOLA DA GAMBA, HARPSICHORD, AND ALUMINUM RODS (1981–1982)

The next year, in 1981, Erickson returned to Carol Plantamura's voice for a cycle of three songs, this time composed for the Five Centuries Ensemble: soprano, countertenor, viola da gamba, and harpsichord. The singers are asked to play in addition Erickson's beloved aluminum rods, rubbed with a rosined glove to produce unearthly whistle-like tones.

The texts were assembled from a number of sources, including Matthias Claudius and Gabriele D'Annunzio. The cycle returns to nature for its subject, and the mood is even more intimate than that of *Postcards*, in spite of the larger ensemble: that cycle was objective in its dramatic portrayal, but *Three Songs for the Five Centuries Ensemble* has an interior, contemplative quality closer to the *Ricercar à 3*. The three titles, "Birds at Dusk," "Night Sky," and "Before Dawn," confirm the nocturnal mood, curiously darker than the instrumentation might suggest; and the time-cycle they represent lends coherence and long-line structure to the set.

"Birds at Dusk" begins low in the viola, its notes curving upward. After half a minute the voices enter with parallel melodies sung to birdsong syllables. The eerie high whistling of an aluminum rod marks the end of the first minute: soon afterward, the music takes on the stalwart open quality of medieval song. The soprano sings a sextolet in French, addressed to a flock of singing birds ("*A vous troupe légère*"), while the countertenor responds in German:

"*Höres klagt die Flöte wieder, und die kühlen Brunneren rauschen....*" The sustained quality of the vocal line is interrupted occasionally: a few low notes on the viola; a sudden harpsichord cluster in an upper register. Half a minute before the end the call of a cuckoo is heard, developing into a lively hocket between soprano and countertenor, again on birdsong syllables, to close the song.

"Night Sky" begins, oddly, with high notes on the rods and viola, but the voices soon enter, with low bowed viola, and quickly build the intense nocturne to a climax of dissonant stroked rods and high soprano. This subsides rather quickly to a long closing passage, ultimately sliding downward in a glissando to a final drone. The text, in French, German, English, and Italian, addresses the absent Moon and invokes the "steadfast lover, Venus" in her "enormous room of sky."

"Before Dawn" opens with a twenty-second introduction of high short plucked notes played on the viola. The soprano enters on a monotone, followed in twelve or fifteen seconds by the countertenor, and the two sing in duet for half a minute after which the introduction is restated. A high metal rod glistens, perhaps suggesting the coming daybreak, and the countertenor recites a French *aubade* below the soprano voice. Recitation alternates with duet singing, and the rods grow in intensity and presence to herald the sunrise.

Retrospection: Late Orchestra Pieces;
Looking to the Mountains

Auroras (1982; rev. 1985); *Taffytime* (1983); *Mountain* (1983) for soprano, chorus, and orchestra; *Sierra* (1984) for baritone and instrumental ensemble

The birds that inspired "Birds at Dusk" produced a big orchestra piece as well: *Auroras*, begun in 1980, completed early in 1982, and slightly revised in 1985. Here we have a hint of what Erickson might have written had he been commissioned to write a Mahler-length symphony. Over twenty minutes long, it is scored for a large orchestra: woodwinds and brass in threes (except the four horns) with an extra playing baritone horn; four percussionists (three of whom play a total of eight timpani as well as other instruments); two sets of stroked metal rods; harp, piano, and celesta; and string sections capable of being subdivided.

Auroras had a long gestation. It grew out of *East of the Beach*:

> The orch piece I wrote for Nee is a testing ground—two specific tests—for some stuff I want to expand in a bigger orch piece that I'm already involved in. All summer I have been doing the getting ready and the study etc., and this school year I'll write it during winter and spring sabbatical. As a matter of fact I might even start before then, because I seem to be very eager to get at it. [Letter to the author, Sept. 18, 1980.]

By June 1981 he had composed about five minutes of the piece, "but I am constantly wondering if it is 'too difficult.' I have composed for semiprofessional groups for far too long, and moving out is not so easy."[1] Ultimately the fears proved unfounded: *Auroras* is effectively written for orchestra, and eminently performable.

Much of the time the music is quiet, with only a few instruments sounding at a time, in chamber-music textures. Yet *Auroras* is big in more than length and numbers, for it expresses, for Erickson, a big awareness:

> I think of my music as simple; easy for listeners though not so easy for the performers. *Auroras* is expressive music—music of feeling. For me

its meanings are non-verbal and non-visual—musical. Nevertheless they
are as precise, definite and rich in detail as visual or verbal meanings,
and for me deeper too, close in ultimate things. [Program note heading
the published score.]

Auroras begins on a drone on D, smoothly alternating among loud brass, quiet
clarinets, and strings, with the trumpets soon joining on A, then E. A filigree
solo on trumpet, echoing *Kryl*, is sounded against a rising chantlike melody in
the trombone, echoing *Garden*. The trumpet filigree is passed to clarinet, then
oboe, and the sweet *Garden*-like melody recurs in the violins, playing in
octaves.

Suddenly, about four and a half minutes in, a new variation of the familiar
microtonal *Kryl* melody is heard, quietly in muted violas and cellos; the
running passage recalls the brook-theme rippling through the finale of
Mahler's Fourth Symphony. Half a minute later this erupts into a rising scale
of quarter tones, twenty-four notes to the octave, with hocketed rests
contributing grain to the texture. A short climax, perhaps ten seconds long,
follows, and the music subsides again to the murmuring Mahler-like tune,
leading to a piccolo solo, birdcall-like, over held notes in clarinets and flutes
and accompanied by whistling rods.

This marks the beginning of the second quarter of *Auroras*. In a minute or
so the apparent tempo has slowed: flutes, high harp and celesta, and rods play
a hushed, glinting nocturne, and the music pauses for nearly a minute on held
Ds and As.

Then, a third of the way into the piece, *Auroras* erupts into a minute of
quick, noisy, low timpani beats, animating growled low trombone drones. The
pulsing continues more quietly in plucked cellos and basses—a distant recollection of *Ricercar à 3*, perhaps—and then, after loud interruptions by the
brass, the pace broadens in a series of chords successively dropped down
through trumpets, oboes, flutes, clarinets, horns, and trombones.

This initiates a three-minute section of solo melodies, all resembling
transcribed nightingale songs, played in turn by horn, clarinet, flute, baritone
horn, contrabass, and cello. The section centers on a striking duet of flute and
baritone horn that again strongly suggests Mahler—the Mahler of suddenly
exposed lyricism in the midst of tumult. (Mahler used a tenor horn to great

effect in his Seventh Symphony, and the baritone horn is frequently assigned that part. But Erickson's choice of the instrument may just as well have been a recollection of the bands he had heard in his youth.)

A short, loud outbreak in strings, trumpets, and high woodwinds interrupts this moment, followed by another birdcall, this time in high piccolo, xylophone, celesta, and harp, then clarinet. The trumpet responds once, briskly, its fanfare irrepressibly calling Wagner's *Siegfried* to mind, to be answered briefly in another hushed three-minute section, again in turn, by solo violins, viola, clarinet, cello, and oboe, ending with another stirring trumpet call and a forceful descending scalewise solo in the contrabassoon.

The final section of *Auroras*, six or seven minutes long, begins with prolonged episodes of held chords, passed among the orchestral sections in the manner of *White Lady*, interrupted by hocketed timpani and trombones. The rarefied high glinting atmosphere of flutes, harp, celesta, and violins returns, dissolving in a very quiet, pulsing, repeated pizzicato hocket dropping by octaves through the strings, then rising more noisily, followed quickly by timpani and trombones. The music closes with two minutes or so of held three-note chords, again drifting among orchestral sections, punctuated a few times by louder attacks in percussion or brass, ending on a high A held in the violins and marked, quietly, with seven downbeats in the harp.

Auroras is exceptional in its structural form. Erickson has left behind any question of conventional forms: the piece simply evolves. The few musical ideas—birdcalls, pulses, held three-note chords, scales, fanfares; successions of timbre; quiet sections animated by louder attack-bursts—these do suggest the recurring sections of such classical forms as rondo. And there are some arbitrary architectural relationships: certain themes, first heard as scalewise filigree gradually climbing through wider intervals, return in reverse order, their intervals narrowing, ultimately to end in scales. But the real structural form of *Auroras* is simply that of an evolving excursion.

Almost reluctantly, in his introduction to the published score, Erickson has revealed the source of *Auroras*, what Henry James would have called its *donnée*, the inspiration providing its "subject":

> In April 1980, I was ill enough so that my mind turned too often to-
> ward matters of life and death. Whatever "aboutness" there is in *Auroras*

has to do with these. As it happened, just at the period when I was full to the brim with these preoccupations, I was invited to California State College in Turlock to lecture. At the Divine Gardens Motel I awakened at about 4:30 am to the sound of birds, lots of them, varied voices, including some that were new to me.... There were enough birds, hundreds, to produce textures of orchestral size and density, all singing against the sort of silent background that, in modern times, is becoming very rare. I hadn't heard birds against such silent backgrounds since I was a boy, and perhaps that was the trigger that brought bird orchestra, things divine, living and dying, closer together, to make a ball of feeling in my belly that was the whole non-verbal source of the musical action of *Auroras....*

Erickson is quick to disavow a literal program:

I have told about a few incidents that are important in my life; but each listener has his own life and death, and his own divine gardens to bring to his understanding of *Auroras.*

But it is clear that Erickson confirms, with this revelation, that since *Summer Music* his work has been increasingly introspective, concerned with ultimate things. There will be diversions, notably in *Pleiades* and *Dunbar's Delight*, but most of the music of his last twenty works is valedictory, autumnal.

TAFFYTIME FOR ORCHESTRA (1983)

Taffytime, the next orchestral score, is the sunlit counterpart to *Auroras*, as *Garden* was to *Night Music*. The instrumental colors are brighter, the textures drier. The form, too, seems less concise, more exploratory.

The music begins in drone again, with quicker inflections than in *Auroras* as the note is handed more often among the orchestral instruments. A steady pulse arises after only a minute, and midrange unpitched percussion instruments are soon heard, as the horn and clarinet stretch the drone to the aural horizon. After three minutes or so a rough low cluster is heard in the contrabasses, soon growing into a complex sonority of pitches—the first in Erickson's music since *White Lady*. The brass single out individual pitches for quick repetitions, and the dry wood-blocks take the texture up to the highest pitches of the violins and stroked rods. The first quarter of *Taffytime* ends with the clarinet weaving filigree melodies out of the horn-sustained pitches, ultimately to play in duet with flute.

Then, about six minutes in, *Taffytime* falls silent. An ineffable kind of rustling is all there is, faintly recalling the much-filtered babbling-brook sound of *Summer Music*. Dry percussion occasionally overlies this: maracas, sandpaper-blocks, hollow wood blocks. The percussion lines extend into unpitched rhythmic counterparts of the complex filigree-tunes of *Auroras*, recalling Erickson's discussion, in *Sound Structure in Music*, of "grain." When the percussion section subsides, the string sections creep in, under the sustained high rods; then the clarinet and oboe, to end this episode.

Then, about ten minutes after it opens, *Taffytime* threatens to fall asleep. Ten seconds of silence are followed by quiet birdcalls in solo flute, then oboe, muted trumpet, and flute again. A noisy timpani break ends this, introducing another coarse drone in the contrabasses, with tunes evolving out of it in bass clarinet, then cello. The melodies climb through horns, tuba, trumpet, and higher winds, then dissolve into cymbals, xylophone, and gongs, the texture still very sparse. The evolving passage is repeated, this time more tensely, with considerable metal percussion, to end in wind-sounds (players blowing tonelessly through their instruments), consonant melodies in woodwinds and trumpets, and fanfare-like calls suggesting great distances. Another percussion break introduces octave drones surrounding a solo bass clarinet and an oddly disconnected harp solo, again subsiding in a high drone shifting from trumpets to oboes, ending in nervous Morse code–style repetitions in the oboe.

At about the seventeenth minute *Taffytime* falls silent yet again for ten seconds, then begins what will prove to be its closing section. The high rods take up the drone to accompany a pentatonic "Chinese" solo in the piccolo. Violins take this up, passing it down to violas and cellos, interweaving simultaneous variations of the idea. From nowhere the Mahler river-warbling appears in the strings, to subside after only ten seconds or so. The drone reappears to climb through orchestral sections for another minute, and then the rough contrabass cluster returns for the first time in nearly twenty minutes. It alternates with other material in a steadily more rhythmic manner: brass drone, bass drum roll, brass burblings, silence, very quiet percussion, silence again. There is one loud interruption, then the quiet sparse percussion continues, lapsing into a solo snare drum whose familiar march rhythm grows steadier, then abruptly ends.

Taffytime is an amazing piece: unmistakably "about" something, something personal, like *Auroras*; clearly referring to other music (previous Erickson scores, Mahler); imaginatively and resourcefully exploring the ideas broached theoretically in *Sound Structure in Music*—but ultimately mysterious. Erickson has revealed its source in cricket noises, analogous to the birdsong source of *Auroras*. *Taffytime* does seem to be a vast panorama of daytime life-activity and certainly balances subjective contemplation with objective description. But it remains, while aurally fascinating, expressively enigmatic. No other music is quite like this: it is heard as a garden is inspected, detail by detail, taking us into new kinds of perception areas. It is as if Erickson had found a third alternative to abstraction and descriptiveness, to object-contemplation and subjective introspection. This kind of music has two older relatives: Varèse's sound-structures and Webern's sound-meditations. The bleak but far from cheerless prospects of late Mahler are not far away, either. But Erickson's music is unmistakably American and late-twentieth-century, out of the main-stream of the European concert tradition, willing to sound awkward, almost adolescent, rather than compromise its openness to the wanderings of a homemade muse.

The title derives from Erickson's meditations on the nature of a composer's interior time:

> *The time between pieces, the empty amorphous, floppy chunks of time, the waiting time, needs filling, and in my case it needs to be filled in a way that invites the next piece or pieces of music. The most important thing about composing is this waiting—waiting in the right way, without fidgeting, respecting the unconscious interior chemistry that will one day fizz up as the decision to compose.*

How can one resist metaphorical extensions of this—the implication that *Taffytime* is about life and death, and man and nature, as well as sound and silence? Yet this is in fact merely Erickson's description of the dry spells that had alternated with his creative activity since the early 1950s. One of the most basic problems facing composers is the problem of the next appropriate sound-gesture, either within the piece under construction, or opening (or driving) the piece to follow. Crickets do not face this problem: they simply continue, as far as we know, or fall silent.

Whereas *Auroras* was "about" hearing birds at night, *Taffytime* is "about" imagining sounds in daytime—imagining them, and waiting for the imagination to find the next one. This makes the music simultaneously awkward, in the listening, and natural. Hearing it, studying it, one can't help think that Erickson is coming close to a basic understanding of what it really means to compose—not *how* to compose, or *what*, but *why* composing *happens*.

MOUNTAIN FOR SOPRANO, WOMEN'S CHORUS, AND ORCHESTRA (1983)
SIERRA FOR BARITONE AND INSTRUMENTAL ENSEMBLE (1984)

Erickson composed *Mountain* in the spring of 1983, immediately after *Taffytime*, "and very quickly too. It was as though some things that hadn't gotten into *Taffytime* needed their own place and time."

What those things may be is a greater sense of spatial dimension. If *Taffytime* is about waiting within a span of time, *Mountain* is about the contemplation of distance and aspiration, as Erickson's text reveals:

> High.
> How high.
> High up high.
> Dim weather.
> Grim gloomy
> Move high
> How high
> High up
> Highest high
> Turn
> Turning
> Turn round
> Turning high
> How high
> High highest
> Sky bright
> Bright sun
> Sun high

How high
High up
High highest
High heaven

Scored for solo soprano, a small women's chorus, flute and alto flute, two clarinets and bass clarinet, trumpet, horn, trombone and tuba, vibraphone and high rods, and solo strings (though all string parts may be reinforced), *Mountain* is the first of Erickson's late pieces to consist almost entirely of long notes. Only the solo soprano and (very occasionally) the chorus is given any note shorter than two slow beats. Virtually every note in the orchestra is held for four beats or longer, and this in slow time. The score is in an uninflected four counts to the measure, its twenty-two pages lasting nearly fifteen minutes.

Furthermore, there are only five pitches in the piece: F, C, G, D, and B flat. (Occasionally there are neighboring-tone ornaments in the solo soprano.) The only events, apart from the unfolding line of the text, are staggered entrances of instruments as they overlap one another, and "hairpins"—the swelling and dying away of loudness conventionally marked in the score by horizontal wedges [<>]. There is little "grain."

Yet *Mountain* evades monotony. The listener quickly understands the point of this music, which is not development or contrast but the marking out of space and of natural changes on a cosmological scale. (Erickson says of the slowly shifting tone-colors that "it reminds me of sunrises and sunsets I see almost every day.") After the introspection of *Auroras* and *Taffytime* this perfect objectivity is perhaps inevitable as well as reassuring.

The solo line, probably written with Carol Plantamura in mind, ranges widely, from the F below middle C to the C above the staff. Apart from the range, the only difficulty in performing *Mountain* lies in respecting the pace and taking care with tuning.

A year after *Mountain*, Erickson again prepared his own text for another contemplation of the land in *Sierra*, commissioned by the baritone Thomas Buckner. If *Mountain* was abstract and universal, *Sierra* is concrete and specific, a contemplation of social history, not natural history.

A slow three-minute introduction opens on a lofty note, setting John Muir's apostrophe to "Yosemite, Tuolumne, Tuolumne Meadows, Tuolumne River: Oh those vast, calm, mountain days in whose light / Light! I live."

In the next nine minutes, though, the atmosphere is anything but tranquil. The solo baritone calls out the towns littering his journey "Down, Down" from Yosemite: *Bootjack. Mormon Bar. Mount Bullion. Coulterville. Moccasin.* The Forty-niner nicknames roll out: *Ground Hog's Glory. Hell's Delight. Ladies Canyon. Devil's Basin.*

There are two greetings along the way: "Hello Helen. Hello Mike" to Erickson's old friends the Czajas; "Hello Terry" to his colleague Terry Riley, born and still living in the Mother Lode.

"Oh Californy, that's the land for me, I'm bound for Sacramento with a banjo on my knee," Erickson sings, and a solo violin and trombone contribute to the old-timey atmosphere—deliberately hokey rather than merely nostalgic.

After twelve minutes, though—on the word "Green," and as the journey begins back up the hills toward Lake Tahoe—the noisy jumble of music settles on a drone, and yet another unmistakably Mahler-like section is heard. Solos in the cello and trombone retain the stalwart tone of the piece but bend it to a more lyrical, contemplative mood. Low clarinet and bassoon extend this mood; then a characteristic upward scale passage takes the piece to its restful conclusion:

> Yuba Pass. High,
> Sierraville. Truckee. High,
> Tahoe. Bliss.

and the final lines are once again Muir's:

> I am always glad,
> To touch the living rock, again

Erickson scored *Sierra* with an ensemble similar to SONOR in mind: flute, oboe, clarinet, bassoon; trumpet, horn, trombone; violin, viola, cello, contrabass; harp, piano, and two percussionists. The piece is very different from the rarefied meditativeness of most of his final music. In both his text and much of the music (notably the fake fiddle-music and Stephen Foster allusions) Erickson's old ironic humor returns, recalling the barrelhouse of *The 1945*

Variations. The trip through the Mother Lode is a good-humored scherzo, bumptiously recalling the homespun litanies of railroad names in Harry Partch's *Barstow* and Ernst Krenek's *Santa Fe Timetable.* But the setting of the framing John Muir quotations reveals Erickson's point of view: he has scaled the mountain and is taking a fond look back at another terrain.

1.   Postcard to the author, June 26, 1981.

Back to the Drums

Dunbar's Delight for solo timpani (1985)

The percussive high spirits of *Sierra* continue in *Dunbar's Delight*, a cheerful toccata—with lyrical, mysterious interludes—for solo percussionist. Like all Erickson's mature unaccompanied solo music, the piece was inspired by the virtuosity and experiment of a colleague, in this case also a student: Daniel Dunbar. Two years of investigation into new techniques for the timpani had led Dunbar to experiment with covering the kettledrums, or "muting" them, in order to dampen their resonance, allowing more rapidly repeated notes to be heard. He had also developed multiple-stick technique (timpani are conventionally played with only two sticks, one in each hand).

In 1984, no doubt delighted with Dunbar's discoveries, Erickson offered to make a piece of them. The result is an extended movement, nearly fifteen minutes long, contrasting the rhythmic reiterations of a fairly small number of pitches with quiet phrases produced by bowing a pair of cymbals. Four timpani are required, and the cymbals are suspended above (and partly overlapping) the smallest two. The bowed cymbals hang only a quarter-inch over the drumheads, so they resonate sympathetically when the higher drums are struck. More importantly, they respond to changes in the tension of the drumheads, controlled by a foot-pedal at the base of each drum. The timpani are struck by hard, soft, and medium timpani sticks, by snare-drum sticks, and by the fingers and hands.

Dunbar's Delight opens with a steady, quiet eighth-note pacing on low E, the octave above added toward the end of the first phrase. The bowed cymbals intervene quietly, and the pacing continues on the upper octave. After a second, similar phrase, the pulse picks up and the "grain" becomes more active, with sixteenth-note hocketing among the four drums and the struck cymbals. This tempo is maintained, articulated every page or so by slower passages on the cymbals, until a minute-long passage for bowed cymbals interrupts the toccata, their tone quality eerily altered by slackening or tautening drumheads below them.

The final section of *Dunbar's Delight* is a steady toccata on the four drums, some of them covered. (Erickson cannily provides just enough time for the percussionist to manipulate these mutes.) The music rarely rises to a fortissimo, though it does end very loud. Interest is maintained through gradual changes in loudness, thoughtfully varied "loops" marked by subtle changes of patterns, and carefully chosen phrase-lengths.

Like *The Pleiades* and perhaps *Sierra*, *Dunbar's Delight* is a diversion among Erickson's deep late pieces—a *divertissement* offered to an enterprising soloist as a reward for having extended a composer's vocabulary. Apart from extending the performer's repertoire, such relatively minor pieces also round off the edges of a composer's work, chasing ideas down into corners that would have been distracting and irrelevant (if not merely unnoticed) had they been investigated in more complex works. They also serve as catalysts, for in composing them one meets ideas that may affect more ambitious scores to come. In any case, *Dunbar's Delight* needs no apology: it is an engaging reminder of Erickson at his most affable, himself delighted to be writing for an immediate occasion.

Strings Again, Two Last Songs, and the Final Chamber Scores

Solstice (1984–85) for string quartet; *Quintet* (1985); *Corfu* (1985–86) for string quartet; *Corona* (1986) for string orchestra; Two Songs: "Days and Nights;" "Seasonal" (1986); Trio (1986); *Recent Impressions* (1987) for piano and chamber orchestra; *Fives* (1988) for chamber ensemble; *Music for Trumpet, Strings, and Timpani* (1990)

If Mahler is still the inevitable witness to a contemporary composer's approach to symphonic writing, Bartók and Shostakovich are not far away when the string quartet is undertaken. And, not much farther off after all these years, Beethoven.

Late in 1984 Erickson returned to that medium for the first time in almost thirty years. As might be expected, some elements of the violin writing in *Summer Music, Garden,* and *The Pleiades* entered this new piece, along with preoccupations from other recent work: hockets, drones, long meditations on the note C. The introspection of *Auroras* and *Night Music* is present, relieved by the optimism of *Mountain.* But *Solstice,* as the new work was titled, has an element of urgency unprecedented in Erickson's music.

Solstice is another single-movement score, divided into three contrasting sections but innocent of conventional form. As the composer says in a prefatory note to the published score, "Whatever its form may be felt to be, it is not something from history, but something *formed.*" [Emphasis added.] In the same note Erickson reveals the importance he had always attached to the winter solstice, "when the days are trying to decide whether to get shorter or longer"; this significance was undoubtedly the more poignant as his health was steadily worsening. "... *Solstice* is not program music. There is no scenario, no plot, no image, only ears and sensibility," he continues, but one wonders how frank the comment is. As Erickson was of course intimately aware, the string quartet has functioned as the musical medium *par excellence* for introspective self-expression since Beethoven's A Minor Quartet, op. 132. Smetana,

Janáček, and Shostakovich continued the tradition up to our own time, and their precedents occasionally come to mind during a performance of *Solstice*.

The opening section is rhapsodic, beginning in trilled octave Cs, continuing with the now-familiar filigree melodies alternating with long-held notes (C and G), developing into broad tunes, often played in octaves, that are composed of only five or six pitches, sweetly consonant, often very high in the violins. The music ultimately falls through the quartet to the cello's lowest note, then quickly rises to a steady patter of repeated alternating Cs and Bs, repeated over sixty times, slowing down, to close the section.

A slower central movement follows without a break: a succession of rather poignant meditations—laments, when played *espressivo*—sounded over long-held drones on C. These are stated first by the viola, but after a minute or two the first violin adds a varied statement to the texture, higher. In a bridging passage a barely audible lament in octaves alternates between higher and lower instruments, still under the droned C; then the viola elegy returns, the section ending mysteriously in slow glides up through octave Cs.

The opening section closed on loud repetitions: now, thirteen minutes into the score, the center section pauses on several seconds of silence. The music then resumes with the expected quicker tempo, first in hocketed plucked sixteenth notes, then settling into a more lyrical, still strongly accented tune that quickly lights on a steadily repeated E.

The pace slows, and extraordinarily harsh discords are heard, all the harsher for having been absent from Erickson's music for twenty years. They are not resolved, but yield to a unison C, held almost a minute, barely audible, and marked "Ghostly" in the score. The dancing motion returns, this time leading to Cs and Es steadily repeated in the violins and viola, two instruments at a time, the other instruments often whirling around them. Previously heard motives are recalled: the repeated C–B figure, and the trills that began *Solstice* twenty-four minutes earlier. The first violin plays one last chromatic melody, ultimately to fall from E to C, which is held twenty seconds to end the quartet.

Once again, the long-held drones function as sonic horizons, or vanishing points to which the ear relates the pulsing repetitions and the broader melodic phrases. Erickson seems to have found a new way of anchoring the pitches in his music: not to a keynote, as is true of conventional harmony, but to some other kind of sonic certainty—devoid of tonal implication, therefore not reliant on formal theory with which the late-twentieth-century listener can no longer be expected to be familiar. This is more apparent in *Solstice* than it was in *Auroras*, for the dramatic expressivity of the quartet, proceeding by contrast of dissonances as well as tempi, demands such recognizable points of rest.

CORFU FOR STRING QUARTET (1986)

Solstice had been commissioned for the Sequoia String Quartet by Betty Freeman. It was premiered in March 1985, and she rewarded its success immediately with another commission, this time for the Kronos Quartet. Erickson set to work in February 1986, after completing the quintet we will consider next, and after revising *Auroras* for a performance by the Los Angeles Philharmonic.

The short preface to the score is laconic but perfectly accurate:

> *Corfu* was composed as a single movement with three divisions. The style is bare and "stripped down," though it is strongly melodic. I have tried to compose a piece that is directly expressive and that goes its own expressive ways.
>
> During the composition of the piece I found myself thinking almost every day of the Greek islands and their ancient civilizations. Hence the title, though I have never been to Corfu.

As had long been his method (except in pieces for soloists), Erickson composed *Corfu* straight through, without worksheets or sketches, dating the pages occasionally as he found time (or inspiration) for the work: 2/9/86, 2/10/86, 3/6, 3/28, 4/14, 4/25. The piece was finished June 19.

It is similar to *Solstice*, in terms of both structure and content, but it is much less urgent and inner-directed. The lyric solos, again played against drones, sound more supple than those of *Solstice*, and the repeated-note articulating points are less driving, more directed to their eventual graceful release. Erickson has again provided a supplementary pair of compositions, and *Corfu* is the gentler, sunnier companion, closer to the calm contemplation of *Mountain* than is the darker *Solstice*.

The opening section alternates extended solo melodies, beginning with wide skips and narrowing to adjacent notes, with held notes (C, G, F). Toward the end the first violin rises to its highest register, often playing octave double-stops, and the section closes, after nearly six minutes, with a calm but mysterious passage in high pure harmonics. The quicker center section is louder, opening with repeated sixteenth notes (E, B), but soon calms down, returning to the harmonics, squeaking now in the faster tempo. After another short flurry of repeated sixteenths the first violin states a fleet-footed melody curving around C, then E, to a background of high drone Es, and this idea is repeated with the melody in the viola, then the cello. The entire section is repeated, ending in a "Ghostly" (it was a favored description of the composer's) pause under the first violin, and ultimately the center section ends with protracted sixteenth-note repetitions on B.

These lead directly to the closing section of *Corfu*, six minutes of slower, more supple melody, first an extended one for cello, then, after a minute of ensemble interplay, a phrase handed from cello to viola and then first violin. A minute before the end a discord momentarily and unexpectedly darkens the sky, but the shadow passes almost immediately as the five-note melody returns, shared hocket-style but calmly by all four instruments, to close the piece quietly on the note F.

QUINTET FOR FLUTE, CLARINET (DOUBLING BASS CLARINET), TRUMPET, VIOLA, AND CELLO (1985)

Before undertaking *Corfu*, and after finishing *Dunbar's Delight*, in March, 1985, Erickson began work on a quintet for mixed instruments, a joint commission through the National Endowment for the Arts for the San Francisco Contemporary Music Players, the New York ensemble Speculum Musicae, and SONOR. Again about sixteen minutes long, the work marks an evolutionary development from the important source that is *Night Music*.

The music opens at a very slow tempo, each beat almost two seconds long, with the trumpet, then flute, then viola extending melodic patterns out from a loud drone E. After over a minute there is a clarinet cadenza, another long minute in duration; and the E is restated, *forte*, by the entire quintet, the flute and cello projecting melodically from it, at the extreme high and low ends of the group range. The viola supplants the flute; another ensemble E interrupts (trilled this time), and a second clarinet cadenza follows, with the close microtonal filigree familiar from *Night Music*, still centered on E, but ultimately leading a minor third away to G.

This opening section is followed, six and a half minutes into the piece, by a supple transition, wind melodies over drones in the strings (G, then E again), to a quicker second section. It begins with hocketed pizzicato notes in viola and cello and continues with duets and trios for changing instrumentation, the melodic lines in quick chromatic thirty-second-note figurations, still over drone E. The strings interrupt this pattern once, with very loud fast passagework leading to a cluster; and then the bass clarinet brings the pitch down to its lowest E to open a more ingratiating dance on E and B, soon supporting brilliant filigree in the flute, then bass clarinet and trumpet. This turns into a trio for the winds, the strings momentarily silent, before a calm close returns to E, now with an A added, in the slow tempo of the opening pages of the Quintet.

A third section follows, again in the quicker dance movement but in angular, quickly shifting meters. It is announced by a trumpet call on E and consists of greater use of contrasting material for the two strings, which are given supple duets and drones, and the three winds, which continue their quickly jointed chromatic melodic phrases. The winds usually play solo but lead ultimately to a flute-clarinet duet, then a trio. A sudden viola solo, forceful in a high register, answered by the trumpet, articulates the movement and leads to a duet in the strings. The winds follow with an insistence on E again, taking up the movement with successive chromatic scalewise passages, the strings reduced to drones (now on B, not E). This ultimately dies away on a slow trill on E, taken up finally by all of the instruments; the trumpet plays a rising scale out of the low range to return E to the highest register of flute and clarinet, and the Quintet ends with two long-held drones separated by a few beats of quick octave alternations swooping down, then back up the register.

For its premiere, Erickson wrote a short program note:

> My quintet presupposes a virtuosity beyond the sound effects and "new sounds" of the fifties and sixties. In the last fifteen or twenty years the manuals and method books have had to be rewritten to reflect technical advances, particularly in wind instrument technique, that are rich in musical possibilities. Each instrument in my quintet employs its full range; each is a soloist and an accompanist; and each plays microtones.
>
> The composition has two main sections, a slow rhapsodic opening, and a faster, rhythmic, longer one in mixed meters. Overall: Slow-moderate-faster.

The score of the Quintet (rather carelessly prepared for publication, with a number of minor errors) carries no program note, and the Quintet is the first piece in Erickson's catalogue to carry a generic title since the *Concerto for Piano and Seven Instruments* of twenty-two years previous. (The *Piece for Bells and Toy Pianos* and the two *Ricercars* may be excepted; their titles carry ironic implications.) In the Quintet, too, Erickson produces a less rhapsodic, more tightly organized structure, though the melodic material continues to sound improvisational and free. It is tempting to read this as a resolution of the personal crises of age, health, and retirement that may have affected the content of the music of the preceding ten years. On the other hand, surprising though it may be, the composer had completely forgotten the piece eight years after its premiere. It is possible—and sad to contemplate!—that it was written and prepared for publication while the composer was under particularly heavy medication.

TRIO FOR CLARINET, HARP, AND CELLO (1986)

In 1978 and 1979 Erickson spent considerable time studying the harp, an instrument he had neglected. He considered including a soloistic part for it in an orchestral piece that ultimately did not materialize (unless it turned out to be *East of the Beach*, which lacks such a part). By 1982 he was thinking of a trio for clarinet, cello, and harp. Finally, in 1986, he completed it—a short, lyrical, rather stately pastorale in three sections.

The first opens on a clarinet drone on middle C, attacked strongly in lower octaves in harp and cello. The clarinet rises one octave, then another, and a full thirty seconds after the beginning the harp enters with another low C, this time answered by tapping sounds on the shoulder of the cello. The clarinet then begins weaving a microtonal web around the middle C, spinning out a melody, soon joined by the cello, that ends in a long-held C. Two minutes into the Trio the harp enters again, first with quiet but sharply attacked Cs, then with a more prominent solo part arriving at a new preoccupation: E. This suggests a fine lyric to the clarinet, answered by cello, always over measured pacing in the harp. An extended clarinet solo begins at the four-minute mark, resolving again in duet with cello, finally closing this seven-minute introductory section on the home C.

The harp begins a quiet, gently rocking central section, and a minute later the cello finds a bolder statement to make—"Bold and Brilliant," the score requests—followed by a calmer duet with clarinet. Then low harp and cello bring back the mood of the opening, complete with quiet but percussive tappings on the bodies of the instruments. Soon, for just a few seconds, the cello recalls its boldness of two minutes earlier; the clarinet responds in kind; and a short, calm ending phrase ("Dolce") rounds out the Trio, which ends in a resonant but very quiet low E in the harp.

CORONA FOR ORCHESTRA (1986)

Erickson next turned to another commission, this time from Betty Freeman's Whitelight Foundation, for an orchestral piece for the Los Angeles Philharmonic. He wrote for a large orchestra this time, the biggest since *Sirens and Other Flyers III*—in fact, a Mahler orchestra, with winds in fours, six horns, but only the standard orchestral percussion: no aluminum rods this time.

Corona is in the now-familiar three sections, increasing in tempo, and linked without pauses. The eight-minute opening section begins with a fast high pulse on F played by xylophone and violins, quickly swooping down, then back up, and answered by the full orchestra (adding C), loud, with whooping gestures from the brass. This forty-five second introduction is followed by a forty-second solo on the timpani (using two players) quickly alternating among at least six drums. The mood then subsides, with the high F on violins and a lower C in the woodwinds covering a sweetly pentatonic duet in the violas and cellos. After two minutes or so, the violins having ascended to a very quiet, very high C, the duet is gracefully dovetailed into a solo for French horn. Trumpets restate the drone F, loud, and the violin sections take up the duet, marked "Sostenuto," later joined by violas and cellos to end the section on a high C.

The quicker, dancelike center section follows, with shifting, angular accents announced by the strings and timpani, taking the drone back to F. Clarinet and bass clarinet play filigrees around C and G over the continuing F drone in brass and strings. A flute solo yields to the subtle transformation of the drone into a cluster, swelling into the full orchestra (without percussion, silent in this central section except for the few opening timpani beats). The melodic lines then move through flute, trumpet, viola, and oboes, ending on a steady trilled F in the violas. The full orchestra takes this up, then the high woodwinds, climbing from F toward C.

The first two sections were each about six minutes long: the final one, faster yet, is not quite four. It begins with fast hocketed pulses on C, climbing to higher octaves and intensifying to "shingled" A and E hanging out of the textures. This is offset by nervous shifting accents in the low strings, harp, and piano. The held notes grow into chords, and hang longer out of the quick texture. The timpani solo returns from the beginning of *Corona*, ending on a rapidly repeated A on the highest drum, reiterated under a quiet held A drone in the full orchestra. The drone grows louder and suddenly breaks off. Barely audible, a mysterious high celesta, accompanied by very high violins, continues the drone, handing it down the octaves to the lower strings. Woodwinds, then brass turn the drone into a pulse, and the beat grows louder and faster in the full orchestra to an abrupt ending.

Here again, title notwithstanding, is a fully "objective," unprogrammatic piece, strong and cheerful. Erickson's driving pulse, as we have noted, began to develop in the early 1960s, at about the same time that Terry Riley composed his revolutionary *In C*. By 1986, of course, this had come to be a cliché of the "minimal" style, a hallmark in orchestral music by John Adams, Philip Glass, and Steve Reich, to name the three best-known younger Americans of the school. (In fact, of course, these three compose very different music: the rapidly reiterated note is the only obvious element they share, and it is no more capable of constituting a "school" than the use of broken chords as accompaniment was capable of overriding the very substantial differences among Mozart, Haydn, and their lesser contemporaries.) The overwhelmingly consonant character of Erickson's melodies—"harmony" is virtually absent, having been replaced by the drones—also has a counterpart in the increasingly tonal, even romantic content of other contemporary orchestral composers whose music was cultivated in the 1980s. What sets Erickson apart from these contemporaries is the individualism of his work, which evolved, as we have seen, through thirty years of study, refinement, experiment, and analysis. Principles of organization that Erickson had learned from his study of twelve-tone music, so long before that they might well have been forgotten, have been completely internalized. His musical form is intuitive; and even melody is no longer sought: it seems to spin its way inevitably out of the drones, on into the pulses. The repetitive cycles of the *Ricercars* and *Loops* well up effortlessly to demarcate the organic sections of music like *Corona*. And the aural horizons of the drones, subtly shifting color as they move among the instruments, counsel a kind of aural patience, not only to the composer as he waits for the next event, but to the listener as well.

TWO SONGS FOR MEZZO-SOPRANO, CLARINET, VIOLA, AND PIANO (1986)

In 1986 Erickson completed two songs to be performed by the New York ensemble Continuum on their European tour. Again, he provided his own texts. They return to the nature-contemplation of *Mountain*, but this time they carry a poignant subtext, concerned as they are with the orderly, inexorable natural cycles of day and night and the seasons. As an indication of his mood, the affecting artlessness of his technique, and his growing skill, the text of the shorter first song is worth citing in full:

> Days and Nights
>
> Dawn. Morning star
> Warm sun rising,
> sliding into blue
> to noon, highest noon.
> Hot zenith of the sun,
> vast sun descending,
> rolling down the sky

slowly, slowly downward,
down to horizon.
Dusk. Darkening night,
deep heaven.
Stars. North star.
Unwobbling pivot,
friend of travelers, counselor
companion of the dark night
be my guide.
Moon. High rider, fair traveler,
where is your home?
Where do you rest
[Do you rest] at the edge of deep night?

"Days and Nights" opens with a slow melodic duet in clarinet and viola. It is a new kind of melody to Erickson, a calm, conjunct, supple melody, like a considerably slowed version of the scalewise filigree that had characterized his music since *Night Music*. After thirty seconds the voice enters, chanting the opening words over the clarinet, now holding a drone, now repeating its web of microtones over slow, wide-spaced notes, marking time low in the piano. A rising trill in the piano illustrates the quick sunrise, then descends. The last three lines of the first stanza are quietly chanted over the measured repetitions of a low chord in the piano.

The supple viola introduces the second stanza, with fixed pitches, repeated in various octaves, illustrating the North Star. At "be my guide" the viola returns companionably, while piano and clarinet share a drone providing the fixed reference point of this aural space, the singer's destination.

The second song, "Seasonal," meditates on each of the seasons in turn, starting with a languorous summer, the high clarinet drone holding the sky above shimmering heat in quickly repeated piano octaves. Here the mezzo-soprano sings wider-ranging intervals than in the first song, arching toward a long wordless phrase ending the stanza.

Autumn begins with a quickly repeated note in the viola. Erickson's ear has noted the appropriateness of the piano tremolo to heat shimmer, the edgier attack of the viola to the description of a brittle leaf about to fall. Erickson depicts the "whispering, crackling, gossiping" leaves in the wind colorfully but unsophisticatedly: the musical treatment recalls the folksy New England pictorialism of Charles Ives's songs, or the wisely naïve, innocent quality of Mahler's *Songs of Youth*, not the lush sophistication of Debussy or even Delius.

Then forward time is stopped by a long-held octave E in the clarinet and viola, steadily and eerily measured by lower octaves again in the piano. This winter is not bleak, but still. Its "blinding white" draws loud, full-throated sound from the ensemble, but the tempo remains glacial for thirty seconds.

Then a steadily accelerating note in the piano announces the spring thaw, and melodic motion returns to describe the "Melting watery spring." The final stanza ends inconclusively, poised on a return to the opening of Summer—a resolution without the negative connotations of finality, appropriate to Erickson's subject (and possibly remembered, if only subconsciously, from the similar resolution at the close of *Finnegans Wake*).

Both Erickson's texts and the musical sound-painting convey something we used to think of as "Oriental." The Ericksons' tour of Japan may have reawakened the nature-contemplation of *Mountain* and these two songs, and this may have been reinforced by his re-examination of Mahler, undertaken at first in preparation for orchestration classes at UC San Diego but continued, probably, through his growing awareness of personal considerations he shared with Mahler: contemplativeness; a love for balancing microscopic sonic detail with big-scale form; above all, awareness of mortality, of the cycles of life, death, and continuity.

RECENT IMPRESSIONS FOR PIANO AND CHAMBER ORCHESTRA (1987)

Continuum made another tour to Europe the following year, 1987, and Betty Freeman commissioned another work for them, *Recent Impressions*. Sixteen minutes long, the piece seems finally to do away altogether with structural relationships; it was probably composed day by day, without sketches or erasures, as the Quintet had been. The result, curiously, is music of utter objectivity: although the material seems to be chosen and shaped intuitively, the sounds, freed from the necessity to relate in any traditionally theoretical manner, take on the vividness and vitality of natural objects.

The music proceeds in a succession of episodes, contrasted through their different textural qualities. We have met these textures before: held notes, quickly repeated notes (pulses); pentatonic "Chinese" melodies; quickly hocketed alternations among the ensemble; filigree-tunes; steadily pacing repeated downbeats. After six or seven minutes, when one realizes these contrasting episodes aren't developing into the two- or three-section form familiar from earlier works of Erickson's, it becomes apparent that the diurnal cycles contemplated in "Days and Nights" constitute a form of their own, and that that form was translated into musical structure by the exigency of writing this music, returning to the penciled score for a few minutes every day at the kitchen table.

Joel Sachs, director of Continuum, has noted a curious contradiction that arises from the simplicity of this daily-life music:

> Although very accessible to the general music lover, its unusual shape demands tremendous concentration from the performer and great placidity from the listener. In fact, the extreme delicacy and transparency of *Recent Impressions* make it one of the most difficult compositions Continuum has ever performed—proving that performance challenges are not the exclusive province of overtly complex music. [Liner note, Musical Heritage Society recording.]

In *Recent Impressions*, though in a very different and personal way, Erickson produces music whose only real analogue is that of John Cage. The composer "finds" this music toward the end of a long lifetime of exploration, trial, repetition, and refinement—finds it with apparent effortlessness, but as the reward for years of discipline. The listener hears this music as an unfamiliar landscape filled with familiar detail. Heard with preconceptions as to how music ought to proceed, it will be either irritatingly contrary or monotonously meaningless; but heard with an open mind and a sense of adventure, it will be delightfully colorful, eventful, absorbing.

The performers must negotiate a middle ground. Sachs is right: this music is hard to play. Musicians are used to having to occupy two states of mind simultaneously, attentive to each event in their own part while aware of the contexts (both immediate and long-term) in which they take place. The relationships among these concerns, in fact, are what constitute the musical meaning of much traditional concert music. But what is the long-term context, the traditional "meaning," of a work like *Recent Impressions*? (Particularly: how can one approach this question while preparing a premiere, perhaps with insufficient rehearsal time, and almost certainly with insufficient knowledge of the body of music that led Erickson to it?) The performers who succeed best will be those who have arrived at a similarly intuitive level, who can take the music—and the individual events and passages within the music—on faith, suspending prejudice, content to let the sounds assume their own careers and take on their own responsibilities.

In *Recent Impressions*, with the attainment of a rare degree of artistic maturity, Erickson has found a way to "let the sounds be themselves," in the phrase recurring so often in Cage's writings. One thinks of Stephen Dedalus's description of the final stage of creativity, after the poet has moved through the lyric and the epic and has reached the truly dramatic:

> The dramatic form is reached when the vitality which has flowed and eddied round each person fills every person with such vital force that he or she assumes a proper and intangible esthetic life. The personality of the artist ... finally refines itself out of existence, impersonalizes itself, so to speak. [James Joyce: *A Portrait of the Artist as a Young Man* (New York: Random House [The Modern Library], 1928), p. 252.]

FIVES FOR ENGLISH HORN, BASS CLARINET, PIANO, VIOLA, AND CELLO (1988)

Apparently some musical investigations remained from the work on the Trio for clarinet, cello, and harp, and Erickson next turned to a chamber piece that took him into a new area. *Fives* is a pastorale, like the Trio, but a nocturnal one, in a slightly more troubled mood. The instrumentation is dark: low strings, low woodwind, and piano. (One wonders if the piano part might not have been influenced by the harp writing in the Trio. It could easily be played by a harp, perhaps to a better effect.)

As in *Recent Impressions*, the form simply evolves in a series of episodes marked by changes of voice or complexity. (In the end, though, *Fives* can be seen as a balanced three-part structure.) The music begins on E again, but darkened with simultaneously sounded D and B flat. The first melody, starting in the second measure, goes to the English horn, whose voice has been associated with seriousness, even elegy, since Haydn wrote so gravely for it in his Symphony no. 22. (That work opens with a sober movement for pairs of English horns and French horns, each pair playing in unison, accompanied by strings.) The opening of *Fives* is immediately imitated by the viola, then bass clarinet, their duet ending in the gently rocking thirds that began the closing section of the Trio for clarinet, cello, and harp.

Then, a minute into the piece, the bass clarinet picks up the tempo to introduce a curiously stern, awkwardly contoured solo in the English horn. The notes are of equal length, for the most part, and detached from one another. Contrary to usual practice, Erickson rarely suggests phrasing to his performers in these late pieces: his notes are set out for their own value, and the performer must find a way to get from one to the next. At first this is disconcerting: we are used to ingratiating musical phrases, whose supple contours cajole a single kind of reception from both performer and listener. This English horn statement sounds stiff, matter-of-fact, perhaps prosaic: its contour is incontrovertible but uncooperative, like a geological feature. Yet since we must make of it what we will, we may make of it what we can: growing familiar with this abstract manner, the listener can find many ways of relating its details, of "interpreting" its shape.

In any case the mood soon changes: at the third minute a more graceful duet appears in viola and English horn, punctuated by piano chords and ending in another extended English horn solo (marked "brilliant" and rising to fortissimo). The cello takes over the viola line and the duet is joined by piano, and gradually the texture rises again to include the whole ensemble in a climax ending the fifth minute of the piece. This introduces complex chords, of the sort we met in *White Lady*, gradually falling in pitch and loudness in the piano to lead to a final section, two and a half minutes long, in which the melodic content is heard in gradually subsiding textures, one instrument at a time dropping away, then returning to close *Fives* on a hushed octave E.

Fives is dark, but ultimately resolved. Only eight minutes long, it stands as an isolated movement in the kaleidoscopic multimovement composition that could be assembled from Erickson's works of the 1980s. It can be thought of as a calmer, less subjective view of the night events of *Auroras*, finally more accepting, therefore more engaged. In returning to the content of *Auroras* and the method of the Trio it turns away from the achievement of *Recent*

Impressions, which is left somewhat isolated in Erickson's catalogue. *Fives* is essentially melodic, however austere and reticent its melody may be. Melody moves the listener through time by clearly relating sounds in a linear fashion. *Recent Impressions* is not primarily melodic. The sounds are heard before or after one another, of course (or simultaneously), but seem to occupy—and to have been intended to occupy—a sound space (as Erickson described it, in *Sound Structure in Music*), to be related or not, to other sounds immediately adjacent or not, as the listener chooses.

MUSIC FOR TRUMPET, STRINGS, AND TIMPANI (1990)

Fives completed, Erickson waited patiently for the next music. His illness was so advanced he was by now, in 1988, confined to his bed most of the time—"imprisoned in his own body," as Alan Rich remarks in his notes to the CRI compact disc. Soon, though, he was reading mystery novels again, always a sign that composition was imminent. And before long visitors noticed a few pages of manuscript paper on the kitchen table. They reported, though, that the music didn't seem to be very eventful, or going much of anywhere: only a few whole notes drawn here and there on the page.

And when the finished manuscript of *Music for Trumpet, Strings, and Timpani* was delivered to Erickson's former colleagues at UC San Diego for its premiere in 1991, a year after it was completed, it was greeted with a certain amount of skepticism. The trumpet part was uncomfortably high; the string writing (thought to be for solo string quintet) rather thin; the piece was quite short; the timpani entered only in the final two or three measures.

In performance, though, *Music for Trumpet, Strings, and Timpani* was very moving, very effective. In its short duration the piece ranges through many characteristic Erickson preoccupations (drone, pulse, microtonal filigree). It seems to allude to Mahler and Copland. And in returning to the solo-and-ensemble format of *Garden, Night Music, The Idea of Order at Key West*, and *Recent Impressions*, it returns to a narrative concept of musical content. It's hard to resist hearing the music as a self-portrait.

Music for Trumpet, Strings, and Timpani opens with a sixty-second solo for unaccompanied trumpet, beginning with a quick scale up two octaves, then down and back up to a higher octave. The familiar microtonal webs of *Kryl* are heard, but in a very high register. (In the premiere Ed Harkins played the assignment beautifully on a soprano trumpet in D.) The strings finally enter with a long, slow, melodic duet; then, after adding to this texture a short allusion to a nostalgic waltz-tune in a Mahler symphony, the trumpet continues into another solo. About two minutes into the score the strings, which have been playing octaves, seamlessly introduce the rocking-thirds idea, soon taken up by the trumpet, which then weaves more tendrils over a duet in the strings.

Halfway through the piece the strings quicken the texture with a steady pulse introducing a new version of the trumpet tune, again set against the strings, in a more chromatic mood. The strings return to sweeter, wide-open intervals leading to a drone over which the trumpet calmly descends. Suddenly, over bare fifths and octaves, the mood darkens; a minor third makes a fleeting appearance. The trumpet seems to modulate to a new key on the fourth note of the scale, beginning a simple martial-sounding tune, but the timpani object to this, quite unexpectedly, with a roll on the keynote, joined by the strings. The trumpet rises to the third note of the scale, drops to the second—the timpani below sounding the minor third once, then the fifth—and the piece breaks off on what in conventional terms would be the unresolved dominant of the key.

Music for Trumpet, Strings, and Timpani is cheerful and outgoing. It makes no attempt to investigate new territory; it is unconcerned with introspection or dark contemplations; it makes few demands of its performers (trumpet part aside). It is engaging and straightforward, as if to close a distinguished, inventive, and finally profound catalogue of over seventy compositions on a note of modest triumph. Music can be complex or simple, expressive or neutral, eventful or calm. It can contemplate things dark or transcendental. It can grieve or rejoice. It is profound solitude or communal cooperativeness. It is everything to its composer, at work on it; to the audience, it might mean anything. In the end—in *Music for Trumpet, Strings, and Timpani*—it is a diversion, notes on paper, then in the air, then gone; six minutes of entertainment at the end of a program. The music is heard; the audience applauds; the performers are content. The music, for the moment, is over. Hearing it changed the way we knew our world.

APPENDIXES AND INDEX

Appendix I: Discography

The CD accompanying this book includes *Taffytime* for chamber ensemble, *Solstice* for string quartet, and *Concerto for Piano and Seven Instruments*.

LP RECORDINGS

• Acoustic Research

AR 0654 084: *Ricercare à 5*. Stuart Dempster, trombones [12:37]. (With Edwin Dugger: *Music for Synthesizer and Six Instruments*; Richard Hoffmann: *Orchestra Piece 1961*.) 1970.

• Ars Nova Ars Antiqua

AN-1001 (SD): *Ricercar à 3*. Bertram Turetzky, contrabass. (With Barney Childs: *Mr. T His Fancy*; Edward Biemanti: *Quartet*; Richard Felciano: *Spectra*; Robert Lombardo: *Nocturne for Contrabass Alone*; Raoul Pleskow: *Bagatelles with Contrabass*. No durations noted.) 1969.

• Composers Recordings, Inc.

CRI 218 USD: *Chamber Concerto*. Ralph Shapey, Hartt Chamber Players [21:00]. (With George Crumb: *Night Music I*.) 1967.

CRI SD 325: *The End of the Mime of Mick, Nick and the Maggies*. Kenneth Gaburo, NMCE I [12:10]. (With John Ferritto: *Oggi*; J. K. Randall: *Improvisation*; Jean Eichelberger Ivey: *Hera, Hung from the Sky*.) ©1974.

CRI SD 494: *Pacific Sirens*. Gregory Barber, The Arch Ensemble [13:25]. *Night Music*. David Burkhart, trumpet; Robert Hughes, The Arch Ensemble [18:00]. *The Idea of Order at Key West*. Carol Plantamura, mezzo-soprano; Robert Hughes, The Arch Ensemble [10:55]. ©1984.

• New World Recordings

NW 254: *General Speech*. Stuart Dempster, trombone [5:18]. (With Harvey Sollberger: *Motet on Doo-dah*; Robert Morris: *Inflections I*; Robert Hall Lewis: *Configurations*; Ralph Shapey: *Three Sketches*.) 1978.

• Orion Master Recordings

ORS 7294: *Oceans*. Jack Logan, trumpet; Robert Erickson, percussion [14:50]. (With Igor Stravinsky: *Fanfare for a New Theatre*; David Ahlstrom: *Scherzo*; Kenneth Gaburo: *Mouth-Piece*; David Ernst: *Exit*; Harry Partch: *Ulysses Departs from the Edge of theWorld*.) 1972.

COMPACT DISCS

- Composers Recordings, Inc.

CRI CD 616: *Kryl.* Edwin Harkins, trumpet [6:15]. *Ricercar à 3.* Bertram Turetzky, contrabass [10:14]. *Post-cards.* Carol Plantamura, soprano; Jürgen Hübscher, lute [13:16]. *Dunbar's Delight.* Dan Dunbar, timpani [14:32]. *Quoq.* John Fonville, flute [8:32]. *Sierra.* Philip Larson, baritone; Thomas Nee, SONOR [15:54]. 1991.

- Musical Heritage Society

MHS 512704F: *Recent Impressions.* Cheryl Seltzer, piano; Joel Sachs, Continuum Ensemble [16:18]. Two Songs: "Days and Nights," "Seasonal." Ellen Lang, mezzo-soprano; David Krakauer, clarinet; Mia Wu, viola; Joel Sachs, piano [4:09; 6:24]. *High Flyer.* Jayn Rosenfeld, flute [6:18]. *Summer Music.* Mia Wu, violin [15:32]. 1990.

Appendix II: Chronology of Compositions

1940	*Three Rilke Songs*: soprano and piano
1943	Motet, "Song of Songs": SATB chorus
1944	*Two Christmas Choruses*: SATB chorus
1944	*The Star Song:* SSA chorus
1945	*Be Still My Soul*: SATB chorus
1945	*Three Contralto Songs*: contralto and piano
1945–46	*The 1945 Variations*: solo piano (with offstage baritone)
1946	*Five Job Choruses*: SATB chorus
1948	*Introduction and Allegro for Orchestra*
1948	Sonata: solo piano
1950	String Quartet No. 1
1953	*Pastorale:* soprano, tenor, chorus, and string quartet
1953	Divertimento: flute, clarinet, string orchestra
1953	Trio: violin, viola, and piano
1953	*Fantasy for Cello and Orchestra*
1956	String Quartet No. 2
1957	*Variations for Orchestra*
1957	Duo: violin and piano
1960	*Chamber Concerto*
1962	Toccata for Piano, "Ramus"
1963	*Concerto for Piano and Seven Instruments*
1963	*The End of the Mime of Mick, Nick and the Maggies*: SATB chorus
1963–65	*Sirens and Other Flyers III*: orchestra
1965	*Piece for Bells and Toy Pianos*: tape and two toy pianos
1966	*Ricercare à 5*: solo trombone with four self-prepared tapes; or five trombones
1966	*Scapes, A Contest for Two Groups:* two groups of instruments, five or more in each

1966	*Scapes II, A Contest for Two Groups*: two groups of instruments, five or more in each
1966	*Roddy*: two-channel tape
1967	*Birdland*: two-channel tape
1967	*Ricercar à 3*: solo contrabass with two self-prepared tapes; or three contrabasses
1967–68	*Down at Piraeus*: solo soprano, chorus, and two-channel tape
1967–68	*Cardenitas 68*: solo soprano, recorder or wooden flute, bassoon, trombone, contrabass, percussion, tape
1968	*Do It*: solo speaker, two choral groups, gongs, contrabasses, and bassoons
1968	*Drum Studies*: two or three sets of tubular drums
1968	*General Speech*: solo trombone
1969	*High Flyer*: solo flute
1969	*Pacific Sirens*: instrumental ensemble and two-channel tape
1970	*Nine and a Half for Henry (and Wilbur and Orville)*: instrumental ensemble and two-channel tape
1970	*Oceans*: solo trumpet and four-channel tape
1971	*Cradle*: three sets of tuned tube drums and instrumental ensemble
1972	*Cradle II*: four sets of tube drums and instrumental ensemble
1972–73	*Loops for Instruments*
1973	*Percussion Loops*: solo multiple percussion
1974	*Summer Music*: solo violin and tape
1974	*Rainbow Rising*: orchestra
1975	*White Lady*: wind ensemble
1976–77	*Garden*: solo violin and small orchestra
1977	*Kryl*: solo trumpet
1978	*Night Music*: solo trumpet and ten instruments (flute, e♭ clarinet, clarinet, bass clarinet, trombone, two percussion, cello, two contrabass)
1978	*Quoq*: solo flute
1979	*The Idea of Order at Key West*: solo soprano, flute, clarinet, trumpet, viola, cello
1980	*East of the Beach*: orchestra
1980	*Postcards*: solo mezzo-soprano and lute
1981	*The Pleiades*: solo violin

1981–82	*Three Songs for the Five Centuries Ensemble*: soprano, countertenor, viola da gamba, harpsichord
1982	*Auroras* (rev 1985): orchestra
1983	*Mountain* : solo soprano, small women's chorus, chamber orchestra
1983	*Taffytime*: chamber ensemble
1984	*Sierra*: solo tenor and chamber orchestra
1984–85	*Solstice*: string quartet
1985	*Dunbar's Delight*: solo timpani
1985	Quintet: flute, clarinet, trumpet, viola, cello
1986	*Corfu*: string quartet
1986	*Corona*: string orchestra
1986	*Two Songs*: soprano, clarinet, viola, piano
1986	Trio: clarinet, harp, cello
1987	*Recent Impressions*: chamber ensemble
1988	*Fives*: English horn, bass clarinet, piano, viola, cello
1990	*Music for Trumpet, Strings, and Timpani*: solo trumpet, string quintet (or orchestra), timpani

Appendix III: List of Works by Title

Boldface page numbers denote major discussions.
† alongside title denotes recording on accompanying CD.

Auroras (1982; rev 1985), 79, **209–12**, 213, 214, 215, 216, 221, 223, 234
> Orchestra (3fl/pic, 3ob/Eh, 3cl, 2bn, 4hrn, 3tr, 3 trb, harp, pno, cel, 4perc, rods, 3vn1, 3vn2, 2vla, 3vc, 4cb)
> Premiere: Thomas Nee, American Composers Orchestra, NYC, February 27, 1984
> Publisher: Smith Publications, Baltimore, MD, ©1986

Be Still My Soul (1945), 28, 86
> SATB chorus
> Text: A. E. Housman
> Publisher: Smith Publications, Baltimore, MD, ©1991

Birdland (1967), 63, 136, **137–39**, 148, 160
> Two-channel tape
> Premiere: Theatre Five, San Diego, CA, August 16, 1968
> Publisher: Tape available from Smith Publications, Baltimore, MD

Cardenitas 68 (1967–68), 62, 63, 73, 86, **151–52**, 153, 155
> Solo soprano, recorder or wooden flute, bsn, trb, cb, perc, tape
> Text: Erickson
> Premiere: Beverly Ogdon; Alan Johnson, ensemble; Univ. of California at San Diego, June 5, 1968 (decor: Lenore Alt-Erickson)
> Publisher: Smith Publications, Baltimore, MD

Chamber Concerto (1960), 14, 38, 47, 53, 85, **115–19**, 122–24, 126, 147, 189
> Fl, ob, cl, bcl, bn, tr, hrn, trb, harp, pno, hrpscd-cel, 2perc, vn, vla, vc, cb
> Premiere: John Silber, Illinois Wesleyan Chamber Ensemble, March 1962
> Publisher: Theodore Presser Co., Bryn Mawr, PA
> Recording: Composers Recordings, Inc., 1967 (CRI 218 USD)

Chamber symphony, 29, 33, 92–93. See also his Divertimento.

†*Concerto for Piano and Seven Instruments* (1963), 14, 38, 53, 73, 88, 90, 121, **122–26**, 127, 129, 132, 135, 136, 139, 147, 148, 226
> Solo piano, fl, cl, bn, tr, trb, cb, perc
> Commissioned: School of Music, Univ. of Illinois, for 1963 Festival of Arts

Premiere: Dwight Peltzer, piano; Jack McKenzie, Univ. of Illinois ensemble, March 1963
Publisher: Theodore Presser Co., Bryn Mawr, PA
Recording: accompanying CD

Corfu (1986), 80, **223–24**

String quartet
Commissioned by Betty Freeman for the Kronos Quartet
Premiere: Kronos Quartet, San Diego, 1986
Publisher: Smith Publications, Baltimore, MD, ©1990

Corona (1986), 80, **227–29**

String orchestra
Commissioned by Betty Freeman for the Los Angeles Philharmonic Orchestra
Premiere: André Previn, Los Angeles Philharmonic, February 1, 1989
Publisher: Smith Publications, Baltimore, MD, ©1991

Cradle (1971), 62, 74, **165–67**, 197

Three sets of tuned tube drums and instrumental ensemble
Premiere: Frank McCarty, ensemble; California State Univ. at Fullerton, May 15, 1971
Publisher: Smith Publications, Baltimore, MD

Cradle II (1972), 62, 74, 167, 199

Four sets of tube drums and instrumental ensemble
Premiere: UCSD Percussion Ensemble, November 27, 1973
Publisher: Smith Publications, Baltimore, MD

Dance score (lost), 50, 86

Divertimento (1953), 33–34, 93, 96, **98–99**

Flute, clarinet, string orchestra
Premiere: ACA Composers' Concert; San Francisco, 1957
Publisher: Smith Publications, Baltimore, MD

Do It (1968), 63, 86, **149–50**, 151, 152, 167

Solo speaker, two choral groups, gongs, contrabasses, bassoons
Texts: Donald Peterson; found material
Premiere: Alan Johnson, speaker; UCSD students and members of the UCSD student ensemble; UCSD, December 3, 1968
Publisher: Okra Music, 1977. Assigned to Smith Publications, Baltimore, MD, ©1991

Down at Piraeus (1967–68), 63, 86, **150–51**, 167, 180

Solo soprano, chorus, two-channel tape

Texts: Plato (*Republic*, Book III); Erickson
Premiere: John Dexter, Mid-America Chorale, 1967
Publisher: Okra Music, 1970. Smith Publications, Baltimore, MD, ©1985

Drum Studies (1968), 62, **164–65**
Two or three sets of tubular drums
Publisher: Smith Publications, Baltimore, MD

Dunbar's Delight (1985), 74, 212, **219–20**, 224
Solo timpani
Premiere: Dan Dunbar; UCSD, San Diego, May 1985
Publisher: Smith Publications, Baltimore, MD, ©1986
Recording: Composers Recordings, Inc., 1991 (CRI CD 616 [CD])

Duo (1957), 45, 101, **111–13**, 116, 126, 132
Violin and piano
Premiere: Robert Bloch, violin; Nathan Schwartz, piano; San Francisco, March 1961
Publisher: Merion Music, Inc., 1962. Assigned to Theodore Presser Co., Bryn Mawr, PA,
   sole representative

East of the Beach (1980), 64, 69, 71, 74, **200–203**, 205, 209, 226
Orchestra (pic/fl, a fl/fl, ob, ob/Eh, cl, cl/bcl, bn, 2hrn, 2tr, trb, harp, 2perc, timp, strings)
Premiere: Thomas Nee, New Hampshire Festival Orch., August 12, 1980
Publisher: Smith Publications, Baltimore, MD

The End of the Mime of Mick, Nick and the Maggies (1963), 63, 74, 86, **126–29**, 138, 155, 193
SATB chorus (capable of subdividing into three voices per part)
Text: James Joyce (*Finnegans Wake*)
Commissioned: Hamline University Choir, Robert Holliday, conductor
Premiere: Kenneth Gaburo, New Music Chorus Ensemble; Champaign, IL, August 1965
Publisher: Smith Publications, Baltimore, MD, ©1988
Recording: Composers Recordings, Inc., 1974 (CRI SD 325)

Fantasy for Cello and Orchestra (1953), 55, 96, **99–100**, 101
Solo cello and orchestra (fl, pic/fl, ob, ob/Eh, 2cl, cl/bcl, 2bn, 4hrn, 2tr, 3trb, tba, timp,
   1perc, strings)
Premiere: Ernst Krenek, Hamburg Radio Orch.; Hamburg, Germany, 1954
Publisher: Smith Publications, Baltimore, MD, ©1989

"Fast Boogie-Woogie," 87. See also *The 1945 Variations*.

First string quartet. See his String Quartet No. 1.

Five Job Choruses (1946), 28, 74, 86
> SATB chorus
> Text: Bible
> Premiere: Hamline Univ. Choir; St. Paul, MN, 1949
> Publisher: Smith Publications, Baltimore, MD

Fives (1988), 80, **233–35**
> Eh, bcl, pno, vla, vc
> Premiere: SONOR, La Jolla, CA, May 25, 1989
> Publisher: Smith Publications, Baltimore, MD, ©1990

Fourth string quartet. See *Corfu.*

Garden (1976–77), 73, **194–96**, 197, 200, 203, 205, 210, 212, 221, 235
> Solo violin and small orchestra (fl, ob, cl/bcl, bn, tr, hrn, trb, cel/e org, vbr/glk/timp, 8-8-4-4-1)
> Premiere: János Négyesy; Thomas Nee, La Jolla Civic Orch.; San Diego, May 16, 1981
> Publisher: Smith Publications, Baltimore, MD

General Speech (1968), 63, 73, **152–54**, 178, 206
> Solo trombone
> Text: Douglas MacArthur
> Commissioned: Stuart Dempster
> Premiere: Dempster; UCSD, March 1970 (decor: Lenore Alt-Erickson)
> Publisher: Okra Music, 1976. Assigned to Smith Publications, Baltimore, MD
> Recording: New World Records, 1978 (NW 254)

High Flyer (1969), 63, **154–55**, 177
> Solo flute
> Text: Erickson
> Premiere: Peter Middleton; UCSD, March 1970
> Publisher: Okra Music, 1976. Assigned to Smith Publications, Baltimore, MD, ©1988
> Recording: Musical Heritage Society, 1990 (MHS 512704F [CD])

The Idea of Order at Key West (1979), 74–76, 79, **198–200**, 201, 204, 205, 235
> Solo soprano, fl, cl, tr, vla, vc
> Text: Wallace Stevens
> Premiere: Bernard Rands, SONOR; San Diego, April 14, 1980
> Publisher: Smith Publications, Baltimore, MD, ©1984
> Recording: Composers Recordings, Inc., 1984 (CRI SD 494)

Introduction and Allegro for Orchestra (1948), 26, 28–29, 55, **89– 90**, 91, 92, 96, 101
Orchestra (fl, ob, cl, 2bn, 4hrn, timp, strings)
Premiere: Dimitri Mitropoulos, Minneapolis Symphony Orchestra, March 1949
Publisher: Smith Publications, Baltimore, MD

Kryl (1977), 73, **191–92**, 197, 200, 205, 210, 236
Solo trumpet
Premiere: Edwin Harkins; UCSD, November 16, 1977
Publisher: Smith Publications, Baltimore, MD, ©1984
Recording: Composers Recordings, Inc., 1991 (CRI CD 616 [CD])

Loops for Instruments (1972–73), 73, **167–68**, 172, 229
Fl, cl, tr, a sax, bn, mar
Premiere: PME ensemble; Monday Evening Concerts, Los Angeles, March 10, 1973
Unpublished (subsequently incorporated as parts of *Percussion Loops*)

Motet, "Song of Songs" (1943), 28, 74, 86
SATB chorus
Text: Bible
Premiere: Hamline Univ. Choir; St. Paul, MN, 1943
Publisher: Smith Publications, Baltimore, MD

Mountain (1983), **215–16**, 221, 223, 229, 231
Solo soprano, small women's chorus, chamber orchestra
Text: Erickson
Premiere: Carol Plantamura; resident musicians; California State College, Long Beach,
    November 29, 1982
Publisher: Smith Publications, Baltimore, MD, ©1984

Music for Trumpet, Strings, and Timpani (1990), 73, 80, **235–36**
Solo trumpet; string quintet (or orchestra), timpani
Premiere: Edwin Harkins; SONOR; UCSD, November 13, 1991
Publisher: Smith Publications, Baltimore, MD

Music-theater piece (lost), 130

Night Music (1978), 64, 69, 73, 74, 78, 79, 80, 135, **196–98**, 199, 200, 202, 203, 205, 212, 221,
224, 225, 230, 235
Solo trumpet and ten instruments (fl, ecl, cl, bcl, trb, 2perc, vc, 2cb)
Premiere: Edwin Harkins; Bernard Rands, SONOR; San Diego, May 24, 1978
Publisher: Smith Publications, Baltimore, MD, ©1984
Recording: Composers Recordings, Inc., 1984 (CRI SD 494)

Nine and a Half for Henry (and Wilbur and Orville) (1970), 136, 144, **159–60**, 195
    Instrumental ensemble and two-channel tape
    Commissioned: KPBS, San Diego
    Premiere: UCSD Players, November 1970
    Publisher: Okra Music, 1976. Assigned to Smith Publications, Baltimore, MD, ©1984
        (film available on rental)

The 1945 Variations (1945–46), 24, 28, **87–88**, 90, 218
    Solo piano (with offstage baritone)
    Text: traditional (Miserere)
    Premiere: Robert Erickson, piano; Hamline Univ., April 16, 1946
    Publisher: Smith Publications, Baltimore, MD, ©1988

Oceans (1970), 64, **160–63**, 164, 167, 192, 199
    Solo trumpet and four-channel tape
    Commissioned: Jack Logan
    Premiere: Logan; St. Paul's Episcopal Church, San Diego, October 4, 1970
    Publisher: © assigned to Smith Publications, Baltimore, MD, 1984
    Recording: Orion Records, 1972 (ORS 7294)

Pacific Sirens (1969), 79, 136, 144, **157–58**, 159, 160, 161, 178, 183, 189, 195, 199, 200, 204
    Instrumental ensemble and two-channel tape
    Commissioned: University of Washington School of Music
    Premiere: New Music Ensemble; Univ. of Washington, Seattle, March 10, 1969
    Publisher: Okra Music, 1976. Assigned to Smith Publications, Baltimore, MD, ©1984
    Recording: Composers Recordings, Inc., 1984 (CRI SD 494)

Pastorale (1953), 33, 74, 86, 96, **97–98**
    Soprano, tenor, chorus, and string quartet
    Text: Jane Mayhall
    Premiere: Hamline Alumni Singers; St. Paul, MN, 1953
    Publisher: Smith Publications, Baltimore, MD

Percussion Loops (1973), 164, 167, **170–71**
    Solo multiple percussion
    Premiere: Ron George; Mandeville Auditorium, UCSD, May 20, 1976
    Publisher: Smith Publications, Baltimore, MD, ©1984

Piano Concerto. See *Concerto for Piano and Seven Instruments*.

Piano Sonata. See Sonata.

Piece for Bells and Toy Pianos (1965), 52, **134–36**, 137, 148, 160, 161, 189, 226
    Tape and two toy pianos
    Premiere: Warner Jepson; San Francisco Conservatory of Music, May 17, 1966
    Filmed and distributed to National Educational Television by KQED, San Francisco
    Publisher: Smith Publications, Baltimore, MD

The Pleiades (1981), 74, **205–207**, 212, 220, 221
    Solo violin
    Premiere: János Négyesy, UCSD, San Diego, April 5, 1982
    Publisher: Smith Publications, Baltimore, MD, ©1984

Postcards (1980), **204–205**, 207
    Solo mezzo-soprano and lute
    Text: Erickson
    Premiere: Carol Plantamura; Jürgen Hübscher; Mandeville Auditorium, UCSD,
        March 4, 1987
    Publisher: Smith Publications, Baltimore, MD, ©1984
    Recording: Composers Recordings, Inc., 1991 (CRI CD 616 [CD])

Quintet (1985), 80, **224–26**, 231
    Fl, cl, tr, vla, vc
    Commissioned by the National Endowment for the Arts Consortium Commission
    Premiere: San Francisco Contemporary Music Players, October 21, 1985
    Publisher: Smith Publications, Baltimore, MD, ©1987

Quoq (1978), 74, **192–93**, 205
    Solo flute
    Premiere: Bernhard Batschelet; California Inst. of the Arts, Valencia, April 28, 1979
    Publisher: Smith Publications, Baltimore, MD, ©1986
    Recording: Composers Recordings, Inc., 1991 (CRI CD 616 [CD])

Rainbow Rising (1974), 61, 64, 70, 73, 75, **173–75**, 187, 189, 191, 194
    Orchestra (2fl, pic/fl, a fl, 2ob, Eh, 2cl, bcl, bcl/cbcl, 2bn, bn/cbn, 3tr, 4hrn, 3trb, tba, hrp,
        hpscd/pno, 5perc, 12-12-8-8-6)
    Commissioned: La Jolla Civic Orchestra
    Premiere: Thomas Nee, La Jolla Civic Orch.; UCSD, March 1, 1975
    Publisher: Smith Publications, Baltimore, MD

Recent Impressions (1987), 80, **231–33**, 234–35
    Fl, ob, cl, bn, hrn, tr, trb, perc, two pno, vn, vla, vc, cb
    Commissioned: Continuum

Premiere: Joel Sachs, Continuum; Cologne, Germany, 1987
Publisher: Smith Publications, Baltimore, MD, ©1993
Recording: Musical Heritage Society, 1990 (MHS 512704F [CD])

Ricercar à 3 (1967), 63, 140, **147–49**, 165, 171, 192, 197, 207, 210, 226, 229
Solo contrabass with two self-prepared tapes; or three contrabasses
Commissioned: Bertram Turetzky
Premiere: Turetzky, for Ars Nova recording
Publisher: University of California Press (University Publications in Contemporary Music), 1973. Assigned to Smith Publications, Baltimore, MD, ©1992
Recordings: Ars Nova Ars Antiqua, 1969 (AN-1001 SD); Composers Recordings, Inc., 1991 (CRI CD 616 [CD])

Ricercare à 5 (1966), 53–54, 63, **140–45**, 146, 147, 148, 149, 152, 226, 229
Solo trombone with four self-prepared tapes; or five trombones
Commissioned: Stuart Dempster
Premiere: Dempster; San Francisco Tape Music Center, March 1966
Publisher: Okra Music, 1971. Assigned to Smith Publications, Baltimore, MD, ©1993
Recording: A/R Records Contemporary Music Project, 1970 (0654 084)

Roddy (1966), 52–53, **136–37**, 148, 160
Two-channel tape
Premiere: Mills College Tape Music Center, January 9, 1967
Publisher: Tape available from Smith Publications, Baltimore, MD

Scapes, A Contest for Two Groups ("a 'contest' with the format of tic-tac-toe") (1966) 54–55, 56, **145–47**, 150, 157
Two groups of instruments, five or more in each
Premiere: San Francisco Conservatory Improvisation Group, May 18, 1966
Publisher: Smith Publications, Baltimore, MD, ©1984

Scapes II, A Contest for Two Groups (1966), 147
Two groups of instruments, five or more in each
Commissioned: University of Illinois
Premiere: Jack McKenzie, Univ. of Illinois Contemporary Chamber Players, July 31, 1966
Unpublished (exists as an alternate performing version of *Scapes*)

Second String Quartet. See his String Quartet No. 2.

Sierra (1984), **216–18**, 219, 220
Solo tenor and chamber orchestra
Texts: Erickson; John Muir

Commissioned by The Arch Ensemble
Premiere: Tom Buckner; Robert Hughes, The Arch Ensemble, January 1985
Publisher: Smith Publications, Baltimore, MD
Recording: Composers Recordings, Inc., 1991 (CRI CD 616)

Sirens and Other Flyers III (1963–65), 56, **129–33**, 134, 137, 144, 147, 148, 189, 203, 227
Orchestra
Premiere: Thomas Nee, Minneapolis Civic Orch.; June 1973
Publisher: Smith Publications, Baltimore, MD

†*Solstice* (1984–85), 79–80, **221–23**, 226
String quartet
Commissioned by Betty Freeman for the Sequoia String Quartet
Premiere: Sequoia String Quartet; California Inst. for the Arts, Valencia, March 10, 1985
Publisher: Smith Publications, Baltimore, MD, ©1985
Recording: accompanying CD

Sonata (1948), 28–29, **90–91**, 92, 96, 98, 101
Solo piano
Premiere: Marjorie Winslow Briggs; Minneapolis, MN, 1949
Publisher: Smith Publications, Baltimore, MD, ©1988

The Star Song (1944), 86
SSA chorus
Text: Robert Herrick
Premiere: Shirley Hammergren, Betty Bronson, June Jeffrey; Hamline Univ. as a trio,
April 16, 1946
Publisher: Smith Publications, Baltimore, MD, ©1988

String quartet, movement (lost), 86

String Quartet No. 1 (1950), 28–29, 91–92, 96, 101, 102n
String quartet
Premiere: Flor Quartet; St. Paul, MN, 1951
Publisher: Smith Publications, Baltimore, MD, ©1992

String Quartet No. 2 (1956), 39, 44, 45, 64, 85, 101, **102–106**, 112, 113, 135
String quartet
Premiere: California String Quartet; San Francisco, 1957
Publisher: Smith Publications, Baltimore, MD, ©1984

String Quartet No. 3. See *Solstice.*

String Quartet No. 4. See *Corfu.*

Summer Music (1974), 5, 62, 64, **189–91**, 194, 195, 212, 213, 221
> Solo violin and tape
> Commissioned: Daniel Kobialka
> Publisher: Smith Publications, Baltimore, MD, ©1984
> Recording: Musical Heritage Society, 1990 (MHS 512704F [CD])

Symphony (lost), 26, 86, 89

†*Taffytime* (1983), **212–15**, 216
> Large ensemble (fl/pic, ob, 2cl/bcl, bn, tr, hrn, trb, tba, 2harp, cel, 4perc, v, vla, 2cb)
> Premiere: John Silber, sonor; UCSD, February 22, 1984
> Publisher: Smith Publications, Baltimore, MD, ©1994
> Recording: accompanying CD

Third String Quartet. See *Solstice.*

Three Contralto Songs (1945), 28, 74, 86
> Contralto and piano
> Texts: Margot Ruddock ("Spirit, Silken Thread"; "Take Away"; "O Holy Water, Love")
> Publisher: Smith Publications, Baltimore, MD, ©1991

Three Rilke Songs (1940), 28, 74, 86, 87
> Soprano and piano
> Texts: Theodor Rilke ("This Is My Strife"; "Thou My Sacred Solitude"; "You Come Too";
> translated by M. D. Herter)
> Premiere: Alice Taylor; Nathan Schwartz; Composers' Forum; San Francisco, 1957
> Publisher: Smith Publications, Baltimore, MD

Three Songs for the Five Centuries Ensemble (1981–82), **207–208**
> Soprano, countertenor, viola da gamba, harpsichord (performers also play percussion)
> Texts: Erickson ("Night Sky," 1981; "Birds at Dusk," 1982; "Before Dawn," 1982)
> Premiere: Five Centuries Ensemble; Salle Pleyel, Paris, November 1982
> Publisher: Smith Publications, Baltimore, MD

Toccata for Piano, "Ramus" (1962), **119–22**, 123, 126
> Solo piano
> Commissioned: Maro Ajemian
> Premiere: Maro Ajemian; New School, NYC, October 1962
> Publisher: Smith Publications, Baltimore, MD, ©1984

Trio (1953), 33, 39, 96–97, 98, 105
    Violin, viola, and piano
    Premiere: Faculty Trio, College of St. Catherine; St. Paul, MN, 1953
    Publisher: Smith Publications, Baltimore, MD, ©1990

Trio (1986), **226–27**, 233, 234
    Clarinet, harp, cello
    Premiere: William Powell; Susan Allen; Erika Duke; San Diego, 1987
    Publisher: Smith Publications, Baltimore, MD, ©1991

Two Christmas Choruses (1944), 28, 74, 86
    SATB chorus
    Premiere: Hamline Chamber Singers; Minneapolis, MN, 1944
    Publisher: Smith Publications, Baltimore, MD

Two Songs (1986), **229–31**, 232
    Soprano, clarinet, viola, piano
    Texts: Erickson ("Days and Nights;" "Seasonal")
    Publisher: Smith Publications, Baltimore, MD, ©1993
    Recording: Musical Heritage Society, 1990 (MHS 512704F [CD])

Variations for Orchestra (1957), 45, 55–56, 88, 90, 101, **106–11**, 113, 116, 117, 122, 126, 132, 138
    Orchestra (pic, 2fl, 2ob, 2cl, bcl, 2bn, cbn, 4hrn, 3tr, 3trb, tba, pno, hrp, timp, 2perc, strings)
    Premiere: Thomas Nee, Minneapolis Civic Orch., 1957
    Publisher: Theodore Presser Co., Bryn Mawr, PA

White Lady (1975), 61, 64, 73, 79, **186–87**, 189, 191, 211, 212, 234
    Wind ensemble (pic/fl, 3fl, a fl, 2ob, Eh, e♭cl, 2cl, bcl, b/cbcl, 2bn, bn/ cbn, s sax, 2a sax, 3hrn, 3tr, 3trb, euphonium, tba)
    Premiere: Larry Livingston, Northern Illinois Wind Ensemble, May 1976
    Publisher: Smith Publications, Baltimore, MD, ©1984

General Index

Abramowitsch, Bernhard, 38

abstract music, 97, 112, 137, 173, 214, 216, 228, 231

abstract painting, 137

academicism, Erickson's views on, 43–45, 58, 68–69, 78, 122

accidentals, 9

accordion. *See* instruments, accordion.

Acoustic Research (record label), 142

acoustics, research in, 168–69

Adams, John, 228

Adjutant General School, San Antonio, Texas, 23

The Adoration of the Magi, 175

African music, xvii, 165–66, 182; West African drumming, 165, 182

Age of Reason, 177, 181

Ajemian, Anahid, 38

Ajemian, Maro, 38, 120–21

Albuquerque, New Mexico, 25, 29

Alembert, Jean le Rond d', 177

Alt, Lenore. *See* Alt-Erickson, Lenore.

Alt, Louise, 11

Alt, William, 11–12

Alt-Erickson, Lenore, 3n, 12, 19–20, 23, 34, 51, 54, 56; art studies, 11–12; artistic career and activity, 12, 19–20, 28, 30, 33, 69; early life, 11; as lighting designer, 63, 153; marriage, 11; miscellaneous occupations, 19, 22, 33; teaching career, 12, 36, 44, 47, 101

American Composers Orchestra, 79

American music: compared with European concert tradition, 43, 214; cross-cultural influence on, 165–66; impact of Charles Seeger on, 42

American quality in music, 126, 191, 214

American society: composers in, 69; concert life in, xiii–xiv; contemporary music in, 93–94, 113, 185, 203

Anders, Detlev, 102

animal sounds, imitation of in music, 142–44. *See also* birdsong.

Annunzio, Gabriele D', 207

Antheil, George, 25–26

Arabic music, 151, 205

Aranyi, Francis, 17–18

Arch Ensemble, 158

arch form, 88, 105

Arhoolie Records, 40

art, awareness of, 93

Art Deco, 187

Art Music (record store, Berkeley), 41

Art Nouveau, 90, 103

artists, position in society, 69, 71

Artists in America (TV series), 160

Aschenbrenner, Karl, 44

Ashley, Robert, *Wolfman*, 53

Asian Art Museum (San Francisco), 72

Asian music, 191. *See also* Chinese music; Indian music; Indonesian music; Japanese music; Southeast Asian music; Tibetan vocal drone.

Asian philosophy, influence on San Francisco Bay Area composers, 50

Atherton, Gertrude, 45n

atonality, 13, 16, 18, 33

attack and decay, in sound, 155, 178

aubade, 208

audience. *See* listener.

Austin, Larry, 184n

Australia, 60

Australian aboriginal music, 180

Austria: banning of music in, 17; Krenek's patriotism, 16; Webern's death in, 17

Avalon Ballroom (rock-concert venue), 68

Babbitt, Milton, 118; Composition for Synthesizer, 49

Bach, Johann Sebastian, 30, 94; cantatas, 8; contrapuntal technique, 108; "Goldberg" Variations, 108; *The Musical Offering*, 94, 141; suites, 106; Webern's orchestration of Ricercar, 176–77, 181

Badlands, 28

Bali, 61; Ericksons in, 66–67

Balinese dance, 66, 166

Balinese music, 61, 66–67; played by American students, 166

band music, 9. *See also* big-band music.

bands, Erickson and, 8, 10, 22, 34, 64, 192, 211. *See also* jazz bands; wind bands.

Barab, Seymour, 15

Barcelona, 14

Bark, Jan, *Bolos*, 142

Baroque music, 53, 115, 142, 148, 183. *See also* eighteenth-century music.

Bartók, Béla, 107; string quartets, 12, 102, 221

bass clarinet. *See* instruments, bass clarinet.

Batschelet, Bernhard, 193

Bauhaus, 15

Bazzini, Antonio, "Dance of the Goblins," 206–207

BBC. *See* British Broadcasting Corporation.

The Beatles, 165

beat generation, ix

beats (acoustics), 52, 178

Beckett, Samuel, *Waiting for Godot*, 145

Beethoven, Ludwig van, 8, 78; "Archduke" Trio, 12; "Kreutzer" Sonata, 12; piano concertos, 12; Piano Sonata in C

major, op. 53, "Waldstein," 68; piano sonatas, 12; String Quartet in A minor, op. 132, 221; String Quartet in F major, op. 135, 15; string quartets, 12, 15, 102, 221; Symphony No. 3 ("Eroica"), 12, 107–108; Symphony No. 5, 12, 175; Symphony No. 6 ("Pastoral"), 71, 138; Symphony No. 7, 12, 106, 159; Symphony No. 8, 159, 179; Symphony No. 9, 12; variation form in, 108; Violin Concerto, 12

bell-lyre. *See* instruments, bell-lyre.

bells. *See* instruments, bells.

Berberian, Cathy, 140, 145, 152

Berg, Alban, 12–14, 15, 22, 44, 99, 107, 115, 183; Erickson's admiration for music of, 13–15, 27, 96, 103; influence on Erickson, 14, 47, 86, 126; and Schoenberg, 103; works: *Altenberg Lieder*, 126; Chamber Concerto, 116; "Lied der Lulu," 22; *Lyric Suite*, 14–15, 71, 103; *Seven Early Songs*, 86; songs, 22; String Quartet, op. 3, 102, 103; Violin Concerto, 14–15

Berio, Luciano, 56, 140, 152, 185; Gazzelloni and, 193; at Mills College, 55; works: *Circles*, 132; *Différences*, 141; *Epifanie*, 132, 152; *Sinfonia*, 132

Berkeley, California, 31, 35, 41–42, 46, 123, 158; fire, 42; social protests, 41. *See also* KPFA; University of California at Berkeley.

Berlin, Germany, 15

Berlioz, Hector, 183, 203; *Harold in Italy*, 73; *Symphonie fantastique*, 71, 72, 179

big-band music, 116, 186

birds, 110, 138, 154, 156, 158, 209, 215

birdsong, 63, 131, 137–38, 155–56, 179, 205, 207–208, 209–12

Bishop, Stephen. *See* Kovacevich, Stephen Bishop.

Bliss, Arthur, 44

Bloch, Ernest, 43–44, 46
blues, 9
boogie-woogie, 24, 87
bop, 108, 124
Borodin, Alexander, *In the Steppes of Central Asia*, 180n, 203
Boston, Massachusetts, 17
Boucher, Anthony, 39
Boulanger, Nadia, 48
Boulez, Pierre, 107, 112, 118, 140, 183; and IRCAM, 168; Gazzelloni and, 193; String Quartet, 49
Boyden, David, 45n
Boynton, Ray, 53
Bradner-Smith Paper Company (Chicago), 11
Brahms, Johannes, 12, 88; Schoenberg lecture on, 18; Symphony No. 4, 89; *Variations on a Theme of Haydn*, 89, 108
brain and music, 179, 180
branching structure, 89, 106–10, 116, 117, 119, 120
Brant, Henry, 183
Braque, Georges, 177
Brautigan, Richard, 187n
Briggs, Marjorie Winslow, 91
British Broadcasting Corporation, 35, 38
Broughton, James, *The Pleasure Garden* (film), 135
Brown, Earle, 118
Bruckner, Anton, 68, 103, 138
Buchla, Don, 137
Buckner, Thomas, 216
"budding" technique. *See* branching structure.

Cable Piano Company (Chicago), 3
Cabrillo Festival (Santa Cruz, California), 38, 79
cadenzas, 197, 224–25; improvised, 124–25, 192
Cadillac, Michigan, 11, 19

Cage, John, xv, 42–44, 107, 118, 121, 126, 132, 145, 184, 232; chance techniques and, 133; Cowell and, 42; group performance and, 48; indeterminacy and, 133; influence of, 50; liberation of sound, 133; at New School for Social Research, 49; Tudor and, 121, 140; works: *Atlas Eclipticalis*, 182; *HPSCHD*, 184; *Inlet*, 158; string quartet, 102; *27'10.554" for a Percussionist*, 171; *Water Walk*, 158
Calder, Alexander, 145–46
California, 70, 70n; Southern California, 201. *See also* specific place names.
California Club, 41, 45n
California College of Arts and Crafts, 47
California Institute of the Arts, 79, 165, 171n
California-Minnesota connection, 48
California spirit in music, 43; Erickson and, x, xvii, 64, 69–70, 201, 217
California State College, Turlock, 212
California String Quartet, 38, 44, 102
Camp Claiborne, Louisiana, 23, 31
Camp Dodge, Iowa, 22
Camp Matthews, California, 61
canon, 94, 95
cantilena, 199, 200
cantus-firmus technique, 108
Cardiff, California, 62
Carmel Bach Festival, 38
"Carnival of Venice," 192
Carter, Elliott, 107, 112, 118, 119; Sonata for Flute, Oboe, Cello, and Harpsichord, 49; string quartets, 102
CCRMA (Center for Computer Research and Acoustics), 168
celesta. *See* instruments, celesta.
cello. *See* instruments, violoncello.
Centaur Records, 184n
Center for Computer Research and Acoustics (CCRMA), 168

Center for Contemporary Music, Mills College, 61
Center for Music Experiment (CME), 61, 169, 171n, 174
ceremony and music, 180
chamber music, contrasted with orchestral music, 115, 209
chamber orchestra, 115–16
Chamberlain Organ. *See* instruments, Chamberlain Organ.
chance elements in music, 50. *See also* indeterminacy.
chant. *See* drones; Gregorian chant; Tibetan vocal drones.
Chez Panisse, xi
Chiarito, Amerigo, 40
Chiarito, Gertrude, 40
Chicago Art Institute, 11–12
Chicago Conservatory of Music, 17–18
Chicago, Illinois, 7, 8, 20, 27; artistic life in, 36; concerts in, 14, 15; Erickson works performed in, 86, 100; Ericksons in, 4, 10–18; New Music Group, 15, 18; Park House (*see* Park House)
Chicago School of Design, 15
Chicago Symphony Orchestra, 14
chimes, stone. *See* instruments, stone chimes.
ch'in. See instruments, *ch'in*.
Chinese instruments. *See* instruments, Chinese.
Chinese music, xvii, 180, 181, 191, 194, 196; ancient, 77
Chinese opera, 152
Chopin, Frederic, 12
chord(s): droned, 150; layered, 185; as organizing device, 88, 185–87; relation to pitch and noise, 177; sustained, 211
"choric" music, 106, 107, 108
Chowning, John, 168, 183
chromatic scale, 73

chromaticism, 8–9, 13, 222, 225, 236
Cincinnati Philharmonia, 184n
cinema vérité, 135
clarinet, bass. *See* instruments, bass clarinet.
Classic period, music, 105, 183. *See also* eighteenth-century music.
Claudius, Matthias, 207
CME (Center for Music Experiment), 61, 169, 171n, 174
collage, 50, 63
collective improvisation, xvi, 38, 48, 55, 124–26
Cologne, Germany, 137
Colorado Springs, Colorado, 29, 30
coloratura writing, 152
Columbia University, 137
communal performance, 139, 167, 169
composer-performer teams, 121, 140, 148, 149
composers: consistent style, 83, 92; early works of, 85; manner of speaking, 83; maverick, ix, xv; as performers, 55, 59
Composers' Forum (San Francisco), 34, 38, 87
Composers Recordings (CRI), 79, 80, 116, 119, 122n, 123, 158, 235
Composers Workshop, 34, 48–49
composition, 13; as collaborative performance, xvi, 48, 55, 86
compositional procedures, 94–95, 214
computer music: Erickson's views of, 169; research in, 168–70, 183
computer technology, 69
concert halls, electronically enhanced, 183
concert life, in American society, xiii–xiv, 93–94
concerto grosso, 115
consonance, 9, 191, 213, 229
contemporary music: commitment to by Oakland Symphony, 55; Cowell's

contemporary music (*continued*)
  encouragement of, 42; place in American society, 93–94, 113, 185, 203
contemporary-music industry, 79
continuing variation, 88
Continuum, 79, 80, 229, 231
contrabass. *See* instruments, contrabass.
contrapuntal organization, 21, 29–30, 47,
  53, 89, 94, 108. *See also* counterpoint;
  polyphony.
Copland, Aaron, 48, 202, 235; *Appalachian Spring*, 9
Corfu, Greece, 223
Cott, Jonathan, 40
counterpoint, 13, 94–95, 96, 141; as clarifying device, 89; in perfection of style,
  96; reaction against, 132. *See also* contrapuntal organization; polyphony.
countertenor, 207–208
Cowell, Henry, xv, 42–44, 48; and Lou
  Harrison, 42; *New Musical Resources*, 42
Craig, George, 136
CRI. *See* Composers Recordings, Inc.
cricket noises, 214, 215
cross-cultural influence, 165
Cross, Laurence, 41
Crumb, George, 173; *Night Music I*, 119
cubism, 39, 177, 204
cummings, e.e., 140
Cushing, Charles, 43
cymbals. *See* instruments, cymbals.
Czaja, Helen, 20, 28, 217
Czaja, Mike, 20, 28, 217

Dadaism, 50, 135
D'Alembert, Jean le Rond, 177
Damon and Pythias, 151
D'Annunzio, Gabriele, 207
Darmstadt Festival, 38, 56
death-life cycles, 212, 214, 231
Debussy, Claude, 12, 126, 231; influence

on Erickson, 196; orchestral sounds of,
  78; works: "Jardins sous la pluie," 8;
  Jeux, 126, 178; *La Mer*, 126, 158; *Prelude to "The Afternoon of a Faun,"* 97
Degas, Edgar, *The Spartan Games*, 146
Del Tredici, David, 38
Delius, Frederick, 15, 195, 231
Dempster, Stuart, 63, 73, 123, 140, 141,
  149, 151; didjeridu and, 180; as Gen-
  eral MacArthur, 152–54; at San Fran-
  cisco Conservatory, 52–53; trombone
  techniques and, 53–54, 153–54
Denny, William, 43
DePaul University, 13
Depression, Great, 19, 31, 35, 42
Deutsch, Eugene, 12
dialectic process, 146
diatonic music, 9, 173
diatonic scale, 67, 173
didjeridu. *See* instruments, didjeridu.
Dillinger, John, 10
dissonance, 22, 191, 195, 208
Dominican College (San Rafael, California), 36, 47
Donaueschingen Festival, 38
Dorsey, Tommy, 141
Dorsky, Aaron, 23, 31
Dorsky, Nick, 23, 31
double bass. *See* instruments, contrabass.
Douglas, Michigan, 19
drone instruments. *See* instruments, drone.
drones, 54, 165, 167, 179–81, 186, 190,
  194, 195, 196, 197, 198, 200, 201,
  203, 210, 212, 213, 217, 221, 222,
  223, 225, 226, 228–29, 235. *See also*
  instruments, drone.
drumming, South Indian, 182; West
  African, 165
drums. *See* instruments, drums.
Duchamp, Marcel, *Fountain*, 50
Dukas, Paul, 43

Duke, George, 52
Dunbar, Daniel, 219
Dvořák, Antonín, 102

Egypt, pre-Christian, 61, 180
eighteenth-century music, 105; theory of, 177. *See also* Baroque music; Classic period.
Eimert, Herbert, 136–37
electronic music studios, 51, 61, 137
electronically manipulated instruments. *See* instruments, electronically manipulated.
electronically synthesized music, 49, 51, 136–37, 185
Elkus, Albert, 43, 46
Ellington, Duke, 144, 186
Elston, Arnold, 44
Elwood, Philip, 39
Emerson, Ralph Waldo, 70
Encinitas, California, 62, 69, 200
Encyclopedists, 177
envelope (of sound), 155
environmental sounds. *See* sounds, environmental.
Erickson, Albertine (aunt), 3–4
Erickson, Andrew (uncle), 3–4
Erickson Celebration, University of California at San Diego, 70n, 80, 88, 100n, 203n
Erickson, Charles (father), 4, 5, 30
Erickson, Edith (mother), 4
Erickson, Ellen Isaacson (stepmother), 4, 7, 30
Erickson, Emil (uncle), 3
Erickson family, musical activities of, 3–5
Erickson, Gus (uncle),4, 51
Erickson, Harold (uncle), 3–4
Erickson, Lenore. *See* Alt–Erickson, Lenore.
Erickson, Robert
  career, xvi
  Center for Music Experiment and, 61

character: American quality of, xv; California spirit, x, xvii, 64, 69–70, 217; individualism, xv–xvii; organizational skills, 22–24, 66; practicality, 31; privateness, 76; questing spirit, x; stability, 31; working procedure, 28–29, 44–45, 62, 214, 223
commissions: Ajemian, Maro, 120; Batschelet, Bernhard, 193; Buckner, Thomas, 216; Continuum, 80, 231; Five Centuries Ensemble, 207; Freeman, Betty, 79–80, 227, 231; Harkins, Edwin, 192; Holliday, Robert, 126; Kobialka, Daniel, 191; KPBS, 160; Minneapolis Civic Orchestra, 106; Négyesy, János, 205; San Francisco Contemporary Music Players, 80; Sequoia String Quartet, 223; SONOR ensemble, 196; Turetzky, Bertram, 147; University of Illinois at Urbana, 147, 123; Whitelight Foundation, 227
composer-performer collaboration, 141, 148, 160, 198
composition, approach to, 141
concern with proportion, 164
concern with structure and technique, 92, 94
conducting, studies in, 29
and Dempster, Stuart, 141
education, 26. *See also* Erickson, musical training.
films on, 52, 80, 135, 160
grants and awards: Ford Foundation fellowship, 30; Friedheim Award, 79; Guggenheim Fellowship, 56, 59, 151; Hamline scholarship, 20; National Endowment for the Arts, 80, 194, 224; Yaddo fellowship, 33, 97–98
influence of, x
interests of, xvi, xvii, 7, 31, 61; ancient Greece, 56, 77, 146, 150–51, 196;

Erickson, Robert (*continued*)

  interests of (*continued*)

    birdsong, 63, 138, 155, 207–208, 211–12, 213; Chinese music, 77, 213; history, 77; home-made instruments, 51–53, 62, 78, 134, 151, 162, 164–65; late nineteenth-century music, 69, 71, 78; mechanical tinkering, 20; non-Western music, 50–52, 61, 66, 152, 165–66, 191; organizations, 22; reading, 7, 75; science, 7, 76; social issues, 69, 76; tuning systems, 66, 78, 169; tuning systems, Greek, 51, 57, 151, 161

    Krenek and, 16, 20–21, 25–27, 29, 58, 89, 92, 99

    left-handedness, 7

    life: army career, 22–24, 31, 45, 62, 153–54; background, xv; childhood, 3–9, 67, 158, 207, 212; family relations, 4; illnesses, xvi, xviii, 64, 69, 74, 77–80, 211, 226, 235; marriage, 11. *See also* (under Erickson, Robert) occupations; residences; teaching.

  and musical complexity, 13–15, 25, 27

  musical style and techniques

    atonality, 18

    classicism, 99

    consistency of, 92, 101

    continuing variation, 88

    counterpoint, xvi, 29–30, 33, 87, 89, 92–93, 96, 101, 113, 129, 147

    development of, x, 24, 28, 33, 45, 47, 57, 85–86, 92, 101, 112, 129, 166–67, 229

    drones, 165, 167, 186, 190, 194, 195, 197, 198, 200, 201, 203, 210, 212, 217, 221, 225, 226, 228–29, 230, 235

    early, 85

    environment, expression of, 157–63

    experiments, sound, 115, 134–35, 142

harmony, 87, 90, 101, 130; absence of, 29, 229; chordal, 183; non-tonal, 87; quartal, 33, 99; tonal, 33, 98

hocket, 139, 167–70, 182, 190, 192, 197, 200, 201, 208, 210–11, 219, 221, 222, 224, 225, 228, 230, 232

hypnotic effect, 74, 158

improvisation, 53–54, 85, 91, 118, 120, 124, 126, 129

influences on, xvi, 14, 21–22, 47, 86, 90, 112, 133, 196

lyricism, 88, 90, 96, 98, 148, 190, 193, 194, 199, 200, 217, 222, 223, 226

maturity, artistic, 233

melody, 86, 90, 103, 110, 113, 116–17, 119, 130, 158, 190, 194–96, 201, 203, 210, 222, 223, 224, 226, 229, 230, 235, 236; avoidance of, 159; consonant, 213, 229

meter, 90

microtonal writing, 73–74, 192, 197, 206, 210, 227, 230, 235–36

neoclassicism, xvi, 34, 90–91, 96, 99

orientalism, 206, 213, 231

pitch(es), 190, 201, 216, 222; high, 132, 183, 190, 207, 224; sustained, 159, 224

polyphony, 47, 86

rhythm, 90–91, 121, 138–39, 150, 189, 191, 198; asymmetrical, 164, 170; motor, 87, 164; overlapping, 138, 165; perpetual motion, 201; slow, 161

rhythmic organization, 138–39, 161, 162, 164, 166, 168, 169, 229

rhythmic polyphony, 165

silence, 190, 213

structure and form, 28, 105; branching, 89, 106–10, 116, 117, 119, 120; exploratory, 211, 212

Erickson, Robert (*continued*)

musical style and techniques (*continued*)

tempo, 105, 116, 120–21, 128–29; changing, 138; proportional, 111–12

tenderness in, 152

text setting, 33, 86, 198, 204

texture, 45, 130, 186, 191, 194, 195, 203, 209, 212, 231, 236

timbre, 45, 61, 64, 130, 157, 170, 176–77, 180, 186, 193, 203, 212, 216

tranquillity, 144, 157, 159, 178, 194, 196

variation form, 106–107

virtuosity, 104, 112, 226

vocal sounds in instrumental playing, 73, 142, 144, 146, 192, 193, 197

voice as musical source, 63

musical techniques. *See* Erickson, Robert, musical style and techniques.

musical thought, xv, 27, 72, 199. *See also* Erickson, Robert, writings.

musical training, xvi, 91–92; in Chicago, 10; as child, 3–9; at Colorado Springs, 29, 97; in composition, 10, 13, 29; at Hamline University, 20–21, 25–27, 87, 89, 92; in harmony, 10; with Krenek, 20–21, 25, 27, 39, 87, 89, 92; with La Violette, 13; with Sessions, 28; at University of Michigan, 17

nature and, 28, 69, 75, 205, 207, 216, 221, 229–31, 232. *See also* Erickson, sounds, natural.

near-sightedness, 22

occupations: army, 22–24, 153–54; Gamble Hinged Music Company, 16; guest composer at Wesleyan University, 50; KPFA, x, 35, 37–40, 75, 122, 136; miscellaneous jobs, 10, 20; potter, 19; printer's devil, 10;

teaching career, 101: St. Catherine's College, 26, 28, 33, 95; San Francisco Conservatory of Music, x, 39, 46–47, 129, 140; San Francisco State College, 34, 39; University of California at Berkeley, x, 39, 41–44; University of California at San Diego, x, 58, 61, 67–69, 74, 78, 109, 140, 164, 226, 231

opera and, 21

orchestra and, 8, 183–84, 203

order and, 199

place in American musical history, x, xi, xii, xv

program notes, 70, 71, 106–107, 119–20, 150, 155n, 174, 191, 199, 209–10, 211–12, 225–26

residences: Chicago, 4, 10–18; Michigan, 4, 7–8, 10–12, 19; Minnesota, 12; New York City, xv, 30, 33; St. Paul, 20, 22, 33–34, 39, 101; San Diego area, 12, 62, 69, 129, 164; San Francisco Bay Area, 34, 47, 164

role as composer, view of, 69

Schoenberg and, 18, 86, 90, 93, 97

sound: fascination with, xvi, 3, 5–7, 12, 14, 72–73, 134; motion of, 130

sound studio in home, 134

students, contact with and inspiration from, 45

teaching, philosophy and techniques of, 17, 26–27, 51, 59, 78–79, 93–95

texts, sources of: advertising, 63, 150; Biblical, 74; California place names, 217; Claudius, Matthias, 207; D'Annunzio, Gabriele, 207–208; Joyce, James, 127–29, 204; overheard comments, 155; poems by friends, 74, 97, 149–50; political speeches, 63, 152–54; Stevens, Wallace, 74–77, 198–200. *See also* (under Erickson, Robert) writings: texts for own works.

Erickson, Robert (*continued*)
travels, 27–28; to Europe, xv, 56; to Greece, 56–57, 151; to Indonesia, 66; to Italy, 205; to Japan, 72–73, 231; writings on, 78
and Turetzky, Bertram, 148
twelve-tone technique, xvi, 13–15, 55, 229
universities, views on, 43–45, 58, 68–69, 78
works: autumnal quality of, 75, 212, 230–31; for bells, 52; for chamber orchestra, 80, 92, 115, 231–33; for chorus, 22, 33, 63, 98, 126–29, 149; for clarinet, 125; for contrabass, 147–49; early, 5, 11, 15, 18, 26, 55, 85–88; eroticism in, 197; exoticism in, 194, 196, 197, 206, 212, 231; for flute, 74, 98–99, 154–55, 192–93; for harp, 225–26, 233; humor and wit in, xvi, 103, 147, 154–55, 157, 192–93, 200, 217–18; introspection in, 86, 148, 152, 157–58, 212, 216, 221; irony, parody, and satire in, 24, 63, 73, 87, 90, 98, 126, 152–54, 156, 217, 226; late, 74, 212; lists of, 24, 32, 40, 45, 57, 65, 81; lost, 86, 89, 130; narrative quality of, 175; for orchestra, 28, 56, 89, 106–11, 130, 186, 194; pedagogical, 164; for percussion, 62, 160–63, 164–71; for piano solo, 24, 28, 88, 90, 119–22, 123–26, 231–33; playfulness in, 24, 139, 140–41; political, 63, 73, 149–50, 152–54, 157; publication of, 79, 88 (*see also* Smith Publications); pulse-pieces, 165, 232, 235; recordings of (*see separate discography*, Appendix I); sense of place in, xvii; for soloists, 95; for speaker, 149; for string orchestra, 80; for string quartet, 79, 101–106, 222; for strings, 235–36; for tape, 52–53, 62, 63, 64, 134–35, 157, 189–91; for timpani, 74, 219–20, 235–36; for toy piano, 52; for trombone, 53–54, 63, 152–54; for trumpet, 64, 191, 235–36; urgency in, 104; for violin, 64, 74, 189–91, 194–96, 205; for violoncello, 55, 99–100; for voice, 62, 63, 74, 86, 97, 151–52, 198, 204, 207, 215–17, 229–31. *For specific titles, see separate list*, Appendix III.
writings, 30, 70–71; *Hearing Things*, x, xiv, 3, 3n, 4, 6–7, 8, 13, 18, 23, 58, 60, 66, 68, 70, 72, 76, 78, 81n, 134, 150, 174, 214; "Krenek's Later Music," 25; "Loops: An Informal Timbre Experiment," 168; memoirs (*see Hearing Things* above); "Other Worlds," 166; *Sound Structure in Music*, 61, 70, 167, 173, 175–86, 191, 194, 213, 214; *The Structure of Music*, 27, 30, 33, 34, 89, 93–95, 97, 101, 141, 173, 185; texts for own works, 74, 128, 152, 155, 204, 215–18, 229–31
establishment, musical, 35, 185
esthetics, 93
European concert tradition: American music and, 43, 214; Balinese music and, 67; in eighteenth and nineteenth centuries, 182–83
European modernism, 13, 132, 191
expression in music, 94, 96, 143, 209, 223
expressionism, 16, 96, 99, 126
extended musical techniques. *See* virtuosity, extended.

fanfare, 211, 213
Fascism, 17; *see also* Nazism.
Federal Arts Project, 12
Feldman, Morton, 118, 119, 126
fiddle music, 217
Fillmore West, 68
filmmaking, 60, 135

films on Erickson, 52, 80, 135, 160
Five Centuries Ensemble, 207
"Flower of Cambodia," 66
flute. *See* instruments, flute.
Foldes, Andor, 42
Folkways Records, 40
Fontainebleau, France, 48
Ford, Henry, 159–60
Ford Foundation fellowship, 30
form, musical. *See* musical structure and form.
Fort Snelling, Minnesota, 22–24, 62
Foster, Stephen, 217
fourths (musical interval), 33, 99
France, 3, 46, 136; modernist music in, 130
Franck, César, 8
Frankenstein, Alfred, 49–50, 122
free improvisation, 124
free-form music, 147
Freeman, Betty, 79, 223, 227, 231
French resistance, 46
Friedheim Award, 79
fugue, 91, 95
fur-lined teacup, 49

Gaburo, Kenneth, 48, 60
Galimir Quartet, 15
Gamble Hinged Music Company, 16
gamelan, 53, 61, 66, 67, 126, 171; in United States, 165
gardens, 117, 196, 212, 214
Gazzelloni, Severino, 140, 193
George, Ronald, 170
Germany, 136; banning of music in, 17; Erickson's music performed in, 56, 80; modernist music in, 130
Gershwin, George, *An American in Paris*, 103
Glanville-Hicks, Peggy, 92
Glasow, Glenn, 48, 59, 72, 80, 88; at

Hamline, 21; as KPFA music director, 39
Glass, Philip, 48, 68, 167, 228
Goldberg, Rube, 62
gong. *See* instruments, gong.
Good Sound Foundation, 183
Górecki, Henryk, 131
Gotham Book Mart, 127
Gottschalk, Louis Moreau, "Night in the Tropics" Symphony, 197
Graham, John, 50
"grain," 178, 183, 213, 216, 219
graphic notation, 124, 143, 145–47, 158
Greece, ancient, 77, 146, 151; Erickson and, 150–51, 223
Greek music, ancient, 77, 164, 196
Greek tuning systems, 51, 57, 151, 161
Gregorian chant, 87; parody of, 24
Griffin, Donald R., 179, 187n
Griller String Quartet, 38
Gropius, Manon, 15
Gropius, Walter, 15
group improvisation. *See* improvisation, collaborative.
growls, trombone, 144, 202, 210
Guggenheim Fellowship, 56, 59
Guillaume de Machaut, 22
guitar, electric. *See* instruments, guitar, electric.

Haas, Berta, 26
Halprin, Anna, 51
Hamburg, Germany, 100
Hamline University, 20, 25, 39, 59; choral groups, 21, 25, 28, 42, 74, 86, 99; Erickson at, 20, 25, 27, 87, 89; library, 30
Hammergren, Shirley, 22, 25
Handel, George Frideric, 8; *Messiah*, 8
Hansel and Gretel, 175
Harkins, Edwin, 73, 192, 236
Harlow, Jean, 187

Harman, Carter, 122n
harmonica. *See* instruments, harmonica.
harmony, 29, 94, 185; in eighteenth- and
    nineteenth-century music, 183; move-
    ment away from, 132, 185; as organiz-
    ing device, 183
harp. *See* instruments, harp.
harpsichord. *See* instruments, harpsi-
    chord.
Harrison, Lou, xv, 42–44, 79; group
    performance and, 48; and Henry
    Cowell, 42
Harvey, John, 92
Haubenstock-Ramati, Roman, 145
Haydn, Joseph, 229, 233; String Quartet,
    op. 64 no. 5 in D ("Lark"), 138; string
    quartets, 102; Symphony No. 22, 234
hearing, experiences of, 176
hearing sound music, 236
Henry, Pierre, 137
Herter, M. D., 86
heterodyning, 138
Hill, Lewis, 35–37
Hiller, Lejaren, 184
Hindemith, Paul, 29, 44
Hink's. *See* J. F. Hink & Son.
hippies, ix
hocket, 139, 167–70, 182, 190, 192, 197,
    200, 201, 208, 210–11, 219, 221, 222,
    224, 225, 228, 232
Hoffmann, Richard, 49
Holbrook, Bob, 51–52
Holliday, Robert, 21, 86, 99, 126
Hopkins, Anthony, 154
Houston, Texas, Pacifica station in, 36
Hujsak, Ed, 151
Humble, Keith, 60

Ilmer, Irving, 14–15
Imbrie, Andrew, 43
imitation (counterpoint), 24, 87. *See also*
canon; fugue.
improvisation, 47, 53–54, 85, 124;
    collaborative, xvi, 48, 55, 86, 124–26.
    See also group improvisation.
indeterminacy, 133, 140, 143, 158, 159
Indian music, xvii, 165–66, 182, 196;
    South Indian drumming, 182; South
    Indian violin improvisation, 189; vocal
    drones, 180
individualism, regional, ix–x, 70
individualists in American art, ix
Indonesia, 66. *See also* Bali; gamelan.
Indonesian music, xvii, 191
industrial sounds. *See* sounds, industrial.
influenza epidemic (1918), 4
Institut de Recherche et Coordination
    Acoustique/Musique (IRCAM), 168
instrument building, 3–4, 51–53, 66,
    151. *See also* instruments, home-made.
instrumentation: of chamber orchestra,
    115; of orchestra, 100, 184, 211, 227.
    See also orchestration.
instruments: accordion, 54; Arabic, 205;
    Balinese, 66 (*see also* gamelan); bass
    clarinet, 115, 116; bell-lyre, 22; bells,
    134–36; celesta, 115, 228; cello (*see*
    instruments, violoncello); Chamberlain
    Organ, 62–63; *ch'in*, 181; Chinese, 52,
    180; contrabass, 63, 147–49, 151; con-
    trabass, extended techniques, 118, 140,
    147–49; contrabass, plucked, 165;
    cowbell, 124; cymbals, 170; cymbals,
    bowed, 219; didjeridu, 180; drone,
    149–50, 180; drums, home-made, 151,
    164; drums, skin, 170; electronically
    manipulated, 64; in Erickson family,
    3–5; flute, Erickson's studies of, 8;
    flute, extended techniques, 118, 140,
    155–56, 192–93; garden hose, 54;
    gong, 170; gong, Balinese, 66; guitar,
    electric, 151; harmonica, amplified, 53;

instruments (*continued*)

harp, 115, 225–26, 233; harpsichord, 115, 207–208; home-made, 51–53, 62, 66, 78, 129, 151, 162, 164; Jew's harp, 151, 180; kithara, 51; lute, 204–205; mandolin, 5; maracas, 213; marble, 62, 151; marimba, 62; metronomes, 132; Near Eastern, 205; "noise organ," 62; oboe, extended techniques, 118; orchestral, 67, 115; oud, 205; percussion, 12, 49, 115, 151, 162, 213, 219–20 (*see also, under* instruments: bells; cowbell; cymbals; drums; gong; marimba; rattles; stone chimes; timpani; tube drums; vibraphone, wind-chimes; wood-blocks); percussion, metal, 52, 64, 170; percussion, tuning of, 161; piano, 115; piano, Erickson's studies of, 7–8; piano, extended techniques, 140; piano, prepared, 52, 136; piano, toy (*see* instruments, toy piano); pitch-pipe, 151; quarreling, 146; rattles, 170; recorder, 151; rods, metal, 52, 64, 151, 173, 195, 207–208, 209, 210, 212, 213, 216; sitar, 165; spatial disposition of, 196; stone chimes, 52, 62; string bass (*see* instruments, contrabass); tabla, 164; tambura, 180; tape recorder, 49–54, 64, 134, 147–48, 157; timpani, 219–20, 228, 235–36; timpani, extended techniques, 219; toy piano, 52, 62, 134–36; toy zither, 151; trombone, extended techniques, 53–54, 140–45, 152–54; trumpet, 64, 160–63, 191–92, 235–36; trumpet, extended techniques, 192; tube drums, 62, 74, 164–65, 197; unconventional, 50, 51, 52, 62; vibraphone, 62, 124, 279; viola da gamba, 207–208; violin, 64; violin, Erickson family and, 4–5, 51; violin, Erickson's studies of, 4, 7, 10; violin, extended techniques, 206; violin, special tuning, 106; violoncello, 99; violoncello, extended techniques, 140;

wind chimes, 52, 134, 137; wood-blocks, 170, 212, 213; xylophone, 227; zither, toy, 151

intervals, musical, 162; fourth, 99; minor third, 206

introspection in music, 148, 216, 221

IRCAM, 168

irony, musical, 87, 90, 126, 153, 217

Isaac, Heinrich, 30

Isaacson, Ellen. *See* Erickson, Ellen Isaacson.

Italy, 157; modernist music in, 130

Ives, Charles, xv, 42, 103, 183; *Central Park in the Dark*, 159; *Concord Sonata*, 87; orchestral music, 42; *Psalm 67*, 42; *Set for Theater Orchestra*, 197; *Set of Pieces*, 48; songs, 231; string quartet, 102; *The Unanswered Question*, 159; *Universe Symphony*, 184, 184n; Violin Sonata No. 4, 42; violin sonatas, 191

J. F. Hink & Son, 41

Jacobs, Henry, 40

James, Henry, 211

Janáček, Leos, string quartets, 102, 222

Japan: Ericksons in, 72; modernist music in, 130

Japanese music, 72–73, 152, 231

Jaynes, Julian, 175n, 179

jazz, 14, 73, 118, 166, 186, and improvisation, 124; at KPFA, 39; Krenek and, 15–16; New Orleans, 124; Polish, 56, 166; variation form and, 108. *See also* boogie-woogie; bop; ragtime.

jazz bands, 186

Jepson, Warner, 135

Jew's harp. *See* instruments, Jew's harp.

Johnson, Alan, 52

Jones, Spike, 141

Jorda, Enrique, 55

Josquin des Prés, 21, 94

journalistic coverage of music, xiii–xiv, 79, 92, 122

Joyce, James, 94; *Finnegans Wake*, 74, 75, 127–29, 133n, 145, 155, 193, 193n, 231; *A Portrait of the Artist as a Young Man*, 152, 233; *Ulysses*, 204

Kains, M.G. *Five Acres and Independence*, 19, 24n
Kakudo, Yoshiko, 72
Kalamazoo River, 19
Kearney, Frank, 12–13, 15, 99, 103
Kenton, Stan, 186
Kerman, Joseph, 58
keynote (harmony). *See* tonic.
Khuner, Felix, 102
Kirana-style singing, 165
kithara. *See* instruments, kithara.
Klangfarbenmelodie, 181, 187n
Kobialka, Daniel, 191
Kontarsky, Aloys, 121, 140
Kotoński, Włodzimierz, 131
Kovacevich, Stephen Bishop, 38
KPBS (TV station, San Diego), 160; Erickson film, 160
KPFA (radio station, Berkeley), x, 21, 35–40, 41, 45, 135, 158; Erickson and, x, 35–39, 67, 136, 122; internal politics of, 36–37, 66; music directors of, xi, xvii, 21, 35–37, 39–40, 76; music staff, 39–40, 80 (Chiarito, Amerigo, 40; Glasow, Glenn, 21, 39, 59; Ogdon, Wilbur, 21, 39, 59; Rich, Alan, 37, 39; Rockwell, John, xi; Rush, Loren, 39, 48; Shere, Charles, xi, xvii, 39; Strachwitz, Chris, 40); programming, 36–39, 31, 157; San Francisco concert hall, 51
KQED (TV station, San Francisco), xvii, 52, 135; Erickson film, 135
Krasner, Louis, 14
Kraus, Karl, 16
Krenek, Ernst, 15–16, 35, 42, 44, 183; in Albuquerque, 29; conducts Erickson's *Fantasy*, 100; death, 17; Erickson and, 16–17, 20, 25–26, 29, 33, 58, 89, 92, 99; esthetics, 93; at Hamline University, 20, 25–26, 39, 87, 89; influence on Erickson's style, 86, 103; life, 15–16, 26; in Los Angeles, 25, 58, 89; musical style of, 16; and opera, 21; Schoenberg and, 17; sources of musical inspiration, 16, 25; as stage composer, 21; John Stewart and, 58; students of, 39; as symphonic composer, 107n; at University of Michigan, 17; at University of New Mexico, 26; at Vassar College, 16; works: *Cantata for War Time*, 25; choral, 21; Concertino, 35; concerts of, 16, 22; *Jonny spielt auf*, 15; *Marginal Sounds*, 48; Piano Sonata No. 6, 99; *Santa Fe Timetable*, 25, 218; Symphony No. 4, 26; *Twelve Short Piano Pieces*, 16; *Twelve Variations in Three Movements*, 16; *Two Suites*, 16; writings: 30; *Horizons Circled*, 107n; *Music Here and Now*, 16, 27, 93
Kronos Quartet, 223
Krupa, Gene, 164, 170
Kryl, Bohumir, 192

La Jolla Civic Orchestra, 79, 173
Lake Michigan, 19
Lake Saugatuck, 19
Lake Superior, 4–5, 7, 157
Lake Tahoe, 154, 217
landscape, music as, 232. *See also* gardens.
Lange, Hans, 14
language: artificial, 168; music and, 166; rhythm and, 166
language poetry, 168
LaSalle String Quartet, 14
Latimer, Ronald Lane, 75
Laufer, Robin, 46
La Violette, Wesley, 13
Lawton, Edward, 43
Leedy, Douglas, *Usable Music 2*, 53

Lewis, Daniel, 59

life-death cycles, 212, 214, 231

Ligeti, György, 185; *Poème Symphonique*, 132

Lincoln Center for the Performing Arts, xi

linear structure. *See* contrapuntal organization; melody.

listener: experiences of, 27, 176; relation to music, 122, 123, 174, 202; relation to sound, 135–36

Liszt, Franz, 12

live-electronic music, 49, 51, 55, 135, 141, 147–48, 158, 189–90

Logan, Jack, 160, 192

Lombard, Carole, 187

London Surrealist Exhibition, 50

loop music, 138–39, 164, 170, 195, 220

Los Angeles, California, 25, 49; Cowell in, 42; as cultural capital, ix–x; Krenek in, 58; Pacifica station in, 36–37; John Rockwell in, xi; Schoenberg in, 17; universities (*see* University of California at Los Angeles; University of Southern California)

Los Angeles Philharmonic, 223, 227

Los Angeles Times, xi

Luening, Otto, 137

lute. *See* instruments, lute.

MacArthur, Douglas, 63, 73, 150, 153

machines, sounds of. *See* sounds, industrial.

MacKay, John, *Music of Many Means*, x, xiv, 85–86, 88n, 104, 158, 167–68, 169, 171n, 190

Maderna, Bruno, 140

Maginnis, Bill, 134

Mahler, Alma, 15

Mahler, Anna, 26

Mahler, Gustav, 12, 26, 103, 106, 148, 210, 235; Berio and, 132; Erickson and, 69, 152, 195, 196, 203, 213, 214, 217, 231; Krenek and, 16; orchestral

writing, 78, 99, 107, 107n, 194, 209, 221, 227, 235, 236; works: *Das Lied von der Erde*, 152; *Songs of Youth (Lieder und Gesänge aus der Jugendzeit)*, 231; Symphony No. 4, 104, 210; Symphony No. 7, 179, 203, 211; *Youth's Magic Horn (Des Knaben Wunderhorn)*, 86

Malipiero, Gian Francesco, 43

mandolin. *See* instruments, mandolin.

maracas. *See* instruments, maracas.

march, 141, 236

marimba. *See* instruments, marimba.

Marquette, Michigan, 4, 7–8, 36; High School, 10; musical life of, 4, 7–8, 192; Northern Michigan State Teachers College, 10

Martino, Donald, 79; Quintet for Clarinet and Strings, 49

maverick composers, ix, xv

Maxfield, Richard, 49; *Cough Music*, 50; *Fermentation Music*, 50; Piano Concerto, 49; tape music, 50–51

Mayhall, Jane, 33, 97

meaning, 23, 50, 93, 145, 146. *See also* music, meaning in.

mechanical songs. *See* sounds, industrial.

medieval music, 108, 139, 205, 207

meditative music, 148, 161, 171, 192, 201

Mediterranean Sea, 201

melody: in eighteenth- and nineteenth-century music, 183; movement away from, 185; orchestral music and, 185; as organizational device, 29, 94, 183; reaction against, 132; in Renaissance music, 21

Mendelssohn, Felix, 203

Menlo Park, California, 42

Menuhin, Yehudi, 46

Messiaen, Olivier, *The Catalogue of Birds*, 138; Gazzeloni and, 193

metaphor in music. *See* symbolism and metaphor in music.

metronomes. *See* instruments, metronomes.

Michigan. *See* specific place names.

Michigan, Upper Peninsula, 30

Michigan State University, Ypsilanti, 17–18

microtones, 73, 74, 156, 192, 206, 210, 226

Middleton, Peter, 154

Milhaud, Darius, 16, 44, 78, 169; at Mills College, 55; *Murder of a Great Chief of State*, 56

militarism, burlesque of, 153–54

Mills Chamber Players, 55, 141

Mills College (Oakland, California), 53, 55, 56, 132; Center for New Music, 61; concert hall, 53; gamelan, 165; student union, 53; Subotnick at, 49; Tape Music Center, 51, 53, 56, 61, 136

Milwaukee, Wisconsin, 4

minimalism, x, 55, 69, 160, 168, 182, 228. *See also* phase-pattern music.

Minneapolis Civic Orchestra, 106

Minneapolis, Minnesota, 22, 91; Erickson works premiered in, 91

Minneapolis Symphony Orchestra, 22, 25, 48, 55, 86

Minnesota, 48; California connection, 48; Erickson works performed in, 29; Ericksons in, 12

Mississippi River, 22

Mitropoulos, Dimitri, 22, 25, 26, 48; Erickson and, 26, 29, 55, 86, 89

mobile form, 124, 143, 145–46

mobile sculpture, 145–46

modernism, x, 6, 13, 105–106, 107, 112, 115–16, 127, 130, 132, 155; craftsmanship of, 195; eclectic, 43; international, 132

modernist composers, 42, 107, 130–32, 171; reaction against, 119, 191

modes, musical, 151

modulation (harmony), 173

Moholy-Nagy, Laszlo, 15

moment-form, 118

montage, 52

Monteverdi, Claudio, 21; *Il Combattimento di Tancredi e Clorinda*, 198

Moog, Robert, 137

Moorer, James, *Lions Are Growing*, 187n

Moran, Robert, 145

Morgan, Julia, 53

Morgan, Robert P., 85

morphing, 173

Morse code, 213

Mother Lode, 217–18

motives, musical, 90, 94, 98, 138, 148, 162, 177, 179, 182, 194, 222; suppression of, 182

mountains, 215–17

Mozart, Wolfgang Amadeus, 8, 229; Concerto for Flute and Harp, 105; *Eine kleine Nachtmusik*, 159; *Musical Joke*, 159; string quartets, 102; Symphony No. 41 ("Jupiter"), 29, 105

Muir, John, 217–18

multiphonics, 154, 156

music: in Balinese life, 66–67; ceremony and, 180; communication and, 166; compared to painting, 183, 185; emotional power of, 175; as entertainment, xiii; essence of, 161; language and, 166; meaning in, 50, 75, 76, 93, 144–45, 146, 166–67, 174, 196, 198, 210, 211, 215, 232, 236; relationship with words, 71–72, 86, 154, 178; speech and, 61, 73, 152–53, 168, 169, 177; spiritual content of, 181; understanding of, 27, 72, 93–94; universality of, xiii; visual experience and, 93, 173; in Western life, 67

music, ritual, 61

music critics, 49–50, 122

music theater-pieces, 49, 51, 54, 130,

music theater-pieces (*continued*) 135, 153–54, 206–207

music theory: eighteenth-century, 177; practicing musician and, 169; twentieth-century, cross-disciplinary, 60

musical expression, 94, 96, 143, 209, 223

Musical Heritage Society, 191, 232

musical narrative, 175

Musical Newsletter, 85

musical structure and form, 88, 92; in Classic period, 105, 182–83; goals of, 93. *See also* arch form; branching structure; mobile form; moment-form; rondo form; sonata-allegro form; variation form.

musicologists, 44, 58, 85

musique concrète, 50, 136–37

mynah bird, 137, 155

myositis, 77–78

Nancarrow, Conlon, xv

narrative, types of, 175

narrative quality of Erickson's music, 174

National Endowment for the Arts, 80, 194, 224

natural sounds. *See* sounds, natural.

Nazism, 17; attacks on progressive music, 46; and Krenek, 16. *See also* Fascism.

Near Eastern instruments. *See* instruments, Near Eastern.

Nee, Thomas, 21, 33, 48, 79, 98, 173, 200, 203, 209

Négyesy, János, 205

neoclassicism, 43, 48, 118; Erickson and, xvi, 34, 90, 91, 96, 99

neo-Dadaism, 50

neo-romanticism, 118, 229

neo-surrealism, 50

New England, ix, 70n, 200, 230

New Guinea, ritual music, 61, 180

New Hampshire, 77; Festival , 71, 79, 200

New Music, 42

New Music Group of Chicago, 15, 18

New Music Quarterly, 42, 49

New Music Quarterly Records, 42

New Music Society, 42

New School for Social Research (New York City): Cage at, 42, 49; Cowell at, 42; Maxfield at, 49

New York, Erickson works performed in, 29, 79

New York City, 30, 45, 56, 79; as cultural capital, ix; Pacifica station in, 36–37

New York *Herald Tribune*, 37, 92, 122

New York (magazine), 37

New York Philharmonic, 26

New York School [of composers], 118–19

New York Times, xi, 40

New York University, 56

The New Yorker, xiii

New Yorkers, view of California, 70

New Zealand, 49

Newsweek, 37

Nin, Anaïs, 43

Nin-Culmell, Joaquín, 43

nineteenth-century music, 106; Erickson's interest in, 8, 69, 71. *See also* Romantic music.

Nobel, Jim, 10

Noh theater, 152

noise, relation to pitch and chords, 177; used as musical element, 6, 178

"noise organ," 62

Nono, Luigi, 107

Nordenstrom, Gladys, 26

Northern State Teachers College, Marquette, Michigan, 10

Northwest German Radio, 137

notation, graphic. *See* graphic notation.

notation of timbral details, 181

Oakland, California, 35, 48. *See also* Mills College.

Oakland Symphony Orchestra, xvii, 38, 48, 53, 55–56, 123; commitment to new music, 55

Oakland WPA Orchestra, 35

oboe. *See* instruments, oboe.

Obrecht, Jacob, 21

ocean, 178, 199. *See also* Pacific Ocean; surf.

Ockeghem, Johannes, 21, 30, 94

Ogden, C. K., *The Meaning of Meaning*, 23

Ogdon, Beverly, 62, 152

Ogdon, Wilbur, 48, 62, 152; Erickson's letters to, 29, 30, 32n, 33–34, 93, 95, 95n, 98–99; at Hamline, 21; as music director, KPFA, 39; at UC San Diego, 58–60, 66; at University of Illinois, 59

"Old Black Joe," 206

Oliveros, Pauline: Center for Music Experiment and, 61; concerts of, 50, 54; Good Sound Foundation and, 183; group improvisation and, 47, 55; as performer, 137; as student of Erickson, 34, 47; Tape Music Centers and, 56, 61, 154; at UC San Diego, 60–61; work with Erickson, 134; works: *George Washington Slept Here Too*, 54; Trio for Accordion and Bandoneon, 137; *Variations for Sextet*, 48

Olshausen, Detlev, 102

op art, 138, 168

open-form music, 124, 145–46

opera: and Erickson, 21; and Krenek, 21

Oppenheim, Meret, *Object*, 50

orchestra: conductorless, 169; large, 130, 227; performing space of, 183; programming for, 202–203; standard instrumentation, 100, 184

orchestra, chamber, Erickson and, 116; instrumentation of, 115

orchestral music, 184, 189; compared with chamber music, 115; late nineteenth-century, 8, 69, 71, 73, 78

orchestration, Bach and, 108; Beethoven and, 108. *See also* instrumentation.

ostinati, 90

Otey, Wendell, 34

oud. *See* instruments, oud.

overtones, 173

Pacific Ocean, 63, 157–58, 159

Pacifica Foundation, 36–37

painting, compared to music, 183, 185

Palestrina, Giovanni, 30, 94

Palm, Siegfried, 140

Palmer, Lynn, 50

Paris, France, 43, 48; Exposition of 1889, 126; Institut de Recherche et Coordination Acoustique/Musique (IRCAM), 168

Park, Dr. Robert, 10

Park House (Chicago), 10, 12, 13, 20, 26, 27, 33, 67, 86, 99

parody, 63, 73

Parrenin Quartet, 49

Partch, Harry, *Barstow*, 218

passacaglia, 89

pastorale, 96–98, 200, 226, 233

Peltzer, Dwight, 38, 53, 121, 122–23

Penderecki, Krzysztof, 118

pentatonic scale, 194, 196, 206, 213, 216, 227, 232

perception of music, 179

percussion instruments. *See* instruments, percussion.

percussion music, 171

percussion sounds, 6, 170–71, 219

performance, collaborative, xvi, 48, 55, 86, 139, 167, 169

performer-composer teams, 121, 140, 149

"Performers' Choice," 38, 123

Perle, George, 13–15, 27, 71

perspective in painting, 177, 185
Peterson, Donald, 63, 149–50
Peterson, June, 22
phase-pattern music, 55, 139
pianist-composer teams, 121, 140
piano. *See* instruments, piano.
piano concerto, 123
piano music, form in, 92
piano, toy. *See* instruments, toy piano.
Picasso, Pablo, 177
pictorial music, 70, 173, 158, 199, 200, 205
Piraeus, Greece, 157
pitch, musical, 154–55, 170, 177, 181, 201, 219, 222; overtones, 173; relation to noise, 177; relation to one another, 161; relation to rhythm, 161; relation to speech, 73; in Western music, 182
"pitchiness," 178, 185
pizzicato, left-hand, 206
Plantamura, Carol, 198, 204, 207, 216
Plato, 25, 150–51; *Republic*, 151
playfulness in music, 139, 141
pointillism, 118, 131
Poland, 46; modernist music in, 130, 131–32
Polish jazz, 56, 166
Polish school (of composers), 118, 132
political expression in music, 17, 63, 73, 149–50, 152–54
politics and music, 17. *See also* Fascism; Nazism.
polyphony, 47, 86, 165; in Joyce's *Finnegans Wake*, 127; rhythmic, 165. *See also* contrapuntal organization.
"Pop Goes the Weasel," 6
popular culture, ix
Port Arthur, Texas, 23
post-Impressionism, 39
Prednisone, 77–78
prepared piano. *See* instruments, piano, prepared.

"primitive" music, 77
program music, 72, 99, 137, 144–45, 187, 212, 221, 229–31
program notes, 70, 71, 127, 232
progressive music, 16, 24, 29, 42, 44, 118; Nazi attacks on, 46
psychoacoustics, 177, 196
pulse music. *See* phase-pattern music; repetitive music.
"pure" music. *See* abstract music.
Pythagoras, 151, 161

quarter tones, 192, 210
queer culture, ix
quotationists, 173, 214

Rabe, Folke, 56; *Bolos*, 142; *Was??*, 180
ragtime, 87
Rameau, Jean-Philippe, 177
Ratcliff, Walter, 53
Ravel, Maurice, 12; *Daphnis and Chloe*, 97
realism, in painting, 177
recorder. *See* instruments, recorder.
Redwood City, California, 28
Reich, Steve, 55, 68, 138, 167, 182, 228; performing ensemble in New York, 56; as student at Mills College, 55; West African drumming and, 165
Renaissance music, 21, 30, 86, 94, 108, 141. *See also* instruments, lute.
repetitive music, 68–69, 73, 139, 149, 158, 167. *See also* minimalism.
Respighi, Ottorino, *The Pines of Rome*, 138
rhythm: asymmetrical, 164; in Balinese music, 67; language and, 166; motor, 164; natural, 162; relation to pitch, 161; in Renaissance music, 21; in serial music, 121; structural, 164; text and, 198
Ricci, Ruggiero, 46
ricercar, 53, 140–41
Rich, Alan, 37, 39, 79, 80, 122, 235
Riley, Terry, 49, 68, 217; concerts of, 44,

Riley, Terry (*continued*)
50; *In C*, 54–55, 56, 138–39, 149, 165,
190, 228; and Kirana-style singing,
165; as student of Erickson, 47; at
SUNY Buffalo, 56
Rilke, Rainer Maria, 74, 76
Rimsky–Korsakov, Nikolai, *Sheherazade*,
201
ritual music, 61
Rochberg, George, 173
rock music, 56, 68, 154
Rockefeller Foundation grant, 60–61
Rockwell, John, 40; as critic, xi, 40
rods, metal. *See* instruments, rods.
Rolling Stone (magazine), 40
Romantic music, 8, 183. *See also* nine-
teenth-century music.
romanticism, x, 71, 78, 99, 106, 195
rondo form, 98, 211
Rousseau, Jean–Jacques, 177
Ruggles, Charles, 42
Rush, Loren, 47–48, 52, 145, 168; as
contrabassist, 123; on faculty at SF
Conservatory, 48, 56; Good Sound
Foundation and, 183; at KPFA, 39, 48;
as student of Erickson, 34, 47; works:
Hard Music, 180; *Mandala Music*, 38
Russia, 3, 46
Russian music, 12

Sachs, Joel, 79, 191, 232
St. Catherine's College (St. Paul, Minne-
sota), 26, 28, 33, 95, 98, 101
St. Paul Gallery and School of Art, 22
St. Paul, Minnesota, 22, 29, 87; concerts
in, 35; Ericksons in, 20, 22, 33–34, 39,
101
St. Paul *Pioneer Press*, 92
Salvation Army, 3
Samuel, Gerhard, xvii, 38, 49, 123, 184n;
Oakland Symphony and, 48–49, 55–56
San Antonio, Texas, 87; Adjutant
General School, 23

San Diego, California, 75, 129; Erickson
works premiered in, 88; Erickson's
musical response to, xvii, 158, 160,
204; Ericksons in, 12, 62, 69. *See also*
KPBS; University of California at San
Diego.
San Francisco, California, 28, 34, 48, 78,
80, 122; concert life, 34–35; Cowell in,
42; Erickson works performed in, 87,
100. *See also* KQED.
San Francisco Ballet Orchestra, 123
San Francisco Bay Area, 12, 28, 36, 39,
56; composers, Asian philosophy and,
50; composers, at San Francisco Tape
Music Center, 51; cultural counter-
current in, x, 48; cultural isolation of,
35, 130; Ericksons' move to, 34, 101;
musical avant garde, 145; new music
in, 132, 141; political climate in, 149
San Francisco Chamber Music Society, 38
San Francisco Chronicle, 122
San Francisco Conservatory of Music,
46–57, 76, 129; Bloch at, 43, 46;
Composers Workshop, 48–49; elec-
tronic music in, 51; Elkus at, 46;
Erickson at, x, 27, 39, 46–57
San Francisco Contemporary Music
Players, 80, 224
San Francisco Dancers Workshop, 51
San Francisco Museum of Art, 34
San Francisco Playhouse, 135
San Francisco State College. *See* San
Francisco State University.
San Francisco State University, 34–35,
42, 47
San Francisco Symphony Orchestra, 44,
55, 102
San Francisco Tape Music Center, x, 51,
56, 62, 68, 81n, 134, 135, 137, 138,
141, 142, 154, 170; synthesizer, 137
San Francisco's Burning (film), 135
San Jose State University, gamelan, 165

San Rafael, California, 36
Santa Barbara, California, Alt-Erickson exhibit, 28
Santa Cruz, California, 79
Saratoga Springs, New York, 33, 97
sarcasm, musical, 87
Satie, Erik, 103; *Socrate*, 25
satire in music, 152
Saugatuck, Michigan, 19
Saville, Jonathan, 198–99, 203n
scale(s), 8, 211; chromatic, 73; diatonic, 67, 173; pentatonic, 194, 196, 213, 232
Scarlatti, Domenico, 112
Schaeffer, Pierre, 136
Schäffer, Bogusław, 131
Schneider, David, 102
Schoenberg, Arnold, 13–15, 17, 42, 44, 88; and Berg, 103; continuing variation, 88; death of, 17; influence on Erickson, 86, 93, 126; Krenek and, 17; lecture by, 18; melody of timbres, 181; orchestral variations, 108; students of, 49; twelve-tone technique, 29–30, 72, 108; works: *Five Pieces for Orchestra*, 172–73, 179, 187, 199; *Gurrelieder*, 12, 18, 35; piano pieces: op. 11, 90; op. 33a, 13; songs, 22; string quartets, 14, 15, 18, 102; "Summer Morning by a Lake (Colors)" (*see Five Pieces for Orchestra*); *Transfigured Night*, 33, 97; writings: *Harmonielehre*, 181
Schubert, Franz, 12, 16, 37, 68; piano sonata, B♭ major, op. post., 12; song, 106; string quartets, 102; string quintet, C major, 12
Schuller, Gunther, *Contemporary Music in Evolution*, 39; String Quartet, 49
Schumann, Robert, 12; string quartets, 102
science and music, 169
sculpture, compared to music, 145–46
Sebeok, Thomas A., 187n
Seeger, Charles, 41–42, 44

Sender, Ramon, 56, 81n; concerts of, 50; electronic studio, 51; *Four Sanskrit Hymns*, 49; San Francisco Tape Music Center and, 51, 68, 154; as student of Erickson, 47; work with Erickson, 134
Sequoia String Quartet, 223
serial music, 54, 118, 121. *See also* twelve-tone technique.
Sessions, Roger, 28, 43, 44; Erickson's studies with, 28
Shere, Charles: Erickson and, xvii; Erickson's letters to, 72–74, 77, 78–79, 81n, 151, 169, 174, 187, 194, 198, 202, 209, 218n; at KPFA, xi, xvii, 39; John Rockwell and, ix, xi
Shere, Lindsey, xi
Shifrin, Seymour, 43
"shingling" of sounds, 185, 194
Shostakovich, Dimitri, string quartets, 102, 221, 222
Sibelius, Jan, 12, 68, 195
Silber, John, 60
sitar. *See* instruments, sitar.
Slonimsky, Nicholas, 42
Smetana, Bedrich, 221
Smith, Patricia, 78
Smith Publications (Sylvia Smith), xiv, 79, 192
society, artists in, 69, 71
Society of Independent Artists exhibition, 50
Socrates, 151
sonata, 92, 105
sonata-allegro form, 90, 105, 112
SONOR Ensemble, 80, 196, 217, 224
sonorities (aggregations of sounds), 178, 183, 186
sound, contemplation of, 136; envelope, 154–55; gradual transformation of, 172
sound-masses. *See* sonorities.
sound patterns, perception of, 179

sound poets, 168

sound sources, 51–52, 62–64, 73, 142, 158, 159, 212

sound, thinking, 148

sounds: aggregations of (sonorities), 178; environmental, used in music, 63–64, 136, 142–44, 157–63 (*see also* birdsong); Erickson's experimentation with, 52, 56, 63–64, 134, 142; Erickson's fascination with, xvi , 3, 5–7, 12, 14, 72; industrial, xvi, 5–6, 63–64, 159–60, 184; liberation of, 132; listener's response to, 176, 179; modes of, 176; natural, 5–6, 158 (*see also* birdsong); natural, used in music, xvi, 63, 75, 142, 143–44, 154, 157–58, 174, 191, 214 (*see also musique concrète*); "shingling" of, 185; spatial distribution of, 183; speech (*see* speech and music)

Sousa march, 141

South American composers, 42

South Dakota, 28

Southeast Asia, music, 180

Soviet bloc, musical life, 132

space, musical, 183–84, 215–16; visual, means of organizing, 177

"spastic" music, 106, 107, 108

Speculum Musicae, 80, 224

speech and music, 73, 152–53, 169, 177

speech recognition, 168

Stanford University, Alt-Erickson exhibit, 28; Center for Computer Research and Acoustics, 168, 183

State University of New York at Buffalo, 56

Stern, Isaac, 46

Sterne, Laurence, 128

Stevens, Wallace, 74, 77, 198; "The Idea of Order at Key West," 74–76, 198–200, 204

Stewart, John, 58–60

Stock, Frederick, 14

Stockhausen, Karlheinz, 40, 56, 107, 112, 118, 121, 136–37, 140, 161, 162, 163n, 185; *Zyklus*, 171

stone chimes. *See* instruments, stone chimes.

Strachwitz, Chris, 40

Strangways, Fox, 166

Strauss, Richard, 69, 97; *Sinfonia domestica*, 71

Stravinsky, Igor, 3, 12, 115, 202; *Agon*, 146, 178; *Concerto for Two Solo Pianos*, 22; *Rite of Spring*, 6, 178; *Soldier's Tale*, 25; string quartets, 102; *Symphonies of Winds*, 107n

stream-of-consciousness writing, 204

stretto, 91, 95

string quartet, 64, 92, 102–106, 221–22

Strong, May, 10

"strophic" music, 106, 107

structure, musical. *See* musical structure and form.

Subotnick, Morton, 55, 141; concerts of, 50; electronic studio, 51; at New York University, 56; Tape Music Center and, 51, 56, 154; Three Preludes for piano, 49

surf, 38, 63, 178, 183, 189

surrealism, 50, 135

Swed, Mark, xvii

Sweden, Ericksons in, 56

Swift, Jonathan, 128

Swift, Richard, 48

Switzerland, Bloch in, 43

symbolism and metaphor in music, 71, 214. *See also* pictorial music; program music.

symphonic music, Erickson's interest in, 69, 71; form in, 107

symphony, in eighteenth and nineteenth centuries, 107

symphony orchestra, 92; sonority of, 64; standard instrumentation of, 100 synthesized music, 49, 136, 172

synthesizers, electronic, 137

Szigeti, Joseph, 42

tabla. *See* instruments, tabla.

tambura. *See* instruments, tambura.

tape loops, 55, 62–63, 138–39

tape music, xvi, 49, 51–53, 63–64, 129, 134–39; combined with instruments, 49, 54–55, 141

Tape Music Center, Mills College, 51, 53, 56, 61, 136

Tape Music Center, San Francisco, x, 51, 56, 62, 68, 81n, 134, 135, 137, 138, 141, 142, 154, 170

tape, prerecorded, 141. *See also* live-electronic music.

tape recorder, as instrument. *See* instruments, tape recorder.

Tchaikovsky, Peter Ilych, 8

techniques, extended. *See* virtuosity, extended.

tempo, proportional, 111–12

Texas, Erickson works performed in, 29

text setting, 86, 130, 153, 154–55, 198, 204

texture, musical: fused, 183, 194; layered, 183; "microscopic," 186; as organizing device, 130, 182, 231–32. *See also* "grain."

theater pieces, 49–51, 54, 130, 135

Thomson, Virgil, xv, 106, 107; *Sea Piece with Birds*, 158

Thoreau, Henry David, 87, 157, 160; *Walden*, 157

"thought-sound" music, 106

thugs, witty, 102

Tibetan religious thought, 181

Tibetan vocal drones, 180

tic-tac-toe, 54, 146

timbre, 61, 64, 154–55, 170, 172; manipulation of, 174; notation of, 181; as organizing device, 130, 168, 170, 175–78,

181–82; pitch and, 177

time, in music, 178–79; nature of, 161

timpani. *See* instruments, timpani.

toccata, 119–22, 170, 197, 219–20

tonality (harmony), 16, 94, 118–19, 173, 177, 223, 229; substitute for, 158, 223

tone color. *See* timbre.

tonic (harmony), 112, 173

train sounds, 6

tribal art, 39

Triest, Bill, 135

trombone. *See* instruments, trombone.

troubadour song, 205

trumpet. *See* instruments, trumpet.

tube drums. *See* instruments, tube drums.

Tudor, David, 137; John Cage and, 121, 140

tuning, 161, 216; role of in musical expression, 9; of violin, 206

tuning systems, 51, 57, 78, 151, 161–62, 169; Balinese, 66; Greek, 51, 57, 151, 161; modulation of, 173; tempered, 178

Tureck, Rosalyn, 59

Turetzky, Bertram, 63, 140, 147–48, 151; and Erickson, 148

Turkish music, 151

twelve-tone technique, 13, 15, 181; Berg and, 15; Erickson and, xvi, 13–15, 55; Krenek and, 16; Perle and, 13; Schoenberg and, 29–30, 48, 108; Ben Weber and, 13

U.S.S.R., conductorless orchestras in, 169

United States: Army, 22–24, 153; concert life in, xiii; culture in, ix; Department of Defense, 168; serious music in, ix

unity and variety in music, 94

University of California at Berkeley, 37, 39, 44, 58; centennial celebration, 45; gamelan, 165; Erickson at, x, 28, 41, 43–45; faculty, 39, 41–45, 49; festival,

University of California at Berkeley
(*continued*)
Department, xi, 41–45, 46–48; noon
concerts, 38; student radio, 40
University of California at Los Angeles,
44; Ethnomusicology Institute, 165;
Schoenberg at, 17
University of California at San Diego:
Buchla synthesizer at, 137; Center for
Music Experiment (CME), 61, 169,
171n, 174; Erickson and, x, 58–59, 63,
67–69, 76, 78, 140, 164; Erickson ar-
chive at, xiv; *Erickson Celebration* (sev-
entieth birthday), 70n, 80, 88, 100n,
203n; Music Department, 27, 58–59,
61, 63, 80, 152, 192, 193, 205, 235;
SONOR Ensemble, 80, 196, 217, 224;
Stewart, John, provost, 58–60
University of California Press, 61, 149
University of Chicago, 10
University of Cincinnati, College-
Conservatory of Music, Percussion
Ensemble, 184n
University of Ghana, 165
University of Illinois, 59, 60, 147; School
of Music, 123
University of Michigan, 17
University of Nevada at Las Vegas, 79
University of New Mexico, 26
University of Southern California, 59;
Schoenberg at, 17
Ussachevsky, Vladimir, 137

Varèse, Edgard, xv, 3, 6, 103, 107, 132,
181; *Déserts*, 178; early works, 85; influence on Erickson, 214; *Ionisation*, 171
variation form, 24, 92, 105, 107–108
Vassar College, 16
Vaughan Williams, Ralph, *Lark Ascending*, 138
verbal narrative, 175
Verdi, Giuseppe, 8

vernacular music, influence on serious
music, 39
vibraphone. *See* instruments, vibraphone.
vibrato, 178
Vienna, Austria, 15, 49, 103
Vienna Conservatory, 46
Viennese School, 44, 48. *See also* Berg,
Alban; Schoenberg, Arnold; Webern,
Anton.
Vietnam war, 149, 154
Vinton, John, *Dictionary of Contemporary
Music*, 136
viola da gamba. *See* instruments, viola da
gamba.
violin. *See* instruments, violin.
violoncello. *See* instruments, violoncello.
virtuosity, extended, 63, 86, 118, 129, 140,
141, 149, 152, 155, 169, 191–93, 226
visual experience, music and, 93, 173
visual narrative, 175
vocal drones, 180
vocal sounds in instrumental playing, 73,
142, 144, 147, 192, 193
vocal techniques, extended, 140
vowel sounds, relation to music, 73, 154–
55, 177

Wagner, Richard, *Das Rheingold*: Pre-
lude, 179, 185; *The Ring of the Nibe-
lung*, 12, 21; *Siegfried*, 211; *Tristan und
Isolde*, 12
Walden Pond, 87
Warsaw Autumn Festival, 38, 56, 131, 166
Washington, D.C., Pacifica station in, 36
Washington University, St. Louis, 12
water, as sound-source in Erickson's mu-
sic, 5, 157–58, 191, 201, 213. *See also*
ocean.
Weber, Ben, 13, 15, 27; *Composition for
Violin and Chamber Orchestra*, 48
Webern, Anton, 13–17, 42, 44, 94, 122,

Webern, Anton (*continued*)
139, 185; influence on Erickson, 126, 214; timbral organization and, 182; twelve-tone technique and, 108; works: *Concerto for Nine Instruments*, 38; early, 85; *Five Pieces for Chamber Orchestra*, 177, 182; orchestral variations, 108; orchestration of Ricercar from Bach's *Musical Offering*, 176–77, 181; String Quartet, 14, 102; Symphony, 107n
Weidlé, Wladimir, 179, 187n
Weimar, Germany, 15
Wesleyan University, 60
West Point, 153
Westminster Chimes, 177
whale song, 179
"When I Fall In Love," 99
Whitelight Foundation, 227
wind bands, 186; sonority of, 64
wind chimes. *See* instruments, wind chimes.
wind sounds, 213
Winkler, Harold, 37
Wolff, Christian, 118

Wolle, John, 41
wood-blocks. *See* instruments, wood-blocks.
words: American public and, 71; relationship with music, 71–72, 86, 154–55
"world music," 42
World War I, 50, 85
World War II, 17, 19, 23, 35, 43, 86, 89, 94
Wright, Orville, 159–60
Wright, Wilbur, 159–60

xylophone. *See* instruments, xylophone.

Yaddo arts colony (Saratoga Springs, New York), 33–34, 97–98
Yates, Peter, 83, 92, 101, 103–104, 105, 119; *Twentieth-Century Music*, 92
Yellowstone Park, 28
Yosemite, 217
Young, La Monte, 44; *Poem*, 44, 50
Ypsilanti, Michigan, 17–18

Zen Buddhism, 31
zither, toy. *See* instruments, toy zither.

Typeset by Thomas Finnegan.
The text face is Adobe Caslon; the display type is Bernhard Modern.
Jacket design by Andrea Sohn.
Illustrations digitally scanned by Peter Tannenbaum.
Printed and bound by McNaughton & Gunn, Inc., Saline, Michigan.